DON'T
FENCE ME IN

Anne with my
best wishes

Wendy x

WENDY McCARTHY

DON'T FENCE ME IN

RANDOM HOUSE AUSTRALIA

Random House Australia Pty Ltd
20 Alfred Street, Milsons Point, NSW 2061
http://www.randomhouse.com.au

Sydney New York Toronto
London Auckland Johannesburg

First published by Random House Australia 2000

National Library of Australia
Cataloguing-in-Publication Entry

McCarthy, Wendy.
Don't fence me in.

ISBN 0 85561 695 4

1. McCarthy, Wendy. 2. Feminists–Australia–Biography.
3. Businesswomen–Australia–Biography. 4. Women–
Australia–Social life and customs. 5. Women–Australia–
Social conditions–20th century. 6. Australia–Politics
and government–1945– I. Title.

305.42092

Cover photography by Louise Lister and Gordon McCarthy
Photograph of Wendy McCarthy and children by Sandy Edwards
Cover design by Yolande Gray
Typeset in 11/14pt Sabon by Midland Typesetters Pty Ltd
Printed and bound by The SOS Printing Group
Reproduction of lyrics from 'Don't Fence Me In' by Cole Porter
courtesy of Warner/Chappel Music Australia Pty Ltd

10 9 8 7 6 5 4 3

To Gordon, Sophie, Hamish and Sam
who gave me lots of room to move

FOREWORD

J ill Ker Conway's reflection on autobiography *When Memory Speaks* asserts that we all practise the craft of autobiography in our inner conversations with ourselves about the meaning of our experience. Yet only some of us set about writing. What is it that triggers the need to do this? Is it vanity or is it making sense of one's life by sharing and exposing it? It is something I have thought much about over the three years spent writing *Don't Fence Me In*. It may well be vanity, but I like the idea that I am part of an increasing group of Australian women from many different backgrounds who are writing their stories into Australian social history. It is a rich and bold inheritance for our daughters' generation, for whom the non-linear careers and feminist stances we adopted may at times have seemed contradictory and confusing.

Yet when first asked to write my story, my immediate response was no. 'It's not over,' I thought. 'I am too young, too busy and I am not sure anyone will be interested.' But in spite of myself I found the idea increasingly present in my mind and at unexpected moments would begin recalling events and unravelling experiences I thought I had long forgotten. My inner conversations were taking over and I decided to take the risk of writing it down.

Our culture offers us an inner script to live our lives by. If women of my age had accepted that script and stayed inside the boundaries it proscribed, Australia would be a very different place. Changing the culture changed the inner script and gave us opportunities unknown to our mothers and grandmothers. I learned to say yes to opportunity and risk and worry later how I would manage it.

The crucible of my feminism was childbirth and fertility and that remains the strongest influence. It connected the personal and political and excluded no-one; every woman had a story to tell and much cultural change was achieved through story-telling. As we shared common experiences we bonded with new insights into what being female in Australia was and might be. Today the narrative remains my preferred and most comfortable way of communicating. I know of no more effective way to set the record straight.

My belief in self-disclosure, especially about sexuality and fertility, is not always appreciated by those who feel that one's private life is sacred. Sometimes telling 'private' stories is out of bounds, especially if it impacts heavily on others. For my family, revisiting events put behind them many years ago may be painful and I hope they will understand that I must write my story as I see it.

There are many people whose names are not here who have been agents and participants in the events that I have chosen to write about. Some will be pleased not to be mentioned, others may feel overlooked and for that I apologise. I do want to acknowledge the constant encouragement and support offered by many older women, like Joan Bielski, Beryl Beaurepaire and the late Edna Ryan. Their commitment to opportunities for women meant they were and are still strong role models.

Thanks to Jennifer Byrne who suggested writing my memoirs was a good idea; to Gordon who came with me on the journey and captured some of my past in the cover photograph of Garema; to Amanda Bilson, my executive assistant, who has endured the emotional roller-coaster that these memories provoke; and to the Random House team who inherited me and offered support and advice.

CONTENTS

THE DECADE OF THE CENTURY

When I tell my children of a world without television, a house without a telephone or electricity, my primary school years at a one-teacher school and a three-mile journey to it on horse or bike, their eyes glaze over. Surely I am talking about the lives of my grandparents? And perhaps I could be, because life in the bush had changed very little in the first three decades of the century. But the forties was a political, economic and social watershed that was to shape us for decades, and yet somehow seems to have slipped from our memory. Professor Geoffrey Blainey, author and historian, called the forties the Decade of the Century.

Seven million Australians made up our nation in 1940. Our identification with Britain was strong then: all our strategic and military alliances were with Britain and it was not until Pearl Harbor in December 1941 that we began to look to the USA for increased support. After six years of war most Australians supported the attempt of the next quarter-century to make our nation self-sufficient. The rise in manufacturing was one powerful expression of this; when the first Holden came off the production line in 1948 the new direction was set.

The Australia my family lived in in the forties was a place where a university degree was as uncommon as a refrigerator, and a family holiday spent more than a hundred kilometres from home was exotic and required elaborate and lengthy preparation. Of every one hundred Australians maybe ninety-nine had not flown in an aeroplane. Probably sixty out of those hundred adults did not touch alcohol more than once a year. Respected information came from

Britain (BBC radio), and our imagination and fantasy were fed by magazines which gave us stories of the Royal family whose lives we followed with great interest. We were loyal subjects and talked of Britain as Home.

Australia in 1940 was a place where forty of every hundred Australians lived in either Sydney or Melbourne, another ten lived in the smaller state capitals, and a further seventeen lived in provincial cities or country towns. Overall, only one in three Australians lived in a rural area. After 150 years of European settlement, white Australians were overwhelmingly a people of the coastal plains.

In the Central West of NSW the impact of war and the changing world was experienced in unusual ways. As a child I was advised to look under my bed in case the Japs had escaped from the nearby Cowra POW camp—they would be looking, I was told, for little girls just like me to kidnap. We were persuaded to eat up and think of the poor British children who had nothing to eat. American blue jeans, check shirts and music became popular in the forties. The Yanks were good guys. Things Japanese were cheap and nasty.

Then, post-war, came the commitment to make the nation a fit place for returning heroes and for some Australians international peace seemed attainable. News in 1948 that Dr H.V. Evatt, then Minister for External Affairs, was to become President of the UN General Assembly was greeted with considerable pride. We mattered in the world scheme of things.

Australians had full employment in the forties, both during and after the war. In 1939 there was twelve per cent unemployment, but as the war effort gathered pace an acute shortage of labour brought hundreds of thousands of women out of the house and into the paid workforce. Nevertheless, when the war ended, Australia escaped the predicted period of high unemployment. In 1946 Prime Minister Chifley said, 'During the past year over 500,000 men and women have been released from defence and other government occupations. Yet at no stage has there been any significant number of unemployed.' Year after year, Australia could boast of less unemployment than the USA.

The shift in Australia's post-war thinking and practice in immigration matters revealed how Australia saw itself as part of the new international order. Immigration was included in the post-war reconstruction planning for national development, and national survival for population was considered to be vital. Fertility rates were low and immigration seemed a better proposition than raising the birth rates.

Continental Europe was accepted as a source for Australian immigration alongside the United Kingdom. The 'white alien' immigration policy reflected a policy shift which changed Australia forever. A target of 70,000 a year was suggested and in 1948 the target was reached, including 10,000 from refugee camps in Europe.

From the mid-forties onward there were at least three decades of favourable weather in the south-eastern corner of the continent, where most of the nation's wool and food was produced. This good weather followed a period of abnormally severe droughts; even in the war years, the droughts had been extensive. The years of increased rainfall brought prosperity to the bush in ways people could never have imagined. My family benefited in those years, and living in rural Australia was seen as truly Australian and desirable.

On 10 December 1949 Robert Menzies became Prime Minister, ending eight years of Labor rule and beginning the longest period of Coalition government in our history. I was eight years old and thought of Ming as king. I was thirty-one years old before another Federal Labor government was elected.

But in the forties Australia had faced extinction. It had not been prepared for war. Much of what has happened since was a response to that threat. Geoffrey Blainey described it as 'the loudest of wake-up calls'. My story reflects how much a child of the forties I was and am.

CHAPTER ONE

FIRST FAMILIES

The number in the birth register is 35,703 in District 493. Wendy Elizabeth, female, was born at Kallara Private Hospital on 22 July 1941 in Orange, NSW. The parents were William Rex Ryan and Audrey McGillivray Taylor. William Rex describes his occupation as a drover and Audrey McGillivray, as was customary for the time, did not state her occupation, simply her maiden name and birthplace. The certificate states they were married at Orange and had no previous issue.

I read my birth certificate for the first time in September 1964 when Gordon, my fiancé, obtained a copy as required for a passport. It made me think how little I knew about my parents' wedding and courtship. Certainly I had absorbed from my mother's mother that my parents were mad about each other; they had been engaged for six months and were determined to be married, although my mother was only eighteen. But I had forgotten that she was christened Audrey, a name she has never been called; my father was always known as Bill.

I was intrigued to read that my father described himself as a drover. Was this his quirky sense of humour or was he still moving sheep from the Coonamble property of his family? I had heard of him being a grazier, a stock and station agent and, for a fleeting period, a commercial traveller, but a drover was not an occupation I was aware of. I did not like the idea at all and filed it away as something to find out about later. At the time I was in the midst of my own wedding plans and it made me think about how we are all recorded and defined in these ways and how much information is missing. My own

5

memory probably reveals my predisposition to romantic interpretations of events and my abiding need to define my own boundaries.

Let me tell you the story of the Ryans and the Taylors as I know it.
It will be no surprise to you to discover that the Ryans came from
Ireland, the Taylors from Scotland and England. For about ten years
they lived across the road from each other in Orange, but saw themselves as quite different people—in country towns the divide between
graziers and townspeople was wide.

The Taylors had a large block of land which included an orchard
and a vegetable garden, as well as a modest but comfortable house
for their six children. They were country town folk. The Ryans were
from Coonamble, their business was sheep and wool. Their cottage
in Orange had been bought as a base for their daughters, who
attended the Presbyterian Ladies College in Orange. It was not until
the death of my grandfather that this place became a permanent home
to my grandmother.

I loved both my grandmothers, different though they were. My
maternal grandmother, Nana Taylor, grew up in Andover, England,
in a comfortable family. She met my grandfather Jock when he was
in England on leave from Gallipoli. Migrating to Australia with no
domestic skills, she became an expert seamstress and provider for her
six children. Her dressmaking was legendary: she made my father's
first long pants and my mother remembers her sewing well into the
early hours of the morning to add to the family income.

Her husband, John McGillivray Taylor, worked in the Post Office
and was passionate about music, especially when he was conducting
any of the various bands he had established. He had a reputation as
a mean and hard Scot. He was of little significance in my life. My
mother always seemed slightly fearful of him and thought him a hard
husband and father. There was no generosity in him, either of purse
or spirit.

In my lifetime Nana Taylor was separated from her husband,
although never divorced. John was transferred to Broken Hill Post
Office. As she had no desire for him, or for life in Broken Hill, she used
his promotion as an opportunity to move to Tamworth to be near her
two favourite, hard-working sons. She was a soft and gentle soul who

asked little for herself and was always generous with what she had.

The last time I saw grandfather John I was about seventeen and attending university, about which he was very proud. He was living alone in an austere, dark farmhouse in Minto, surrounded by books. My mother felt she should visit him, and so we went together. He gave me a silver vase and his copy of Boccaccio's *Decameron Nights* when we left. I treasure them as a family link and often wonder who he really was.

Will Ryan, my father's father, died before I was born, so his influence survives only in family folklore, and in a few photographs and some stories. A piece, written after his death in 1934 at the age of 58, is treasured within the family. It was written by his former teacher Mr William Hagen in a letter to *Country Life*.

> 'Billy and I were great mates in the grassy west in those days of the early nineties. He was the apt and big-hearted pupil and I was the newly-appointed teacher. Elsie Phelps was also a pupil of the old Milchomi and Cashel half-time school. Since then I have been in many centres from Come-by-Chance in the west to Longreach in the north, at times like Wolseley riding the waves of glory, but more often like Hopeful, on the rocks of despair, and if I were asked to write a name in letters of gold it would be "Will Ryan of Cashel".'

It is family folklore that for a long time Elsie Mary Phelps and William Ryan were engaged to be married, but as she was Methodist and he Catholic, a common religion could not be agreed. Marrying across religions, then, was akin to marrying across cultures now. Finally, Will Ryan and Elsie Mary were married on 22 December 1910 at the Pilliga School of Arts with the Reverend Bonner of Coonamble officiating. It had been agreed that the children would be christened Methodists but that, when his time came, William Ryan would still receive the last rites and be buried as a Catholic in the family vault at Rookwood. The local paper described the bride as looking charming in 'a trained white ivory Japanese silk gown trimmed with white silk fish-wife net of real lace. She was attended by three bridesmaids'. The report notes approvingly that the presents were numerous, and in some instances 'costly'.

Will and Elsie had three children between 1914 and 1920. My father William Rex, or Bill, was the middle child and only boy. He grew up on the Coonamble property Ellim-eek, an environment of horses, wide open plains and an annual cycle of life which followed sheep. But when he was only eighteen, his father died, and he assumed the responsibility for the family property. During those Depression years he drove mobs of sheep for months at a time and survived by buying and selling sheep which he fed and agisted on the public stock routes. In his own terms he was, as he wrote on my birth certificate, a drover.

Bill's sister Bubbles (christened Myra) was 'a bit funny'. She had meningitis when she was a baby—something for which Coonamble could offer little medical attention. Bubbles often had convulsions and certainly suffered from epilepsy. She couldn't read or write, but loved stories being read to her. As children we had to be nice to Bubbles, even when she was mean to us. The worst thing that could happen was that—even though she was so much bigger—you would have to take her down the street and risk meeting someone you knew who would laugh at her or feel sorry for you.

My grandmother's life in Orange revolved around Bubbles' needs and she led a frugal life so that when she died, Bubbles would be provided for. Her constant anxiety was that Bubbles would be put in Bloomfield Mental Hospital because no-one would know how to manage her.

In Nana Ryan's house the radio was a constant companion and the ABC was the voice of authority. Her days began and ended with the ABC news. It was on her kitchen radio that I heard Sedgeman and McGregor win the Davis Cup. And it was there that I became addicted to my first soap, *Blue Hills*. When the *Blue Hills* theme music started, all other activities were suspended as we sat down for the daily episode.

My mother didn't listen to soaps and was rather dismissive of them, especially when I announced that I wanted to listen to *Portia Faces Life*. She suggested I return to *The Search for the Golden Boomerang*, which I thought was childish. Indeed, it is here that I should confess

I was not an ABC Argonaut and actually thought *The Argonauts* rather silly compared with the grown up dramas I was listening to.

Soon after Nana Ryan died her eldest daughter Shirley, left with the care of Bubbles, admitted her to Bloomfield. After a stay of twenty years, when I was forty-six, Bubbles died there. It remains a source of pain to me that I did not visit her, that I didn't even know she was alive, until notified by the Office of the Public Defender that she had left her cumulative pension to me.

My father was witty, entertaining and fun and liked to be the performer at the party. It's easy to see how he swept my mother off her feet. She was beautiful, very young and inexperienced. Against her wishes, my mother had to leave school early to contribute to the family income. She has always had good taste and great style and, I think, would rather go barefoot than wear the wrong shoes. She has an abiding fear of not looking right or, worse, looking like someone who was disadvantaged. In our family, poverty, or the look and smell of it, were to be avoided no matter what. Looking your best was next to Godliness and when we got new clothes we kept them for best. Even now I often keep new things for weeks before I wear them, much to the amusement of my friends.

My father was called up in 1940 and joined the Light Horse Regiment. Some of his peer group have told me he was a larrikin in the army, alternately engaging, charming, and not amenable to authority. When I was working at the Bicentennial Authority I met war historian John Laffin who later wrote to me about him, recalling their time based at Orange Showground in 1944:

> Bill was a militiaman, that is he had an N army number and was expected to fight only in direct defence of Australia. He was a sergeant member of the instructional staff. Bill's job was to convert the men at Orange into competent infantrymen. These men were not exactly ideal soldiers; some of them were tough, rough and rebellious. Some hated the army, and all had been guilty of some army crime or other.
>
> Bill Ryan's great strength in approaching this job was that he could talk their language. Though always firm, he had a

quick, easy smile and a casual manner. I thought several times that he would have made a fine Light Horse trooper of the World War I type.

Bill had more than a streak of the rebel in him and he understood our soldiers better than nearly all the staff. Nothing much worried or frightened him and under pressure he became more relaxed.

There was a streak of the larrikin in him and he did not always stand to attention when speaking to an officer if he did not respect the officer. His salute left something to be desired too. It was rather on the casual side. But his friendly manner showed that he meant no insult or flippancy.

Bill was a happy-go-lucky man and he laughed a lot. He certainly liked to be popular and he was generous and gregarious. The roots of his liking for drink lay in these traits. He just liked to yarn and he did this best with a glass in his hand. The trouble was that he reached the point when he did not know he had had enough. Actually he had quite a capacity ... basically he seemed happy when he had had too much to drink.

He had some fanciful ideas about how he would earn his living after the war. Most soldiers had such ideas. Bill's probably concerned activities in which he would be his own master because the army never owned Bill Ryan.

Bill liked the open country life, and though he was in the army with three stripes, he was not cut out for responsibility. While he did a good job as an NCO, he was really at heart one of the boys. He was a man who loved children. I recall him with affection because of his genuineness and sincerity. He put on no airs and graces and there was no pretence about him. He was just Bill Ryan.

My father wanted us to think of ourselves as country children. Every Saturday morning, from the age of three, I was taken to riding school in Orange, a block away from the main street. I loved the smell of the place, the gentle horses, my jodphurs, and riding on the front of the saddle with my father who would make everyone laugh.

Those early years were precious. Always there were horses, and I remember only happiness. When we moved into our little, modern, brick semi in Prince Street there was even room in the yard for a fat white pony called Judy to stay overnight. Our family friends, the Kables, whose father Viv was in the infantry with Bill, lived not far away. I adored their children, Jan, Alistair and Fran—they were a little older and took me everywhere with them.

It seems in my life I've never been far away from schools. They are places I mostly love and respond to. Their camaraderie and sense of order make me feel secure. I was usually a happy schoolgirl. My own school life began when I was three, in a little bluestone building next to the Holy Trinity Anglican Church in downtown Orange. To give a child a pre-school experience was, in the forties, an enlightened decision. I can't imagine how my very young mother, who had not had that benefit herself, could have been so persistent and far-sighted. I loved the brown uniform, the school badge, the sense of belonging to something special and having friends. I am still in touch with my first and best schoolfriend, Gael Knepfner, and our mothers remain in contact.

The Principal of Trinity Grammar was a large, noisy woman, Mrs Pender-Brooks, whose double-barrelled name helped cover up her educational deficiencies. She ran a rigorous campaign to convert my left-handedness, despite my parents' advice that it would be a waste of time. And, indeed, I remain left-handed. Yet she ran Trinity as a free-flowing school where we were encouraged to read and tell stories—still my favourite pastimes. Classes were arranged to suit the skills of the children and we could be in different levels according to the activity. I had three happy years there and when I left, at seven, I had already skipped one class and established a reputation as an enthusiastic schoolgirl with a 'retentive memory'.

In 1945 my brother Kerry was born. My mother was very sure that she wanted her children well-spaced. Her own mother had six children in seven and a half years and she didn't want that happening to her. So I had been an only child for four years, accustomed to being the centre of attention. But I did not resent the move off centre-stage when Kerry arrived. I thought him adorable, but was not excessively interested in him—involved as I was in grown-up things like kindergarten and birthday parties. He seemed to make my parents happy and that was fine.

My mother was finding her feet socially in Orange and flourishing in her role as young wife and mother. My father, however, was not content to live a town life. Work post-war was uncertain, but eventually he found a job with Farmers and Graziers, a stock and station agency, where at least he worked with country people and stock. His performance skills were useful for his auctioneering role, but he really wanted to be back on the land. When Bing Crosby and the Andrews Sisters crooned 'Don't Fence Me In', my father sang along with passion and I absorbed that yearning and love for space and endless horizons.

Years later, ABC Television broadcast the BBC production of *The Singing Detective* and I found the soundtrack extraordinarily poignant, as so many of the songs were songs my father sang. Most of all I remember 'Don't Fence Me In'. When I was asked to identify some desert-island discs for a radio program I surprised myself by nominating it. I know it as well as the Twenty-Third Psalm.

> *Oh give me land, lots of land under starry skies above*
> *Don't fence me in*
> *Let me ride through the wide open country that I love*
> *Don't fence me in*
> *Let me be by myself in the evening breeze and*
> *Listen to the murmur of the cottonwood trees*
> *Send me off forever but I ask you please*
> *Don't fence me in.*
>
> *I want to ride to the ridge where the West commences,*
> *And gaze at the moon till I lose my senses,*
> *I can't look at hobbles and I can't stand fences*
> *Don't fence me in.*

I have not found a cottonwood tree, despite a lifetime of searches. The song has always been a theme for me. I don't want to be fenced in—I need room to move.

CHAPTER TWO

GROWING UP IN COUNTRY NSW

Some years ago I was asked to open an exhibition called 'My Mum Stayed at Home'. Since then that's been my metaphor for the fifties, the decade of my adolescence. Everyone's mum aspired to stay home and have a real man provide for them. This was the model family, the one to covet. Two parents, a stay-at-home mother and three children. We reflected that family formation and aspiration, and I knew of no women who worked for money. Similarly, one assumed without question that one's mother would be there at all times. Many men called their wives Mum. But that did not happen in our family.

Though the assisted immigration scheme of the previous decade continued in the fifties, it had been so successful that the government had to cut back the intake from 170,000 in 1952 to less than 80,000 in 1953. In Central Western NSW we saw no evidence of these profound changes, for life on the land was prosperous and graziers were still seen as a cut above the average in social terms. When wool prices hit unknown heights in the fifties, we rejoiced that we, like our nation, rode on the sheep's back, and praised the government that had introduced the soldier settlement scheme so that men like my father had the opportunity to be farmers and graziers again.

By the end of the fifties the car had become the symbol of prosperity. Even young people coveted and acquired them. In 1955 the law changed in NSW and permitted hotels to stay open after 6 p.m.— a sign of decadence if we had ever seen one. Worse was to come, as we abandoned Howard Keel and the crooners for 'Rock Around the

Clock', sung by Bill Haley and the Comets and, not long after, our own Wild One, Johnny O'Keefe.

In 1956 Australia had two firsts: television was introduced and the Olympic Games were held in Melbourne. Australians revelled in the Games and the success of our competitors. Overnight we found new heroic models and reaffirmed our love of sport. For Australians like us, these were good times and we believed without question that this was the best place in the world.

Change in our life came quickly. Security and certainty disappeared overnight. My father was offered a job managing a sheep station called Nanangro, on the Murrumbidgee River south of Goulburn. But as the property was remote and my mother was pregnant, it was agreed that my father would work on the property and we would stay in Goulburn. This sounded exciting. And we would have our own horses.

Looking back now, it seems that this was my father's first serious escape from domestic responsibility—it began a pattern he would repeat for the rest of his life. But we could not recognise those signs then. We settled in Goulburn in a little brick cottage in the centre of town, and my sister Deborah was born there soon after. Betty the 'mother's help' joined us. I was seven and a half years old and Kerry nearly four. My memories are almost all of my mother, an attractive young matron enjoying the life of picnic races and the polo scene. I remember her as glamorous and wearing beautiful clothes. I have little memory of my father's presence in Goulburn during the six months we lived there.

At Goulburn North school I was told that I was not clever, cute or appealing, and that I would be repeating third class as I was far too young to enter fourth class. Goulburn North was a shock, my first public co-educational school, an unhappy place of which every memory is negative. I was teased for being different, I hadn't been to a state school before, and the kids said my mother was a snob ... yet I do not recall her ever being at the school. The playground was a tough place. I was not the only child tyrannised: the Balts had a hard time too. This was my introduction to 'Balts' and 'reffos' and it took me quite a while to work out who they were and why they were despised.

It was especially hard to understand why these girls, with their thick blonde plaits like Heidi in *The Swiss Family Robinson*, could not be admired. To a girl like me, with thin brown hair, they were gorgeous. The children of workers on the Snowy Mountains Scheme, they came with different accents and different sandwiches. In the classroom I sat next to a beautiful girl from Estonia who was clever and friendly, but our parents made it clear that this friendship was not to continue outside the school fence. After school we dispersed to different lives. Goulburn, like most Australian country towns, was fearful of difference and the local children reflected and articulated the prejudices of their families. I hated the place.

I can recall visiting my father at Nanangro only a couple of times. Nanangro was remote and scary. Visits were a major expedition that involved driving to the Murrumbidgee River, and boarding a punt to cross the river. Then a horse and sulky journey on narrow, hilly tracks for miles to the manager's house where my father was living. The river there was turbulent, cold and pristine and the trees were tall and ghostly. I'd never seen alpine country, and even the horses seemed different.

My father was rounding up wild brumbies and had chosen one, Bobtail, to break in. This involved chasing him and then strapping up one of his legs to get on him. Invariably it attracted an audience. Bobtail terrified Kerry and me, so we were given quiet ponies to ride. Even if they were not very well-mannered, these ponies would be ridden constantly before our arrival so that they would be too exhausted to bolt with us.

Nanangro was not a happy place for our family. We could sense the tension between our parents. It was a life for single men and, I suspect, a life not unlike the life my father had enjoyed as a young man. To my mother, with two children and a new baby, life in Goulburn must have looked a lot better than life at Nanangro.

In no time at all my father received a letter to say that he had won a block of land in a soldier settlement ballot. The block was a subdivision of the Boyd Estate and was part of the post-war soldier settlement scheme. We were off to a place called Garema, seventeen miles west of Forbes. It was totally unknown territory.

My mother was apprehensive. She had three young children and had moved only six months before but my father dismissed all objections. He had won the ballot and, I think, considered it his natural entitlement to be back on the land and have us together as a family.

We arrived at Garema in 1948. It was yellow, brown and flat—just one hill could be seen on the horizon. Our 1000-acre block was fenced, but had no buildings, no sheds and of course, no house—not even a post box where the mail could be delivered. The dominant buildings of Garema village were the wheat silos on the railway siding. To me as a child they seemed enormous. Our block was best suited to mixed farming, which meant that my father couldn't be the grazier he wanted to be. For a couple of years in the wool boom he concentrated on sheep and wool, but it was a short period of good times, and those of our neighbours who planted wheat prospered.

Our property was named Ellim-eek after the Coonamble property of my father's family and our first home was a large tent with an outside fire and a copper. We kids thought this was fun for a week or so, but as it rained and rained our 'home' lost its appeal and we fantasised about a real house. So my father organised for us to live in a long row of shearers' huts on a property some miles away, until we could afford to build a house.

We set up house in the long, dark green, wooden building. Shearers' accommodation was not designed for a young family and it required a great deal of ingenuity to reach the degree of comfort my mother established. From a child's perspective, being near the creek was fun and a source of endless entertainment. This view abruptly shifted, though, whenever the creek flooded the place and we had to be rescued—usually by the neighbours, as Daddy would be 'away', our code for on a drinking bout. When not 'away' he would be the rescuing hero and we would be so proud of him.

When we arrived at Garema it was suggested that Kerry and I would do school by correspondence. This had been a hugely exciting prospect for us—we reckoned we would mostly play, as our mother would be too busy with Deborah to teach us anything. Alas it was not to be, as correspondence lessons were not allowed because the Garema school was within the qualifying distance.

Garema Public was a one-teacher school in the little railway-siding village and welcomed us warmly—the school population was in need of extra pupils to remain viable. Twenty-five seemed the base number, but there was always a floating number of five to seven pupils whose fathers were railway fettlers.

Imagine a weatherboard portable building with an entry porch, one classroom and one teacher. In the playground there were two lavatories—one for the girls and one for the boys—and a weathershed. Most of my time here was spent reading, singing along with ABC radio or helping the smaller kids with their spelling and their tables. It was a happy time. Our teacher, responsible for all grades, was always busy, so I played the role of good girl and the teacher's helper, or retreated to my own world of books.

I rode my black Malvern Star bicycle three miles there and back from third class—yes, I had to do third class again—through to sixth class. At special times, when the road was wet and my bike would get bogged, I was allowed to ride my favourite pony, Stella. She was a grey pony over twenty years old and didn't mind having three or four on her back, so sometimes I would double Kerry on her. When we arrived at school she would be happy to be tied up at the fence for the day, with a break for rides for kids who didn't have a pony.

I don't remember there ever being more than one other person in my class at primary school at Garema. My classmate and best friend, Sue Tout, came from a well-established property, 'Uah', some miles away. We competed for first and second place more or less evenly—but could say we'd always come first or second in our class! After she went to a Sydney boarding school at the end of fifth class I was the only pupil in grade six.

As well as the children of the railway fettlers, the Garema school pupils came from the families of graziers, wheat cockies and the village shopkeeper and postmistress. The teachers (always men) struggled to be part of the local community and to apply a veneer of civilisation to their students. This was a melting pot of Australian rural society, and the social and class distinctions were drawn early—only those who left Garema would make it, and they were the graziers' children.

Years later when I read Sally Morgan's book, *My Place*, my brain went *click* as I realised that the black children at Garema school had been Aboriginal, not Indian. Told that they were Indian, we had had no reason to disbelieve it. Now I wonder how Australia kept those secrets about blacks. What conspiracy was it that had us all thinking that Aboriginal people were Indian? Why was it better to be Indian?

The Dunn family was a large Aboriginal fettler family. School attendance for the Dunn kids followed the rhythm of their father's work cycle on the railway. We loved it when they were there for the school picnic day because they could all run fast. Reggie Dunn was my special friend for a while, and he was always in demand for the football and relay teams. In 1999 at a conference on Reconciliation where I was a speaker, a woman in the audience said she was related to the Dunns and their mother actually was Indian.

Other exotic people passed through Garema. At the creek near the school we would often see caravans of 'gypsies'. Their society was absolutely off limits to all local children, whose mothers warned them of unknown terrors that would befall those who played with gypsy children. This, of course, added mightily to their attraction, and often I would go down and peep at the exotic haberdashery in the caravans.

Eventually, my pony Stella died a legendary death. When sheltering against the outside dunny one night she slipped in. Early the next morning, as my father entered the toilet, he was terrified and distressed to hear the sounds of her suffering. Sadly she never came out of the dunny. It was filled in on top of her and relocated. That ended school pony rides.

By the age of ten I knew, albeit in a childish and inarticulate way, that my father drank too much and could not accept prolonged responsibility. Country children are either at school or at home, and so see a lot of their parents. My father was often moody and violent. He lied about his drinking, which made me angry and sorry. Travelling back from Forbes could take hours while he made short stops to examine 'engine problems'. It was clear to us children that the journey home from town did not require ten engine checks. After each swig beneath the bonnet, his driving became more erratic and we would cry and ask him to stop. We could never rely on my father.

On one memorable day my mother was sewing and asked me to keep an eye on Deborah, my little sister, who was crawling everywhere. I was only half concentrating, when I heard a dreadful scream. My horse Starlight was tied up at the fence. My sister had crawled between her legs and had been kicked in the head. She was unconscious, and blood was pouring out of her head.

We had no vehicle on the place, so my father hopped onto Starlight and galloped over to the neighbour's place for help. Our neighbour's car took Deborah and my parents to the hospital. There my sister battled for her life and the doctors warned of brain damage.

It was too much for my father. After the first few hours he disappeared—on a bender—leaving my mother to handle things. The biggest thing was to be there when Deborah regained consciousness: we would find out then if she was brain damaged. Amazingly she wasn't. But when it was time to return home, my father was still nowhere to be found. One of the neighbours took my mother to the hospital to bring Deborah home. A day or so later, my father returned—contrite, remorseful, hung-over but sober . . . what puzzled me was that he adored his little girl, yet he had abandoned her. I think this added to my understanding that he couldn't cope with stress. I was very happy to see Deborah home—she had looked so frail lying in hospital on sandbags, which immobilised her. I often think of this incident and think how well my parents handled my feelings. I was meant to be watching her and I could have been blamed. I wasn't—it was treated as an accident.

A social worker today might describe our family life as dysfunctional: the family income was unreliable and unpredictable, my father had a drinking problem. And yet that doesn't really tell much of the story. It doesn't tell you that I felt loved, encouraged and nurtured by both my parents. Oh, yes, we learned to stay out of sight and never provoke our father when he was drinking, but we were encouraged to read books and to dream of other lives we might lead.

We often played our favourite game, 'What Would We Do If We Won The Lottery?' Our wishes were simple: a new house, a car (not a truck), boarding school fees—and a father who didn't drink. Our world was divided into two zones of experience and they demanded different behaviours. There were clear distinctions between when Daddy was drinking and when he was sober.

Initially the drinking sessions were few and far between. Those were the good times, when we'd be laughing, singing, playing games, joking—in many ways the model of a happy family. The good times were seasonal, a common story for country children. A good season could cover up many tensions with the cushion of money. We would have new clothes and books, and summer holidays were planned at the beach. Our parents would go to parties and our father would sing.

Then there were the dark times, when he'd come weaving up the road, the truck going from one side to the other. We would run to bed and pretend to be asleep—but really we were lying there ready to defend Mummy if he flew into a rage. Sometimes he would stay away for days and the neighbours would come and check on us. They would have seen him somewhere on a bender. Don and Dulcie Doust and Bruce and Val McDonald were great friends, wonderful neighbours. We adored them and I loved listening to Val talk of her war service and Dulcie of her pre-married life as a nursing sister at Manly Hospital—romantic, adventurous, exotic occupations. They fired my imagination.

As the end of our days at Garema came near, my parents were getting anxious about secondary school. Mr Kay, my teacher, thought I should sit for a state bursary, to help with the costs of secondary education. No one doubted that I would be successful, so I was not prepared in any way. I sat for the exam feeling confident. It was a shock to open the mathematics paper and find it almost incomprehensible. Knowing my tables did not seem to be much help. I didn't win a bursary.

There was now palpable anxiety about where I would attend secondary school. Only one thing was certain: I had to leave home. There was no school bus into Forbes, which was seventeen miles away, and most of the boarding schools of choice were in Sydney. The last-ditch option would be the local convent. But that represented desperation—the Anglicans hated the Catholics, whom they saw as socially inferior.

My mother still desperately wanted me to go to boarding school in Sydney. So although my father's financial position made it increasingly unlikely, we persevered with the enrolment. Queenwood at Balmoral was the chosen place. Then, out of the blue, they decided to close their boarding houses. Schools of similar price range were explored then, until Claremont at Randwick was chosen. The maroon and grey uniforms were bought—and I thought them fantastic. I could see myself as Wendy of the Upper Fifth, just like all those books I had read about smart English schoolgirls called Hilary of the Upper Sixth.

But reality finally set in. A Sydney boarding school was not affordable. The uniforms and the hat were returned to David Jones and a far cheaper place was found for me. I would board at St John's Anglican Hostel and I would be a pupil at Forbes Intermediate High School, which was adjacent to the hostel.

Garema Primary proved to be a suitable cultural preparation for secondary school. In both places we sang 'Rule Britannia', 'Land of Hope and Glory' and 'God Save the King'. We celebrated Empire and Arbour Day and joined the Gould League of Bird Lovers. Our elders still referred to England as Home and hoped one day to visit. Our literature was English, with the exception of *We of the Never Never* and *The Man from Snowy River*. At home I was reading *The Cruel Sea* (unexpurgated edition) and *The Dam Busters*.

It was 1952 when I began my secondary education at Forbes Intermediate High School. I was thrilled to be back in school uniform. In first year there were three streamed classes, of which only IA took Maths 1 and 2, French and Latin. I was placed there, but the year I started there was no Latin teacher. It's one of the great regrets of my life that I didn't study Latin.

All girls did Domestic Science, a subject I loathed. The cooking and sewing teachers were prissy and I could not see the point in making bloomers large enough to cover two people. Those teachers did not like the A-stream girls and tried to cut them down to size. But this only made me determined to show them—and I did it by coming first in domestic science in the year, as well as by being cheeky.

Forty-odd intermediate high schools were scattered throughout

New South Wales. They struggled to offer the teaching options of larger schools. Their objective was to educate and retain children until the end of compulsory school age—then fourteen years and ten months. To have a full high school was a source of pride to a town. When Forbes Intermediate High became a full high school in 1953 and prepared its students for the Leaving Certificate, the Forbes *Advocate* was fulsome.

By good fortune, there were some very able children in my intake at Forbes High School. We pushed each other along, with much help from our skilful teachers. Of the fourteen people out of that first year intake who ended up presenting for the Leaving Certificate, more than half are university graduates and/or successful corporate and civic leaders. There are some distinguished Australian achievers among them: Bruce Mackellar and Phillip Shirvington are two who enjoy international recognition in science.

School was all consuming. There was no activity that escaped my curiosity and engagement. I loved the opportunities offered for team games, opportunities denied children in schools with tiny populations. I turned out to be competent at hockey and softball, which meant I could play in the local town competition. It provided a sense of community and belonging that I craved, and it helped ease my anxiety about my mother's position at home. When my father went on a bender life was hard, money was scarce, and it was my mother who had to hold it all together. Simple but drastic inconveniences occur for a family with one vehicle living in a fairly remote place. If the vehicle is away the family is grounded, and for some time there was no telephone service.

By 1953 I was swimming well enough to get into the school swimming team. My moment of great glory was winning the 33–yards breast stroke final. Such achievement was rewarded by selection for the interschool team—and many bus trips to towns that were nearby but seemed faraway because we had heard of them but never been there. Parkes, for example, was only twenty miles away, but far from my experience. This was a pre-travel life. These trips were coveted for the competition they provided, the adventure, and the journey home in the bus when it was dark and boys and girls snuggled up together. It was a powerful incentive to succeed at sport.

I loved living in St John's Hostel. Established by the Anglican Church to assist rural families educate their children through secondary school, it was a remarkable and idiosyncratic experiment. There were forty boarders—twenty girls upstairs and twenty boys downstairs. We all shared the domestic chores. Our Warden was Don Shearman, an Anglican minister aged twenty-seven who had been a Bush Brother and had had a short time in the airforce. He and his wife Faye were newly married when they were posted to St John's. We were, to a girl, in love with him and with their young marriage.

My arrival at St John's coincided with a rush of Wendys—there were four, so I was called Chick at the hostel. Life at St John's offered experiences that I'd only known from books. I listened to my first classical music on Saturday nights there. And Don Shearman, also called Padre, introduced us to many aspects of life we knew little about, including religion. What an unusual education it was, to be boarding at a co-ed institution, attending a co-ed school and establishing relationships so early in life. At the time it seemed perfectly normal. We were encouraged to have friendships with both boys and girls, and from the age of eleven I always had a boyfriend. These boyfriends could be met at drama, sport or the school social.

The monthly school social was a very serious event, for it was there that girls particularly were taught their social roles. No dancing until the teacher said, 'Gentlemen, take your partners.' The twelve-year-old gentlemen slid across the floor, made slippery by a preparation known as Pops, to grab a girl for the Foxtrot, the Pride of Erin or the Barn Dance. Our teachers had impressed on us those lines: 'Girls, don't be bold. Wait to be asked to dance.' They stayed with me throughout life, and even at eleven I knew that to be a wallflower was social death.

School was a seemingly endless time of learning, friendships, dances, sport, playing by the river, belonging to teams. I was so happy in the conviviality of the boarding situation that I usually chose not to go home for the weekend.

In the fifties the Education Department provided incentives for its teachers to do country service; those who wished to progress in the system embraced that option to increase their opportunities for promotion. Forbes Intermediate High would not have been a particularly desirable post, as Forbes was a small town and the school was not classified as a full high school. Yet I think we were blessed with our teachers who worked hard to broaden our horizons. We had an Indian geography teacher, Frank Brown, who also ran the local amateur dramatic society *and* coached our hockey team with great skill. Our maths teacher, who was German, was determined that we would not leave school without being numerate, and our French teacher struggled with our pronunciation and imagination.

During this period I received an unexpected bonus—a Christian education. At the hostel we attended church three times a week, and as I prepared for my first communion, I moved easily into the language of the High Church mass and evensong. My mother swears that it was during this period that I talked about becoming a nun. Each week a few of us went to church and polished the altar brass with great love and devotion. The legacy is an ease and familiarity with the worship of the Anglican Church.

There were growing pressures on my family. My father's drinking had worsened, the time between benders was decreasing and money was an issue. If I thought my father was in town, I was careful not to go past any of his favourite drinking spots in case I ran into him.

I worried constantly about how my mother was managing with Kerry and Deborah. At some stage when I was in high school, the telephone was connected at Ellim-eek and she and I would have long conversations in semi-code about 'how things were'. I knew that my part of the deal was to be a good girl—to succeed at school and St John's, so that I could stay there.

After the first year, my father couldn't pay the fees at the hostel. Padre (Don Shearman) and my mother searched for funds for my schooling. They discovered the Canteens Trust Fund, set up from the proceeds of the staff canteens during the Second World War for the children of ex-servicemen. School reports had to be provided and reviewed each year. This was a strong reason for me to succeed at school—and the fund supported me to the end of my fourth year at high school.

After the Intermediate Certificate at the end of the third year many of my friends left school. It was easy to find work in banks, on the farm and in local shops. Leaving school at Intermediate level was the preferred option in most families. Many people questioned the need to waste education on girls, when they were going to get married anyway. My mother, though, supported by Padre and the teachers at school, ensured that I would stay on to finish high school, even though things were fairly tough at home. And so I went into fourth year at fourteen, making subject choices that gave me the broadest possible opportunity for further education.

This was a great year. There were only fourteen in our class. I was a prefect both at school and the hostel, and cherished the responsibilities. In retrospect I was lucky to have the experience so early, since 1956 was a year of family tumult. At Garema, Ellim-eek had to be sold as the debtors were circling. To this day I cannot recall our departure from Ellim-eek as I was left at the hostel. Amazingly, my father was offered a position as manager of a large remote sheep station, Gunyawarildi, at Warialda in north-western NSW. Full of contrition and with promises to stay sober, he persuaded my mother to go to Warialda with him. Kerry and Deb were to attend the little bush school there.

But Warialda was a nightmare. My father's drinking was right out of control and it was clear he would not last in the job very long. He was frustrated, humiliated, self-reproaching and violent, especially towards my brother Kerry. My mother, in searing heat and ugly circumstances, was doing her best to make a home out of the manager's residence, which turned out to be a horrid little fibro house.

It had been agreed that for my last year of high school I would board with some family friends, the Beckenhams, and attend Tamworth High. It was not a prospect I looked forward to. I had been happy and felt a great sense of belonging and security where I was, and to move for the last year of secondary schooling was very unsettling. Any rewards that would have been offered at the end of school were denied to me now, as I was starting all over again. But I can't remember feeling any particular resentment, just acceptance, since I wanted to be near my family. At the end of the school year I said my farewells to Forbes and headed for Warialda for the Christmas holidays.

I was immediately confronted by what I'd conveniently forgotten while at school. The deterioration in my father's behaviour was shocking, and I begged my mother to leave him. I was truly frightened he would hurt her. A couple of times we did abandon my father, when the pressure got too heavy and there was no money to live on. But we invariably returned, because we believed that he cared about us and wanted to be better. And we wanted to be a family.

At last, though, my mother packed up again and left Warialda. It was a dramatic exit and done in secrecy. Again my Nana Taylor took us in. And again Bill sobered up and found a job managing a property at Breeza, near the village of Currabubula. Seduced by the promises, the lack of options and the pleasant living conditions there, we all agreed to try yet again. The place had a marvellous house. For a while things seemed to be working. Deb caught the bus to the village school at Currabubula, Kerry went to Farrer Agricultural High School at Tamworth and I continued to board privately in Tamworth with Wal and Ruby Beckenham and their three boys. We played tennis on the property, Kerry and Deb had their tonsils out, and there was a breathing space.

Being a new girl in fifth year at Tamworth High was a culture shock. I had left a group of fourteen in the fourth year at Forbes High School and moved into a group of more than seventy students. These Tamworth students were light years away from my peer group in Forbes. They drank, smoked, drove cars and listened to *My Fair Lady*! I might have come from outer space in terms of my experience. Even my subject choices were not compatible with the timetable of Tamworth, and parts of my physics and chemistry course had to be individually supervised by a science teacher who made it clear that it was a total waste of his time. It was bad enough to have a girl doing physics and chemistry. Any boy who chose to be my partner in the experiments was treated as a sissy or a sex maniac. It was my first experience of an ugly teacher. It made me determined that I'd get a better pass than the rest of the class and when the numbers went up at the end of the year, I had got an A-level pass in Combined Physics and Chemistry.

My history teacher, Mr Dooley, taught by dictation, a method I'd never come across before. His wife, who did my career counselling during the year, advised me strongly to apply for physiotherapy because it was, she said, the most 'marriageable' course at Sydney University. I wondered what she was talking about.

Tamworth High School was my first experience of a community where girls were groupies and observers rather than participants. At Forbes there hadn't been enough boys to play in the team, so we had to have girls. But in Tamworth the clever girls chose not to play sport—they saw sport and drama as opposites. This was incomprehensible to me; I represented the school in hockey, swimming and ball games but did not make the school play that year.

Although I was self-conscious about my father and his unpredictable behaviour, my classmates at Tamworth thought it quite exotic that he managed a property and that we lived in a homestead out in the bush. As the year came to a close, there was a lot of pressure on me to have an end-of-school party. Ours was a lovely house and garden, and I wanted to share it ... but I was afraid that my father would not be able to manage forty eighteen-year-olds and would retreat into alcohol.

In the end my mother and I decided to take the risk, and I asked forty people to the party. At midday, my father started drinking. I became deeply anxious. When it began to pour with rain—an inch of rain on the road between Tamworth and Breeza would make it impassable—I sat in my room praying that the rain would continue.

And it did. At about 5 p.m. I rang up one of the sensible boys who had a car. I said he couldn't possibly make it, we'd have to do it another time. He agreed. But about half an hour later he rang back and said, 'No, we've decided to come anyway, we can't bear to think of you sitting out there on your own with all the party prepared.'

I protested, but to no avail. The slippery roads were seen as a challenge. Most of the guests turned up. My father skulked around, much to my embarrassment. But he was not as visible as he might have been. My mother, feeling extremely anxious, got very stroppy when she found people kissing in the garden. When the last one left after midnight, my sense of relief was overwhelming. That was my school finale.

I've never discussed the party with anyone who attended it. I have no idea whether they knew or felt anything of the background drama. An interesting feature of living with an alcoholic is that while you're totally tuned in to what's going on and aware of his behaviour, many other people don't notice it and just accept it as part of the person. One also needs to decide on tactics for managing life with an alcoholic. Right from the time I was aware of my father's problems, and probably knew that other people knew our awful secret, I never ever spoke to any of my friends about it. The exception was Padre, in whom I could confide—indeed I had to, because of the fees. But I acted as though we were a regular and intact family, not at all dysfunctional. It was our problem and we did not want to talk about it. I didn't want to hear 'Poor Wendy'. That strategy of survival paid off. We might have been down and out at times, but we never looked like it for we were always well fed and well dressed. Success at school was a wonderful buffer against pity and disparaging comments and we were all competent and well behaved at our various schools.

Despite Mrs Dooley's advice on taking a 'marriagable course', when the time came to put the applications in for scholarships I applied for Arts, with Rural Science as a second preference. I also applied for both Commonwealth and Teachers College Scholarships. The application for the Teachers College Scholarship caused great drama in my family, as it required guarantors in case you forfeited your bond. My father, who disliked authority of any kind, initially refused, and my mother ended up persuading one of my aunts to sign the form with her. But I was disappointed with my Leaving Certificate results: an A in Combined Physics/Chemistry and five Bs—I'd hoped for six As. Still, news came a couple of days later that I had won both Commonwealth and Teachers College Scholarships to the University of New England. It was agreed that I would go.

*

Click to 1997 and I'm driving back to Garema with my husband Gordon to check my memories. At the one-teacher school, only the loos remain to remind me of this place which opened in 1941 and closed in 1971, when the school bus took the local pupils to Forbes. But the wheat silos still dominate—they remind me that this country is best suited to cropping, the activity my father hated.

CHAPTER THREE

ON MY OWN

University in northern NSW in the fifties meant the University of New England in Armidale. Armidale was considered a safe place for country kids. In its favour, it wasn't Sydney, where a girl could easily get into trouble (read: pregnant), and it had an established reputation as a conservative educational centre. 'The city of schools and churches' was its tag.

For many country parents whose daughters were the first generation of girls to attend university, UNE at Armidale was a wonderful option. Professor James Belshaw, Dean of the Faculty of Arts, wrote in the orientation handbook:

> The University of New England is the only university in Australia outside the capital cities and the large urban centres. Because of that it was once described as our 'bucolic University'. Certainly it is a university in a rural environment. It is inevitably, therefore, a residential university. That alone would be enough to set it apart from other universities. Certainly there is no other Australian university that is a university community in quite the same sense.

That made it sound safe for parents who were sending their young daughters. A residential college community was an incentive, as perhaps it was more like a grown-up boarding school.

Over the long post-secondary school vacation, my future had been discussed and the mysteries of university courses had begun to unravel. The attractions of Rural Science were extolled by my father, but Arts was finally agreed upon—once it was established that Arts had nothing to do with drawing, for which I had no aptitude. The next decision was whether to accept the Commonwealth or the Teachers College Scholarship. There was glory attached to winning a Commonwealth Scholarship, but it faded when it was realised that the living allowance would not cover the boarding fees. The £500 teaching scholarship offered a job suitable for a girl. Its drawback was the bond which required repayment or five years of service. Women could marry out of it after three years and everyone assured me that I would easily be married by then so it did not present as a major risk.

Life was sounding better by the minute and I accepted the four-year Secondary Teachers College Scholarship to complete an Arts degree and a postgraduate Diploma in Education. I was on my way to a world no-one in my family had experienced. It was exciting and scary, and yet I was buoyed by the fact that my family was proud of me and were sure I would succeed.

On a hot day in February 1958 my mother and father drove me in our small family car to the University of New England to begin my life as an Arts student. My mother had made me clothes which we hoped would be right for the life of a student, and I wore my new pigskin stacked-heel Bedggood shoes. My father, who was in a sober phase at the time, handed me ten pounds, which he predicted would do me until the May vacation. It seemed generous but, as I recall, lasted only two weeks. Without the Teachers College Scholarship I would have been on the streets. That twenty-eight pounds a month was manna, and when the book allowance of forty pounds arrived I was in heaven.

First impressions were not stunning, as I was placed in Bellevue, a house on the outskirts of both the town and the university. It looked disappointingly domestic, not the Oxbridge spires of my dreams. What did I expect? I know not, for there was no university experience in our family or immediate friends. Perhaps the English images created through our literature classes fuelled expectations beyond an average house in a country town. It was not until we saw the main building, Boolamimbah, with its sweeping grounds and deer park, that the mood changed. This had the sense of place I had hoped for in a university.

A senior student on the Orientation Committee greeted me at UNE. Don Aitkin, a history honours student, seemed extraordinarily sophisticated, mature and handsome. He became a friend and mentor in my first year. Now, forty years later, we share the governance of the University of Canberra, where he is Vice Chancellor and I am Chancellor, still friends and mentors to each other.

But then, I was sixteen years old with ten pounds in my pocket, a new wardrobe and a Teachers College Scholarship which provided an allowance I could live on for the next four years. As my family drove away I felt alone and exhilarated. Life looked good. I already felt grown-up, despite being told by the Registrar that, with two others, I shared the distinction of being the youngest in the year. I really didn't have a clue about what courses to choose, so I stuck to English and History as subjects I knew, and chose Economics, because it sounded smart, and Psychology, because it sounded exotic and people-focused.

First lectures were a surprise. It seemed that lecturers were not teachers. They read their notes for an hour and reminded us that only one in three students would be there next year. I thought this was a weird way to welcome us, but was not too bothered. I told myself that I had really intended to go nursing and had I been the required age (seventeen) and accepted by Royal Prince Alfred Hospital as a nurse trainee, that's what I would be doing. Meanwhile a year at uni sounded good and I would keep the idea of nursing in my head as a defence, just in case I didn't make it. But still, those first lectures were not promising. I hoped university life was going to be more fun than university lectures.

My last advice from my father had been, 'Be careful of mixed drinks. It's a good idea to drink beer.' It turned out to be good advice. Within days I was plunged into a whirl of social activity. Freshers were inducted into university life through every conceivable activity. I joined the Uni Revue and the Hockey Club and attended endless parties. I developed a taste for Pimms, gin slings and any other cocktail some boy was offering me. Three months into the year, as I threw up from an overdose of gin slings, I got smart and learned to love beer. Strangely, given the drinking problems in my family, I don't recall considering abstinence as an option.

That was a fun year of emotional and social, if not intellectual, growth. I enthusiastically threw myself into university activities, learned to smoke and have sex without intercourse. Learning to smoke was a complete turnaround for me. I had spent years nagging my parents about smoking and drinking. However, such is the vulnerability to peer pressure that within weeks I was smoking Stuyvesants and looking very cool, I thought.

The variations on sexual thrills were endless and keeping one's virginity was important for your own self-esteem as well as your reputation. With each new relationship my heart beat faster and I got closer to 'going all the way'. I have no doubt that such lovemaking has wonderful benefits for women's sexuality, as the learning is gradual. I was never burdened by guilt about sex and I was never coerced into sex. I went all the way, as we so quaintly called it, when I was ready and an equal partner.

But intellectually I was struggling. I found Economics dull, so I skipped many lectures; English required a mind more mature than mine and struggling with Chaucer and Middle English was soul destroying. My intellectual curiosity was nurtured only in my History and Psychology courses, both of which I enjoyed. About the beginning of third term, as we began to think of exams, I realised I might not pass. The implications were awful: my first public failure, and loss of my scholarship. Nursing suddenly lost its attraction as an alternative career. Worse still, I might have to get a job, in a shop.

Then my father started drinking heavily again and was fired from his job at Breeza. Amazingly, he found another job, this time at Blayney, near Orange, with a stock and station agency. In fifteen years he had gone full circle. I went to Blayney to visit my family only once, in my first uni holidays. Life there was out of control. Our family had rented half a house in the wrong end of town. My heart ached for my mother and Deborah who had to endure it. For Kerry and me, it was a place to visit in school and university vacations. My mother and Deborah were stuck there. This time Daddy's job lasted for only a few weeks, and as his drinking became acute, he was admitted to Bloomfield Mental Hospital suffering from the DTs. I visited him after he was admitted. He looked pale and sad. I begged him to go to Alcoholics Anonymous, to give himself a chance. He said it was for drunks, not him. He said it would be silly for him to stay in hospital because he really didn't need this sort of treatment. One could only place people in mental homes for a limited period of time, after which they had to agree to remain in, or leave voluntarily. He refused to stay.

That really was the end of the road for our family. After Blayney, we never again lived with my father. He left Bloomfield to stay with his sister and brother-in-law at Manildra. My mother stayed with friends at Garema and then moved to Sydney with Deborah to work. I went back to university, my brother to boarding school. The Canteens Trust fund had come good for Kerry's education too.

At university I made a strategic decision to work hard in History and Psychology, make a last-ditch stand in English and assume Economics was a write-off. For more than half of third term I studied conscientiously and, to my surprise, remembered I liked learning. Assignments were completed. I left the union café scene for the library. In a final flamboyant effort to stay awake longer and study more, I swallowed the then fashionable No-Doz before my first exams. It made no difference except that I felt awful. I left the Economics paper after an hour. Some of my colleagues who stayed have done remarkably well—Don Stammer, Chief Economist at Deutsche Bank and Bernie Fraser, former Governor of the Reserve Bank, to name just two.

My homecoming that Christmas, to the Dousts in Forbes, just a few miles from our old property, was hardly triumphant. I had to decide what to tell my mother about my likely failure at university. How was I going to explain that I had wasted my opportunities when she was struggling yet again with the departure of my father. It was also becoming clear that we could not depend indefinitely on the generosity of our friends the Dousts and the McDonalds.

So it was agreed that I should go to Sydney and find work over the summer break. My Tamworth boarding family, Wal and Ruby

Beckenham, arranged for me to stay with their relatives in Manly. Before the end of December, I was interviewed by the Manly Unemployment Bureau and had found a job as a mother's help for three weeks at Dee Why. For the next three months I worked with four different families, minding their children for five pounds a week and board. The bonus of sorts was that I lived on the northern beaches of Sydney, an area I had very limited experience of until then.

None of this was going to save me. When the names went up, mine appeared in two places only, History and Psychology; I had failed Economics and English. I was now in grave danger of losing my scholarship. That would mean no university life, and no degree. I rang the Department of Education and made an appointment, to ask them for a second chance. I pleaded that the instability of my family circumstances were a contributing factor and, given a second chance, I would do four subjects so that I could still complete my degree in the three years the scholarship offered. Eventually the Department agreed. I returned to UNE in 1959 knowing that I was there by the skin of my teeth. I must now become a proper student, so immediately on my return I knuckled down to work and replaced my Economics course with Geography.

In March I was selected to play for the uni hockey team at Intervarsity in Hobart. Needing money to fund this, I was desperate to find a job when the vacation began. As luck would have it, I noticed a sign asking for domestic help at Dalcross Private Hospital, just a couple of blocks away from Killara, where my mother and Deborah were living at a friend's house. Within a day, I became the hospital cleaner. According to my calculations, I would earn just enough to get me to Hobart for Intervarsity. Even the task of cleaning the theatre after a tonsillectomy failed to deter me.

Then, one week later, my father was dead from a haemorrhaging gastric ulcer and Intervarsity became a distant dream. His death was sudden—we had a phone call from Nana Ryan saying he was in hospital and very ill and wanting to see us. Mummy and I flew to Orange to be with him. He was very ill and frightened. As he worsened, the doctors decided he needed to be in a large Sydney hospital. The ambulance brought him to Royal Prince Alfred Hospital, Ward

C1, in Camperdown. It was dark and frightening. He was remorseful and loving when my mother and I said goodnight.

We were barely asleep when the phone rang at midnight to say he had died from a massive haemorrhage. He was forty-three years old. My reaction was relief—no longer any need to feel guilty or worried about him, just thank God it's over and we are all free. It was better to be a widow than a divorcee and better for one's father to be dead than alcoholic. No more cover-ups and explanations, just the simplicity of the statement: my father's dead.

Family life, family dynamics changed after that. Over an extended period I had been my mother's confidante and adviser and she had been my emotional support. I still played that role—but, eventually, there would be the arrival of a new man on the scene. I would be very happy to withdraw and focus on my life. No Ryan man in the last three generations has lived to sixty. We Ryan children grew up not knowing our grandfather. Now my own children would never meet theirs.

I promised myself again that I would pass my exams in all four subjects so that I wouldn't be a burden on my family. The hospital matron, Olive McIntosh, produced fifty pounds to help our family, and guaranteed work for me. When I returned to UNE I was exhausted but determined to get on top of my academic work.

What is missing from this story so far is the romance and freedom of uni life. Toasting bread on one-bar radiators and talking all night. Walking around the grounds early in the morning hoping no-one would notice you were wearing last night's clothes. Slipping out of men's colleges, and slipping men out of your window when the Principal knocked on the door. Most of all, being in charge of your own life and living with the consequences. Meeting people far removed from our prior existence, French soirees, uni revues, visiting lecturers, my first protest march, football and hockey parties. Wonderful enduring friendships with girls I may never otherwise have met.

Three of my close friends studied Rural Science and had been boarders at Ascham, a Sydney girls school; two others did Arts with me and had been educated in the public school system, like me. We came from all corners of NSW. How could I have thought that I wouldn't miss this life if I failed and went nursing.

And the New England landscape: snow gums and mountains, exotic trees, freezing mornings, amazing stars, frost and snow, deer in the park. All so different from life on the plains of Forbes and Breeza. My first impressions of New England had been misleading, for I had seen only a summer Australian landscape. Living there drew you into a seasonal rhythm I had not experienced before.

Inevitably I fell in love. In 1959 I met a city man/boy who had been sent to Armidale to pick up some extra subjects so that he could return to Sydney and do Law. Alas for his parents, he was a romantic and a dreamer who loved boats, women and the theatre. Law proved an elusive idea. We were a couple within a week of meeting, and remained that way for the two years he attended UNE.

I kept my commitment to the Department of Education. I passed all my subjects, while being fully involved in college and university life. At the end of 1959 I was able to return to Sydney for the summer vacation, happy with my life and looking forward to a vacation job as a nursing aide at Neringah Home of Peace, a home for the terminally ill. There I would learn to pack bed sores, lift immobile people and lay out corpses. I also learned a lot about compassion.

The family was living at Chatswood now, and my mother was involved in a relationship with a man she would subsequently marry. I didn't want her confidences about him and I wasn't really interested in him, but as long as she was happy I didn't think my opinion mattered. He was a lawyer and offered security and a chance for a new life. I spent the four month vacation between the nursing home, my boyfriend and my family. It was a great summer. When I thought of my father it was still with a sense of relief that the struggle was over and we were free of that oppressive and constant gnawing worry that he provoked.

In 1960 I was a member of the Orientation Committee. My descriptor read thus: 'Wendy Ryan Arts III—History and Education. Wendy is Treasurer of the Women's Hockey Club. The Revue is one of her main interests and much of the social program is Wendy's work.' By then I was in love with university life and was convinced that UNE was a special and unique place. In 1960 I was also in love with History especially, because I had Russell Ward as my Australian history lecturer. He was an extraordinary teacher and a gifted communicator who encouraged us to be proud of and curious about our history. It was the beginning of my interest in the intellectual experience of being Australian. My Education and Geography lecturers were creative, and I flew through the year to graduation. At the end of 1960 I had completed the requirements to graduate in Arts. It had been a rocky academic journey, but once I learned to cooperate intellectually it was satisfying, stimulating and exciting.

After the rigour of final year Arts subjects, fulfilling my Teachers College Scholarship commitment by studying for my Diploma in Education was intellectually dreary. Dip. Ed. students were infantilised in the way we were taught. Had I not had positive experiences in my first teaching practice, I would have abandoned teaching as a career.

But the Dip. Ed. year was valuable. It enabled us to make our worst mistakes under the guidance of experienced teachers. It prepared us for the rigid structures of the schools we were to teach in. When you taught beside teachers with no professional training, the differences were obvious. We were taught to teach, to engage pupils, to be methodical in lesson preparation and disciplined intellectually. Graduates without a Dip. Ed. missed this learning experience.

While these studies may not have been intellectually challenging, my role as a moral tutor in Duval College was confronting and engaging. I was responsible for the pastoral care of sixteen young women housed in a portable hut called Carramar. This I found immensely satisfying. And I enjoyed the responsibility and collegiality of the College tutorial team.

We were inspired and led by Audrey Rennison—she was fun, fair and unshockable: for me the first really powerful role model who was a single woman. Of this time Miss Rennison wrote:

> During Mrs McCarthy's final year at Duval College when she was still a student taking her post-graduate Diploma in Education, she was trusted with the care, as tutor of a residential unit of the College, in which about sixteen young women were housed. They were an ill-assorted group, mostly first year students who had by no means

settled down to university life, and one or two rather immature and undisciplined students from more senior years. I knew they would give Mrs McCarthy a rough time of it and they did, but had no other tutor available who combined her qualities of youth and maturity, and I thought this may be the only authority the group would come to respect. This proved to be the case and Mrs McCarthy justified my faith in her. I think also that she gained something from this experience.

Nineteen sixty-one was my last year of university. By now our group of six best friends was changing. One had married, another had dropped some subjects and managed to get a teaching job in a local private girls' school so she could complete her degree part-time. We four who remained became closer as we took on more responsibility in university life. All of us were in steady relationships apart, we thought, from our friend who was teaching. Mine was suffering the tyranny of distance, though: my boyfriend had decided that UNE was not for him. He had returned to Sydney to live.

Our teaching friend managed to stay in touch. We would meet at the Union for coffee when she came to uni for lectures. On one particular day I remember thinking what a stunning looking young woman she was. She was wearing a long, bulky amethyst mohair sweater, rather like the ones I was knitting throughout my Dip. Ed. classes. But she seemed a little preoccupied. When I asked what was worrying her, she said she had a medical problem. She needed to see a doctor in discreet circumstances. Would I borrow our friend's car and drive her to Guyra (a small town about thirty miles away)? She thought she was pregnant.

I was astonished. I hadn't known she was having a relationship with anyone. But she was adamant that I was not to ask her about the man involved, nor tell anyone else. I agreed and we arranged to meet the next day. It was a tense journey. So many questions and fears were spinning in my head. This was my first real confrontation with the universal terror of single girls. What would or could she do? Vague memories stirred about who you went to to fix this—the woman who ran the local bookstore, for example, was said to be sympathetic. But the truth was I had no idea.

I waited in the car while she went in to the doctor's. She came out white-faced and crying. The doctor had established that she was five-and-a-half months pregnant and there was nothing to do about it except have the baby. We sat in the car and talked about what next. It felt surreal. The Guyra doctor had suggested that she tell her parents so they could help. But she desperately did not want to do this—she was an only child and thought it would break their hearts. Nor did she want to tell the man involved. Clearly, he was not part of her life, or the rest of us would have known him.

By the time we were back in Armidale we had one good idea: to contact some gynaecologists we had met in Townsville at a friend's wedding. This wedding had been a wonderful ceremonial affair, complete with jet flypast in honour of the groom, who was in the RAAF, and attended by officers from the local RAAF base. There had been two doctors from the Sydney University Medical School at the wedding. They were attending a Sydney University Regiment camp. We three single girls had spent time with them, and thought them charming and fun. I would approach them for help.

The response to my first phone call was positive and generous. My friend must come to Sydney immediately, she could live with the doctor and his wife and children until the baby was delivered and adopted. He would make arrangements for the management of the confinement. It seemed like a miracle. Within days she left for Sydney. I was to meet her parents, who would be arriving the following weekend and packing up her gear. But I was still sworn to secrecy. The official story was that she had been offered another job in Sydney.

My friend Prue came with me on Saturday morning to help pack our friend's things and meet her parents. Prue was offered no special explanation for the hasty departure. Early in the morning we set about disassembling our friend's Armidale life. Prue began on the clothes. I had been asked to go through her desk and pull out her papers, check them, throw them away or package them. When I opened a drawer of her desk on the right hand side, I saw a telegram.

Telegrams were the most serious way to communicate and were invariably thought to bear bad news, even though they were also sent for congratulatory purposes. Of course I read it.

I can't remember it verbatim. It was from my boyfriend. Its significance was clear—he was the father of the child. I was dumbfounded, and all the cliches jumbled up in my brain. 'It can't be true. It must be a mistake.' I put the telegram in my pocket and said nothing. I kept going to the toilet to re-read it, just in case I had it wrong. It had said he was accepting responsibility and that he would meet her at Central Railway Station in Sydney.

By the time the parents arrived they knew of the pregnancy and asked who the boyfriend was. I said I did not know and that she had refused to talk about it. They kept insisting that, as her best friend, I must know. Obviously they were hoping for marriage. I assured them I had not been aware of any relationship and kept longing for them to leave so I could deal with my own terror.

We drove back to college and I burst into the safest place I knew—Audrey Rennison's office. She listened to the story, and let me weep for hours. She served brandy and coffee. I remember waking up in her apartment on the sofa the next morning and wondering what I was to do. Perhaps it wasn't true? So when Miss Rennison suggested that the first sensible thing to do was to establish the truth, I clutched at that straw—everything might not be as it seemed. I rang my boyfriend and asked him.

It was as it had appeared. He was the father of the child. It had been an affair that had begun when the two of them became close after visiting me in the hospital when I had Asian flu earlier in the year. Somehow it sounded like my fault and I remember the line he used. 'We only had sex once. It was just bad luck that she got pregnant.' I desperately wanted to believe this. I certainly didn't hold my girlfriend responsible. I remember with great clarity asking whether he had told his parents. When he said no, I extracted an agreement from him that he would. Then they could offer her some financial support through the rest of the pregnancy.

This period was a nightmare time. I tried to make sense of it all. When my friend realised that I knew who was the child's father, she refused further contact. We have never met since, although in a scene worthy of the lowest script, we passed on the escalators in Grace Bros, Chatswood, some months after the baby was born. And for a time in the late seventies, we had a mutual friend who would chat about her occasionally.

I had lost one friend, and now had to work out what was happening with my boyfriend. The conventional advice was 'never speak to the bastard again', as I was the wronged woman. That didn't feel right. And in any event, few people knew anything of this. So once again I took the advice of Audrey Rennison. Her view was that the whole affair could only be understood if he and I spent some time together and talked it through. After all, we had been together for over two years.

Some weeks later we met for a weekend in Tamworth. Our relationship was finished, we knew, and we were not planning a future. However, we assumed we would stay close friends, and I agreed to speak with his mother to encourage her to support our friend during the pregnancy.

It was a profound experience for the three of us. The remarkable thing about it in retrospect is that life just chugged on. I continued in my role as the resident tutor at Duval College, caring for my bouncy students. I worked at my Dip. Ed., did my first teaching practice, had two or three love affairs and prepared for the world post-university.

Of course the pregnancy was not even obliquely referred to after those first couple of painful weeks. The times insisted on secrecy. Amazingly, it was a five-minute wonder and to my knowledge only two or three people knew. My friend simply disappeared from sight.

It was not until years later that I thought consciously about the social cruelty and injustice of this. I have no sense of bitterness or betrayal about the experience, but I was sad about the loss of friendship and to an extent the loss of innocence. I also understood that my friend's experience could have been mine. An active sexual life for two-and-a-half years, with no contraception except withdrawal, meant that I had been truly lucky. And I could see that she paid a much higher price than he did. It was many years before I thought about the baby.

The summer holidays were spent at the new family home in Roseville, my teaching notice arrived in mid January 1962: I was to report for duty at Telopea High in the ACT. I was incredulous. I had made a special plea to be appointed to a school in Sydney so I could live at home with my mother, brother and sister. I had never been to Canberra and knew no one there. It sounded like Siberia.

I called the Department and begged for a Sydney appointment. The appointments clerk suggested I find someone who had compatible subjects and a swap would be considered. Extraordinarily, I did find someone. By day one of the school year I was reporting to Cremorne Girls High as a Graduate Assistant, Level 1.

That first day in the classroom was like coming home. I had forgotten how much I loved the shape, smell and energy of schools. Cremorne Girls High was a small school of five hundred girls in the pretty lower North Shore suburb of Sydney. It had long suffered from the dominance of North Sydney Girls High, the nearby selective academic school for the area.

My first year out (when out meant out from university) was also the first year of the implementation of the Wyndham Scheme, which restructured secondary education in NSW. It decreed that there would be no streaming; all schools would be comprehensive and serve the children in the local area. That single edict changed the student intake for Cremorne significantly. The school had to respond to many disappointed parents whose daughters would previously have been assigned to North Sydney. They were very concerned that Cremorne would not offer the intellectual rigour and status of North Sydney Girls. Quite a few of these parents had come to Australia after the Hungarian Revolution in 1956, and were anxious that their daughters had the best intellectual education available.

I was assigned to the History/English department, despite my majors being in history and geography, which were the subjects I wanted to teach. I thought it ridiculous that a history major was assumed to be competent in English, and although I had passed English in my second year, I was still bruised from that failure in first year. However, no first-year-out teacher would dare to argue with a senior teacher, so I started preparing for my English classes.

At that time I was counselled that this was the only way to go if I wanted to make subject mistress. Such an astonishing thought had not occurred to me. I was not the slightest bit interested in promotion—this was a job, not a career. I would be married before such issues were relevant, and then I would not work. What would promotion matter to me?

I turned twenty-one in July of my first year teaching. As we celebrated at school some of the girls in my fifth-year History class reminded me that they were already eighteen. It meant that I had to approach them differently. I couldn't pull rank based on years of experience. We learned together and it was exhilarating. I had rarely worked so hard; night after night until midnight and beyond, I read history books and prepared lessons so that I had something to offer.

It was good, too, to be living at home and getting to know Kerry and Deb better. Kerry was finishing high school at James Ruse and Deb was in primary school at East Lindfield. It was a long time since we had lived together. My mother was generous with her car and in providing meals and space for me to work, and I had a wonderfully productive first year out. Only the presence of Geoff Lewis, my mother's new husband, was negative for me as there was so much friction between them, and yet he was the provider and for that I was grateful.

Cremorne Girls High School was ruled with a rod of iron by its Principal, Gwen Colyer. She inspired fear and terror in both her younger teachers and her pupils. One of her more unusual habits was to walk around with a hairbrush and flatten any offending teased beehive hairstyles. On the other hand, she could be capable of extraordinary compassion. She was truly the woman principal of her times—hierarchical, authoritarian, and determined to do the best as she saw it for her pupils.

The teaching profession operated on seniority. As the most junior teacher, I was assigned 2C, the naughtiest class in the school. My girls were always in trouble. Lateness, rudeness, beehives, heavy make-up and truancy were the regular repertoire; in the class and house-points competition we were the school liabilities. I would despair of making a difference, while secretly thanking Audrey

Rennison for the experience of managing Carramar and the naughty girls at UNE.

One day, sensing my anxiety about them, one of the ringleaders said to me, 'Don't worry, miss. It's not your fault, we were like this before you came. You'll get a better class next year.' I told her I liked this class and wanted to stay with them. I just needed some encouragement from them. Slowly it happened. My roll class and I learned to trust each other, and 2C became a cooperative part of the school. I loved them for their loyalty and support and their ability to see right through the system.

All this was a wonderful entry to the profession. There were some outstanding teachers at Cremorne and the staffroom was a stimulating and friendly place. I quickly made enduring friendships with the Latin teachers, Trish King and Margaret Maguire, one of them sadly cut short by the early death of Margaret from a brain tumor.

There were many different role models of women in that staff: the young first or second-year-out teachers, the married women with children who belonged to an underclass of permanent casual teachers (classified thus because they'd committed the unpardonable sin of interrupting their careers to marry and have children), and the single women in senior positions, such as Hazel Logan, our English mistress, who had made career decisions.

We younger teachers were fascinated by the single women who had responsible senior jobs, and we created fictions and fantasies about them losing their fiancés in the war. Otherwise they'd be married, wouldn't they? It never occurred to us that this might have been their choice. When we discovered that our Principal went to symphony concerts with a man we were astonished. It did not fit the stereotype we were creating.

Most of us were on the marriage track. Those whose prospects were not looking good required sympathy and understanding. I recall no working mothers in senior responsible positions; the demarcation lines were clear and eventually choices would have to be made between careers and motherhood. At no time did it occur to me to challenge that. The future seemed a long way away and the classroom fun.

Meanwhile, all first-year-out teachers were reminded they were on probation—and had to be inspected. This could be intimidating and we prayed for a good inspector. When I heard that Leo Payne would be inspecting me everyone was pleased—he was thought to be genuinely interested in young teachers. One of the scary aspects was the lack of feedback until the written report arrived. What a relief when I received Leo Payne's report! On 3 December 1962 he wrote:

> Miss Ryan has shown pleasing development as a teacher in her first year of service. Both the Principal and her Subject Mistress speak highly of her interest and enthusiasm for teaching, the very good relationships she has established with her classes and her ready participation in all school activities.
>
> Miss Ryan plans her lessons carefully, ensures the continuing participation of her pupils in them and strikes a very good balance between oral and written work. Her supervision of regularly given written exercises is most conscientious.
>
> Miss Ryan has shown initiative in her successful use of the Reading Laboratories and is adept in the handling of such mechanical aids as the projector and the tape recorder.
>
> It is recommended that her efficiency be determined as meriting the award of a Teacher's Certificate.

The Director General agreed and on 17 January 1963 my probationary period was over. I was a proper teacher. I was thrilled. But one of the senior women said to me, 'You'll be a very good teacher and you could probably end up as a school principal.' Now I was shocked. That anyone would see me as principal material suggested Unmarried and Childless—social death.

In 1962 men and women teachers were still paid different rates and the equal pay campaign was a constant source of discussion in the staffroom. I cringe to recall that I initially accepted the argument against equal pay, on the grounds that men who had to support wives and children needed the bigger pay packet. Phrases such as 'a rate for the job' were not in my consciousness. I thought I was well paid.

Why did I need more? I listened carefully to the discussion in the staff room, particularly to the views of the Teachers' Federation. It was my first experience of a union and the constancy of political activity. I recall only one teacher, a new geography mistress, who was outspoken about the justice of the equal pay argument and urged us to support the Federation's case.

In my first three years of teaching there was no public Wendy Ryan. I was utterly absorbed in my job, and public sector behaviour did not include a public profile except through the Teachers' Federation and that was not a likely prospect. The only organisation I played any role in was the History Teachers' Association. This was in response to an invitation from a history teacher I admired, Ian Vacchini. I did general dogsbody work, but I doubt I would have joined without being pushed or invited. I was happy to be concentrating on my job and I did not imagine I had anything to offer.

About the time these arguments were raging I decided to buy my first car—a pale blue second-hand Mini Minor. I went to the manager of the local Bank of New South Wales. But not only did he refuse the loan because I had no male guarantor (could I help it that my father was dead?), he strongly advised me against buying a car independently: I would probably get married, he said, and my husband would have one. I changed my mind on equal pay overnight and went and borrowed the money from a finance company while refusing the salesman's invitation to dinner. I was surprisingly accepting of the bank's decision. I just don't think it occurred to me that I could do anything about it. Indeed, that bank refused me credit three times before I decided to move my account.

I was consumed by teaching in my first year out. My old boyfriend reappeared somewhere during the year and our relationship was re-established. We never spoke of the child he had fathered. In the September school holidays of 1963 we went on a holiday to pre-fashionable Noosa with my little brother and sister, Kerry and Deborah, and Peter Chadwick, a friend of long standing.

It was a happy holiday and at the end of it my boyfriend announced he was off to England to live, to go to London University. Only days later I was waving him goodbye from Pier 11 at Pyrmont as he sailed

away on the *Patris*. I promised to be in London in three months'
time. The Noosa holiday had lulled us into a sense of fantasy about
resuming the affair. It didn't last long.

Three weeks later I met Gordon McCarthy on a blind date arranged
by a temporary flatmate, Helen McFie. She had arranged to go to the
pictures with a man who lived in Blues Point Tower, and asked that
he bring his flatmate and make a foursome with me. This was not
matchmaking but the kind of protection we organised when we did
not want to be with the man whose invitation we had accepted. I
decided it was time I expanded my circle of friends, and agreed. He
sounded OK, quite different; attractive looking with an economics
degree from the Australian National University, and now working as
a chartered accountant with Cooper Brothers.

I was at this time conscious of the fact that I was single and most
of my friends were couples. It sounds silly today. I don't recall panic
as I was only twenty-two, but I knew that I wanted to create a family
and I could see no prospects. All the conventional people I knew
didn't interest me. I wanted to find a partner for both my heart and
my head. I wanted romance and sex, but most of all I was looking
for a soulmate. I wanted to be married but I had not seen a marriage
that I really admired. I wanted to build and grow a family with a
partner whose values about families and life matched my own and I
was prepared to wait to find the right person. I was not going to
settle for second best. I also observed that my major love affairs had
been with men who were engaging rogues: charming, intelligent,
witty, unreliable, unpredictable, unfaithful—hardly life partnership
material.

Gordon was different from any man I had met, but our first date
could easily have been a disaster—he arrived late and disappeared
early, promising to ring me. He called the next day and suggested we
go to the movies to see *Knife in the Water*. It was October and I
remember I wore a cream and caramel dress and jacket with matching
shoes. So often I remember events by the clothes I was wearing. Does
this make me a clothesaholic or is it that my view of how I present
externally defines the moment? I am not sure but I can retrieve memories through my clothes.

Gorden remembers none of this. He checked the ferry timetable and coordinated the arrangements so well that our ferries passed each other on Sydney Harbour twice. We made the late show and agreed to meet again. This time it was dinner at The Fiddler's Three, a local Cremorne restaurant. Three nights later we were in bed and planning a wedding. Wisely we decided to keep this to ourselves for a while as he had a girlfriend in Canberra and I had to settle the loose arrangement with the London-bound man. When these past liaisons were ended in the next week we embarked on a wonderful love affair and started planning our future.

For the next six months Gordon and I were inseparable, and despite the learning experiences of unplanned pregnancies we continued to use the combination of withdrawal and rhythm that had worked to date. It was a shock to discover early in 1964 that I was pregnant. I could see my life disintegrating. It was not the time to become parents. We agreed that we should find someone to fix it. 'Fixing it' was the language, and Gordon went on the great abortionist chase. This, curiously, was still seen as men's business; men managed and paid if they wanted to stay in the relationship. Gordon remembered a pharmacist friend from school and university who was said to have contacts. When he called him, he immediately volunteered the contact number for a clinic at Malabar, with the recommendation that only Macquarie Street gynaecologists worked there. He stressed that his name was not to be mentioned and that all phone calls had to be made from public phone booths. In blind faith and mounting terror, we agreed and made the appointment for the following Tuesday. Before then we had to raise sixty-three guineas in cash, which was to be paid at the door before entry.

That weekend we drove out to Malabar to check the place, an ugly block of liver brick flats which did not look clinical and seemed terrifyingly near Long Bay Gaol. Gordon, a modest share investor at the time, sold his Channel Ten shares to pay. I rang school to say I was suddenly unwell and on Tuesday morning we set off in the red Volkswagen beetle to Malabar to join the endless number of women who sought abortion, the unspeakable crime.

I walked up the stairs with the money in my purse and rang the bell. A woman came to the door and asked me for the password and to identify myself. Satisfied with my response she asked for the sixty-three guineas, which I passed through the slight opening in the steel grille door. After it was counted she let me in and directed me to undress and put on a green gown. I was shocked at her dismissive attitude and immediately got the message that she was doing me a favour.

A query about allergies prompted my usual response that I was thought to be allergic to cocaine, a legacy of a strong reaction to a dental injection in my teens. With that she pronounced that I would have no anaesthetic, as they could take no risks. This was scary but I had little time to appreciate what it meant because I was told to get up on to the table. Once I was on the table with my legs in stirrups a reasonably kindly man approached and said, 'This will hurt a little without anaesthetic, but we can't do much if you are allergic to our medication.' Again I was overwhelmed with a feeling of guilt and self blame. The doctor then assured me that he was a qualified practitioner, and repeated that it would hurt 'a bit'.

Perhaps to divert me the nurse said, in a conspiratorial woman to woman sort of way, 'Who's the mongrel who did this to you?' I thought I was drowning: the pain was sweeping over me and I was being asked to denounce the one person in the world about whom I cared, as well as to define myself as a victim. I answered tearfully, 'My fiancé, and he is not a mongrel. He is down there in the car waiting for me; he's probably throwing up with nervous anxiety. And I did it too.' The sister, from her superior vertical position, said in a world-weary and rather malicious tone, 'Oh young lady, we've heard those words before, just make sure the bastard doesn't get you back here again.' I closed my eyes and stopped responding and was soon in the recovery room. After half an hour's rest I was given antibiotics and the emergency phone number and told I could leave. As I gathered my clothes I glanced at the entrance, to see one of my star school pupils approaching. I raced to the toilet and stayed there until I heard her go into the theatre. Then with thumping heart I fell into the arms of a white-faced Gordon.

I have never felt the slightest regret or grief about this abortion, even later when I was finding it difficult to conceive. Yet, not only did I not discuss it with anyone, I lied about it for years. As part of my pre-marital preparation some months later I presented for the customary gynaecological checkup. When asked if I'd ever had a pregnancy, I looked the doctor straight in the eye and said 'No'. I didn't bother to confide in this doctor that I was already taking a friend's oral contraceptives, that I'd had a termination of pregnancy, that I'd been sexually active since I was seventeen. It didn't seem worth it really. Nevertheless, I felt the proper process had been followed. I'd had my gynae check, I had my own Pill prescription in my very own name and I could join the ranks of all the other young brides-to-be who'd done the right thing.

For years, when I went to gynaecologists, obstetricians and family planning, I denied that pregnancy. Curiously it wasn't something I grieved about. The issue was utterly clear-cut. I was not ready to be a parent and nor was Gordon. We both wanted to be, but not then. We managed the circumstances ourselves and in many ways that experience of trusting and sharing became the metaphor for much of our life together. We depended on and supported each other and didn't often feel the need for further support.

A decade was to pass before I spoke about my abortion and then I flaunted it by joining with a group of other women and signing my name on a petition published in *Nation Review*. We took the centre page and invited the police to arrest us as we disclosed our unlawful terminations of pregnancy. None of us was arrested, but my mother was outraged to read about it; outraged because I had not trusted her or enlisted her support. I thought I shouldn't bother her.

Years later, when I worked in Family Planning, it became an important part of the Family Planning process to insist on counselling women who came for pregnancy tests and termination referrals. I was a lone voice pushing the view that we can overdo counselling because many women have made up their minds before they come to the clinic. They don't need intensive counselling, but expert and sympathetic service.

All my legacies from this experience are positive, with the important exception that I had conceived in the first place. I became a sexually responsible person and in time found my voice so that I could become an advocate for choice and recognition of the need for abortion to be a safe and available medical procedure—but that belongs to my family planning story.

In March 1964 Gordon and I became engaged. I was sure that this was my life partner and even deferring our wedding until my mother's pregnancy was over did not put a cloud on the horizon. It gave us time to plan a December wedding followed by an ocean voyage to London. Being engaged increased my interest in marriage.

In 1964 two of my favourite fellow teachers, Jean Dunlop and Helen Johnman, recommended that I read what they believed was an important book. It was *The Feminine Mystique* by Betty Friedan. This was a book that changed my life because it mapped out a future and its possible repercussions. It challenged all my assumptions about life after teaching, which I still saw as an interim activity. *The Feminine Mystique* provoked me to think about both my mother's life and the lives of all my friends. When I compared their lives with the women of their age I taught beside they seemed nowhere near as full, varied and interesting. Curiously, many of them felt sorry for those women who 'had to go to work', or dismissed them as being rather clever. This was not a compliment. It seemed to me the working women were better off and generally happier. They had made a decision about the quality of independence in their lives and they chose to go to work, even under punitive industrial conditions which denied them superannuation and permanency. They were powerfully contrasting role models, and this was highlighted by my mother announcing she was pregnant, a pregnancy she was very happy about. As for many women of her generation, a pregnancy consolidated a family. My feelings about the pregnancy were ambivalent as I thought it was a destructive relationship with no future. In my view, she and Geoff were so ill-suited; he was a club man and she was a creative home-maker. They had incompatible expectations. Still, she was my mother, and if that was her choice I would support it, and I knew we would all love the baby. Once, when asked if I was embarrassed by it, I remember being shocked that anyone would think that. Today, no one would question a pregnancy decision for a forty-one-year-old.

Teaching proved to be a lot more than history and English. In my first year out one of the girls kept falling asleep in class. I responded by threatening her with a suitable punishment if she didn't wake up and pay attention. At the end of the class one of her friends said she wanted to see me after school. In a very direct manner she said, 'Just lay off her will you? Her old man's rooting her all night and she's exhausted. If she doesn't come to school she gets in trouble from the social worker and if she stays home he is at her again. And Miss, you're not allowed to say I told you.'

Dip. Ed. had not prepared me for this. There was no method teaching on incest. I barely knew the word. However, I did understand that this girl was at risk and I was not prepared to leave her without a lifeline. After a lot of agonising, I talked to the Headmistress who helped find her another place to live so that she could stay at school. Experience such as this put into perspective some of my own embarrassment about my father. A drunk was nothing compared to a child molester.

I loved the girls at Cremorne and still take pride in following their careers. Cathy Gee became Kate Grenville the writer, Pam Swain an ABC producer, Dorothea Schultz a senior person in DOCS and some, like Mary Vallentine of Sydney Symphony Orchestra fame, remain my friends today. They were generous with me and my struggles to be a good teacher. They were far more worldly than girls I had gone to school with and it was my first experience of a single-sex school. I have a cherished photo of some pupils standing outside the church at my wedding and they epitomise golden young womanhood.

However not all the girls were princesses who wished me well at my wedding. One pet at Cremorne told me to 'get fucked'. She was thirteen years old and my jaw dropped to the ground in astonishment. No-one had ever said that to me, let alone in the classroom, and I thought I deserved better. After all I was the teacher. It was a salutary moment for me as I began to understand that respect has to be earned—position is not sufficient.

And then there were the parents. Dip. Ed. method hadn't paid any attention to them either. Why were we not advised about pushy, lecherous and patronising parents? Twenty-year-olds were ill-equipped to deal with these. Of course there were others who redeemed the awful ones. At my first Parents Night a father who was very ambitious for his daughter said, 'My daughter's going to be a doctor and I don't want to hear any nonsense to the contrary.' He was strenuously advised by the school to encourage her into another career as her IQ consistently tested below 100. He refused to accept the judgment and insisted that, even if she had to repeat, that she be enrolled in maths and science to prepare her for medicine. Years later when I was resting post-labour we recognised each other. She came over to say hello and said, 'You see, Miss, I did it.' I have never forgotten that family's tenacity and insistence that their daughter be given extra support to succeed. Since then I've never underestimated a person's ability to succeed if they are focused and determined.

It was at Cremorne that I had my first contact with indigenous people's political struggle for recognition. The previous history mistress came back to visit and introduce her two adopted, coloured children. I was astonished and enchanted by this commitment and nurtured a desire to do a similar thing at some future time. Not long after, a black woman, Faith Bandler, was the guest speaker at school assembly. She had a profound impact on all of us and remains one of my heroines. *Langunyah*, the school magazine, of 1962 described her visit as follows:

The White and Brown Australians

Mrs Bandler, who is a Torres Strait Islander, appealed to the girls to foster better relationships between the brown and white Australians by breaking down existing prejudices.

Speaking very fluently and charmingly and then answering almost thirty questions asked in the Senior Assembly, we learned about the difficulties surrounding the Aborigines. Each state has different laws, for instance privileges gained in Victoria, where there are 2000, against 140,000 in NSW, cease to exist the moment the Aborigine crosses the border into another State. If you want to visit on a reserve you have to seek permission and then you cannot be entertained overnight. Voting rights are being given without citizenship rights.

Families often have to travel with the father to seasonal jobs, the only ones available, from the Irrigation Area to the South Coast and then to the Central West. By so doing, the children's education naturally suffers. Often families on a reserve have saved enough money to build a house elsewhere, but the white man's prejudice soon drives them back to the reserves. The pay for the indigenous population is often only a seventh of the pay for the white man doing the same work. In twenty-one schools there is segregation in teaching, as the schools are especially for Aborigines. This does not help assimilation.

The indigenous Australians only want to be treated as human beings. The protection laws of 1909 are no longer necessary. The usual arguments of dirtiness, untidiness and lack of education result from the conditions under which they are forced to live. Appreciation of their difficulties will certainly help us to understand and assist our Australian Aborigines.

It was a powerful message and I was impressed that these seemingly conservative women on the staff were concerned about social justice.

Cremorne was a traditional school that aspired to academic excellence and resented the second-rate tag assigned to it by virtue of North Sydney Girls' High's dominance. It provided an all-round education and teachers were encouraged to take responsibility for other activities. I coached hockey and debating and developed history excursions into an art form. Three years there flew and when I left in 1964 I felt secure that I was a good and competent teacher and would be able to teach anywhere. In order to help me find a job in London I asked the Department to forward details of my service and Miss Colyer to write a reference. She wrote as follows of my three years at Cremorne:

I have known Mrs Wendy McCarthy (nee Ryan) as a member of staff of Cremorne Girls High School. During this time she was a teacher of English and History, taking students to

Honours Standard in History for the Leaving Certificate Examination.

She showed keen interest in debating and under her guidance the Senior Team won the Competition arranged for Departmental Schools in the Sydney and Newcastle areas in the state.

In addition Mrs McCarthy trained girls for a Hockey competition on Saturday mornings, and her organising ability was shown in arranging House Functions. In all I have found Mrs McCarthy an enthusiastic, energetic and willing member of staff.

CHAPTER FOUR

COLONIAL TEACHER,
CORPORATE WIFE

At 5 p.m. on 18 December 1964 Gordon and I were married at St David's Anglican Church, Palm Beach. Our reception was held at Jonah's at Whale Beach, a truly magical place overlooking the ocean. We had chosen that church as my family was living at Avalon, and we had no connection to any other. I asked Padre (Don Shearman), my mentor from St John's Hostel who was now a bishop, to officiate and was disappointed when he was unavailable. Despite not being regular churchgoers we would not have considered being married anywhere else than a church.

December 18 was a perfect Aussie summer day. I went for a swim at Avalon beach in the morning. Swimming is my favourite way of relaxing, and I wanted to have that rosy glow that a couple of hours in the morning sun produces. Over lunch my mother and I had one of those unfortunate discussions that can occur on a wedding day, in which she expressed her doubt about Gordon being the right person for me. I was aghast and remember thinking not only was she wrong, but at twenty-three I knew what I was doing. Such is the confidence of youth, and as life has evolved we would now both agree that Gordon has been and continues to be a wonderful life partner.

Gordon and I have always loved giving parties and we carefully planned our wedding. I thought we were lucky to do this and we were more than happy to accept the financial responsibility, unlike some of our friends who had to fall in with their parents' wishes. Although he offered, I thought it would be unfair to ask Geoff to contribute just because he was married to my mother. My brother

Kerry walked me up the aisle and gave me away. Some of my Cremorne pupils had gathered outside the church.

It was a traditional event; I wore a simple, long Empire-line silk dress and bridal veil. There were three bridesmaids, a page boy, a bridal waltz and a wedding cake. In the fashion of the day, I departed the reception in a going-away outfit, which was a very pretty pale pink silk shantung coatdress made by my mother, complete with white Oroton bag and the obligatory white slingback shoes. I cannot remember if I promised to obey. If I did, I broke the promise.

There were unusual aspects—the photographs with a beautiful baby, my sister Sarah who was four months old and for whose arrival the wedding had been deferred. I often wondered if some of the more conservative members of the congregation thought she was mine, as it was not so unusual for daughters who had babies out of wedlock to ask their mothers to raise them. My mother's joy at this baby should have dispelled such thoughts. To the consternation of some members of our family and friends, Gordon wore a wedding ring. This was visible proof of unmanly behaviour and I was advised by many that forcing a man to wear a ring would do me no good in the end. Of course it begged the question about whose choice it was. It mattered to me as a symbol of commitment and equality.

After a night at the Newport Arms we drove to Berowra to collect the Halvorsen cruiser we had rented for the first week of our honeymoon. It was an opportunity to enjoy our last Australian summer for some time and was a wonderful first week of our marriage. As we returned the boat to its mooring, we began to focus on the next water adventure, a boat trip to London.

It is almost impossible for anyone now to understand the enormity of travel at this time. In a sense we were leaving indefinitely, for another life. On 28 December we boarded the *Fairsea*, a Sitmar line boat, for England; a journey that would take five and a half weeks. We took with us our suitcases of clothes, the money we had been given as wedding presents and a total trust and belief that we could manage on our own. We knew no-one to whom we could turn on the other side of the world. We were on our own together and it was powerfully exciting. The only security at the other end was Gordon's job as a chartered accountant with Cooper Brothers in London. While I was confident that I would find teaching work, I had nothing organised.

The voyage was a continuing cultural encounter. We visited ports with exotic names and smells and the ship ensured that we had plenty of time there. We shopped for cameras, and a tape recorder. We ate food prepared in the street. Singapore, Colombo and Aden made powerful impressions and began my love affair with Asia and Asian food.

Life on the ocean was all the cliches we might have imagined: endless sunny days, Italian food, dancing or playing bridge for hours each night, hours of time at our disposal to talk and dream. By then we had made friends with other young couples—Allan and Maureen Baxter, Graham and Tania Teague and John and Lois Ellis. Because of the restrictions on the Suez Canal we bussed through the desert into Cairo and made the pilgrimage to the pyramids and the Nile. Walking up the pyramids and shopping in the Cairo bazaar remain highlights of the trip. There is still a copper pot as evidence of shopping in the bazaar.

Travel at this level was a spiritual experience of great rarity, and for us there was the overlay and adventure of a new marriage and the feeling that we could be anything we wanted. Not for us the suburban houses of our friends; we were curious about the rest of the world and we wanted the adventure of living on our own in a new environment. Just don't fence us in.

The light and energy of the desert gave way to the turbulence and greyness of the Bay of Biscay, and I always think of our arrival in England as a grey experience. As we approached the southern coast the sea was grey and merged into an endless grey sky. We caught the train to Waterloo Station; the sky was overcast and we saw black people everywhere. The Commonwealth was here in force and wanting its share of the action.

Observing some of our travelling companions at play had confirmed our intention to live outside the well known Australian ghettoes. The McCarthys would not be living in Earl's Court with Barry McKenzie. We needed neither the security nor the restriction it might impose. After checking in to a pub in Kensington we went in pursuit of accommodation and finally rented the basement apartment of a handsome terrace house, 26a Bark Place, which was just off Queensway. At eleven guineas a week it was expensive, but it was only a block from Kensington Park and it was our first house together. We decided we wanted to live with some style and while short on sunlight (we decided it would primarily be a night-time house for us), it was cosy and well equipped for entertaining. A bonus was the discovery that Spike Milligan lived close by. Just seeing him occasionally made me smile.

We had arrived in England at an extraordinary time. We heard of Winston Churchill's death on the way over, so we went to live and work in the London of Harold Wilson and the Labour Party. Within a week Gordon was at work with Cooper Brothers in the City and I was applying to the Greater London Education Authority for supply (relief) teaching assignments. Professionally, our lives were miles apart. His firm was busy seeking work with the new government while wishing to maintain its Establishment status. There were dinners at the Café Royal to introduce him to English professional life. I doubted that this would be part of my work experience.

By the second week of February 1965 I was assigned my first job, and it was a long way from the City Establishment. Wearing my white kangaroo-skin coat, a wedding present from my darling husband, I caught the train to Hackney Marshes to report as a supply teacher to Hackney North Secondary School. The clerk at the Greater London Education Authority had assured me that this was a good posting and that they loved Australians. The school was three blocks from the station. Everyone seemed to be West Indian or English and their clothes were drab, black or grey. I looked utterly ridiculous in a cream fur coat. Had they opened it, they would have seen my initials embroidered in the silk lining.

The principal greeted me by saying, 'Oh God, another Australian. Oh well, I suppose you can teach, they mostly can. What do you teach? It doesn't matter really. Here, take the Maths and the Religious Instruction.' By the time I opened my mouth to explain that I was neither religious nor mathematical, she'd gone. I tentatively inquired from one of the teachers in the staffroom about suitable texts for teaching. One of the friendlier ones said they were all West Indian or Cypriot and weren't much interested, so for Religious Instruction I should read the Bible and for maths do shopping arithmetic.

'Tell them they have two pounds to buy the weekly groceries. List the prices of the goods they are to buy and then calculate how much change there is. That should take all the time of the lesson.' I thought she was being facetious. I went into my first class and introduced myself to guffaws and interested comments about what a funny accent I had, and yes, they loved my fur coat which they thought was rabbit. They were shocked to discover it was kangaroo fur. 'You don't kill them kangaroos for that, do you, Miss? Didn't think you had white ones.'

Somehow it seemed that what I'd learnt at Cremorne Girls High was not going to be much use here. We went through the exercise suggested in the staffroom and I prayed for the bell to ring. For the rest of the day I looked after other people's classes. This was sophisticated baby-sitting, not teaching.

The next day I was given the Religious Instruction classes. This seemed to consist primarily of colouring in what I remembered as Sunday School-type comics. At one stage I read something from the Bible and mispronounced Job, which sent them into convulsions of laughter. 'Don't you have the Bible where you come from, Miss?'

This was an environment without hope; everyone had given up. Keeping the girls there until they turned fifteen was sufficient challenge. A few extra life skills were a bonus. I decided to get out before I lost my own life skills.

I had met a couple of other supply teachers who told me that going to the Greater London Education central office to get work meant you were always sent out to places like Hackney. It was far smarter to go to the area office closest to your home. This I did and a week later I was sent for an interview at Gilliatt School for Girls at Fulham. Meeting the Principal, Miss Kindred, was a good beginning. She was kindly and direct: 'I like Colonials,' she said, 'they are usually very good at what they do. But I do want you to understand that this is an amalgam of schools, a secondary modern and a grammar school brought together to be a comprehensive school, and our task is to provide a comprehensive education for the benefit of all the girls. We have a very distinct philosophy, we don't say no to our girls. Too many of them have lived their lives with people saying no to them. Society says no all the time. We try to understand who they are and encourage them in what they do so they can achieve.' I am thinking, 'We don't say no.' Hmm. Another educational philosophy I'd not heard of, but it seemed a lot more promising than shopping lists and baby-sitting at North Hackney. I took the three-month temporary job on offer.

Gilliatt was a school on two campuses divided by a park. This provided endless diversion, as despite the best timetabling efforts, both teachers and girls invariably moved from one campus to the other. Reasons for being late for class included, 'I met this dirty old man in the park, Miss. He didn't half frighten me. I had to hide.' Reports of what he flashed could easily engage half the lesson, which was about all that was left after the stragglers arrived.

The school's mission was to succeed as a truly comprehensive school. It invited all comers. The British secondary school entrance exam, the 11 plus, had recently been abolished. This was to be a place where everyone had a chance, not just early developers. A major objective was to get its first girls through A levels and off to university. Universities were the targets because so few of the working class reached further education. Many teachers saw education as the only way out of the class ghetto, and were dedicated to the task. It was a great Labour experiment, with much at stake.

Gilliatt School was closely connected to the British Labour Party, as the chairman of the school board, Mary Stewart, was the wife of the Foreign Secretary, Michael Stewart. Both Michael and Mary Stewart took a close interest in the school. They made Gilliatt teachers welcome at official receptions at Whitehall, and talked up the importance of teaching and teachers in the new order being established by the government of Harold Wilson. We were encouraged to think of ourselves as professionals who were leading a new social agenda. Such political savvy and involvement I had not seen before. Nor had I ever thought of myself as having political significance.

As outsiders we found we could bring people from different

backgrounds together, and we did it often. We became friends with the Beevors, whose eldest son, Nigel, worked with Gordon. His parents welcomed us into their homes in Eaton Square, Belgravia and a country house in Sandwich, Kent. There we mixed with the Establishment, while at Gilliatt my teaching friends had two jobs and were doing up flats in Clapham.

After being at Gilliatt for two months as a temporary I was encouraged to apply for a permanent assigned position, which meant that I would be employed by the school rather than the London Education Authority. The interviewing committee made it clear that they would be delighted to have a young Colonial on the staff. One of them kindly pointed out in the interview that many of the girls at Gilliatt were from families who had been moved from the East End to the North End Road at Fulham. He observed that they were not dissimilar in attitudes and accents to those people who'd gone to settle Australia and that I would undoubtedly have a real empathy with them. I wisely refrained from commenting.

My appointment as the Geography Mistress made my educational future in London secure and I moved into the school community life very easily. One day it was announced that Anthony Wedgwood-Benn, the Minister for Education, would be visiting the school. He was admired by the teachers and there was great excitement at our staff meeting to discuss how to manage his two-hour visit. I was seen as an important part of the Wedgwood-Benn day, a way of demonstrating how they accommodated Colonials to be part of the educational experiment of egalitarianism.

This was the time in my life when I learned to live with tokenism and turn it to advantage, even under extreme provocation, as when it was casually mentioned in the staff room that my degree could not be compared to any UK degree because it was from a colonial university. This was followed by, 'But it's OK, she teaches well'. I learned to smile. Internally I raged and wanted to yell that most of my university teachers were English, that standards were high and how dare they say and think that.

So it was with mixed feelings that I told Miss Kindred that I had a problem with the Wedgwood-Benn visit as Gordon and I had been invited to Buckingham Palace for a garden party on the same day. Choosing a garden party over the great Labour leader seemed frivolous, but not to Miss Kindred, 'Oh, my dear Mrs McCarthy,' she said, 'this is not a problem. You have not been invited, you've been commanded. Of course you will go to Buckingham Palace. Your class can prepare their work and they can tell our minister where you are. He'll be thrilled to know.'

At the next school assembly she announced, 'Girls, we are so proud of Mrs McCarthy. She and her husband are going to Buckingham Palace to meet Her Majesty. Girls, what do we think? Is this not wonderful news?' Rounds of acclamation. I was a star, I had been chosen, and this in a Labour stronghold. The girls thronged around me after assembly. 'Miss, you'll see the flamingos.' 'It won't half be nice there.' 'Aren't you lucky, Miss.' 'Do they eat off gold plates?' 'Do you think you'll see the children?' 'What's she really like?'

Anthony Wedgwood-Benn became a marginal event. The hot topic for the next few days was what Mrs McCarthy would wear to Buckingham Palace to meet the Queen. Should I wear a hat and what would the Queen be wearing? Mothers from all backgrounds sent their advice through their daughters and girls encouraged me to practise the curtsy. I didn't, but I did wear the going-away outfit of pink shantung and prayed the weather would stay dry.

At Gilliatt the children of the Commonwealth and the lower classes were learning or at least being schooled with the backdrop of Swinging London and Carnaby Street. The North End Road was a block away, and Chelsea the next suburb. Hammersmith Odeon, where the Beatles played, was within walking distance and all the girls saved up for concerts.

It was a time to marvel at the British welfare state acceptance of the children of the Commonwealth; backs, eyes and teeth were straightened. As school medical and dental services took over from years of neglect, hot school lunch and school milk provided the basic diet. If anything was missing it was sport and exercise, and this was to be rectified in part by the sporting Aussie Mrs McCarthy, who was assigned to teach rowing on the Thames.

'Australians can do all sports, can't they?' 'Of course, Miss

Kindred,' I responded, as I contemplated with terror the fragile craft I would be travelling on. As barges and boats went past us on the water, the men who were coaching us would roar instructions. Somehow we never capsized and we all learnt to row. In May 1999 I returned to the rowing club on the Thames and marvelled that I ever had the courage to get in a tiny craft on that river.

This was a happy school and parents were encouraged to visit. Indian mothers who were worried that I didn't know how to make curry properly would send their daughters to school with freshly ground spices so that my curries would taste just right. The West Indian girls showed me not only how to put on false eyelashes but how to straighten my hair. 'First of all the straightener, Miss, then you iron it with brown paper on top.' I was desperate to have my hair dead straight and followed their instructions carefully.

One day I suggested a school excursion on a Saturday afternoon to see *Othello* at the cinema in the West End. 'Oh Miss, we ain't ever been to the West End, what's it like there?' I couldn't believe they had not been there. The Number 14 bus went past the door and it was a short trip to the West End, but it was cultures away and I was beginning to realise that class was a strong inhibitor. They did not think they had the right to be there.

It was agreed that we would go together, and there was much exuberance when we met at school at midday Saturday. However, as my noisy, uppity, quick-to-give lip girls got closer, they became quieter. When we reached the foyer they were silent. One asked if she could touch the velvet curtains so she could tell her mum what real velvet felt like. As we took our seats I wondered if I was pushing them too far, but I had underestimated the power of Will Shakespeare. Laurence Olivier's *Othello* filled the screen and engaged them to tears.

This was the first of many excursions as we learned history and geography together from both books and places. One Saturday we went for a boat trip along the Thames, another unknown experience at their back door. Although they were outspoken about their rights and the football teams they supported, they were without confidence in new situations, and this I took on as a challenge.

Gilliatt School changed my professional approach to teaching.

The philosophy of constant positive feedback was powerful and pervasive. We were strongly encouraged to look for the positive aspects of girls' characters and abilities and discouraged from extolling traditional hierarchical obedience. Teachers too were encouraged and it was a wonderfully supportive environment to work in. The aim was to break the cycle of negativity. It's worked for me ever since.

Australian teachers did well in London. They were considered reliable and well trained; they were well paid and their earnings were tax-free for two years, which was a real bonus. The holidays were better distributed than those in Australia, so the opportunities for a second job and/or a long holiday were good.

These years of living in London were extraordinarily different from our previous lives. Weekends were for us; there were no family commitments and we could do as we pleased. We bought a green Morris Mini van and equipped it so that we could sleep in it. We had two Li-Lo's and two sleeping bags which joined together, and by pushing the seats forward we could stretch out and sleep in the back. We had a gas stove for cooking breakfast. Almost every weekend we were exploring the English countryside and sleeping in country lanes and byways. We drank and ate in pubs and talked to whoever was available.

Some weekends we played golf at Richmond Park, and we usually went out at least three nights a week. We heard Andrés Segovia and Jacqueline Du Pré at Festival Hall and saw *The Homecoming* and *Look Back in Anger* at the Royal Court. Our curiosity and tastes were eclectic—movies, ballet at Covent Garden, concerts at the Hammersmith Odeon and endless movies. (We especially loved those movie theatres where you could smoke all the way through.) Sometimes I thought we were like two pieces of blotting paper, absorbing everything.

We spent hours in antique markets and shops; collecting silver cutlery became a passion. As we lived close to Portobello Road, we did our regular shopping there and as I learned to expand the housekeeping budget I often blessed Amrey Commins, who extolled the virtue and dignity of good housekeeping. Complete with *The Joy of*

Cooking by Rombaur and Becker, I developed into a good housewife and giver of dinner parties, things I still love doing.

My first Christmas in London was not a culinary triumph. I went to the markets to buy my Polish butter and English turkey. We decided we would have a traditional English turkey by ourselves, splash out on some Spanish wine and then visit friends who'd invited us for drinks. I remember the man in the market stall explaining how I should hang the turkey outside overnight on Christmas Eve if it was cold. It was, and, persuaded that this was a truly wise and sophisticated European thing to do, I hung the bird on the clothes line thinking food writer Elizabeth David would be proud of me.

Next morning I thought the turkey had a very gamey smell and as it was cooking it became apparent that it was off. The smell permeated the house. Our landlady, Mrs Rosenthal, either smelt the vile smell or heard me crying and saved the day by inviting us to her Christmas lunch. Her turkey was perfect and her guests were from all over the world. One, a German Jewish lawyer with an enchanting, café-au-lait baby boy, Daniel, described herself as a single mother. I couldn't think of this happening in Sydney. She explained she was not interested in marriage and had chosen a diplomat from Ghana to father a child for whom she would accept responsibility. I marvelled at her confidence and bravery.

During 1966 Gordon's mother, Ruth, came to visit us for a few months and we all went to Ireland where we looked for the Ryans and the McCarthys. Despite a wish in the McCarthy family that we were of Scottish ancestry, McCarthy was as visible as Ryan in Ireland, and both appeared frequently as the names of publicans. I was very sure of both my Irish and Scots ancestry. When I walked down the streets of Irish towns and saw people who looked just like me, I understood a lot more about my heritage.

And of course there was travel. London was truly the centre of the universe. In our first holidays in Europe we had gone to Scandinavia for a month and learned to travel cheaply by camping in designated camping areas. Gordon had been in love with Sweden for years and we were enthralled by Swedish design, technology and social democracy. I vividly remember the impact of the realisation that the Danes and the Swedes thought that children were important. Their best designers designed furniture, toys, schools and kindergardens. They were committed to the power of a creative environment.

The arrangement of school terms in England was based on a long summer holiday in July and August and even celebrations such as Christmas were a minimal interruption. In our second year there I decided to find a holiday job. I wanted to share most of my sight-seeing with Gordon and I did not want to be scratching around and unemployed for the months of July and August. The more money we saved, the longer we could travel when Gordon finished his time at Coopers and I completed the school year of 1966.

Most teachers worked for at least half of their vacation, partly because they were poorly paid, but also because the Greater London Education Authority encouraged it. Experience in community-based programs was well regarded and many teachers worked abroad in holiday programs. This was very different from my Australian pro-fessional experience, where holidays were prized as time to go to the beach.

I decided to do what the Londoners do and before the end of the term I went to see what was on offer. Within a couple of days I was offered a job as Assistant Director of an adventure playground at Ravenscourt Park in Shepherd's Bush. This meant I would work after school from 5.00 p.m. to 8.00 p.m. during daylight saving, and daily from 8.00 a.m. to 5.00 p.m. through the school holidays. I grabbed the opportunity. Ravenscourt Park was only a couple of stops on the tube from our place, and working outdoors for a change was very attractive as, like most Australians in the northern hemisphere, I was longing for the sun.

Adventure playgrounds were invented by the Danes after the Second World War and had their origins in the creative play move-ment, which recognised a child's need for adventure play. The first parks in Europe were in bomb sites, which kids chose as play spaces in preference to manicured parks, which were generally hostile to children. European and English parks were covered with signs that said Keep Off the Grass, the very place urban children wanted to play. Adventure playgrounds took part of that manicured space and dedicated it to play that could be mucky and creative.

Ken Roberts, an artist, was appointed director of the park. There were just two of us and our brief was to establish a creative adventure playground for the local children. Ravenscourt Park was an elegant and traditional English park, surrounded by a concentrated West Indian population who lived in crowded circumstances. It was close to Wormwood Scrubs Prison, and families whose fathers were inside gravitated to rented flats in the area.

We were catering for children aged five to fifteen, and we set about developing programs that would appeal to them. Ken set up painting and craft activities and I organised games and storytelling. Outdoors our ambition was to build a permanent structure of cubby houses and a flying fox. But almost every morning when we came to open up, the place had been trashed. It was heartbreaking.

Gordon McCarthy's carpentry skills were enlisted and we started on an ambitious ship, built around a tree, with a plank to walk. It was a daily race to get enough built to make it too hard to pull down, and to get enough boys (I regret that only boys were using the carpentry tools) using the tools and making an investment in the structure. Every day for weeks we'd start again. Then one wonderful day we arrived to find it as we had left it. It seemed to be under the management of a couple of the bigger boys whom we had suspected of the trashing. They told us they were minding it and their mums had asked whether their little brothers and sisters could come each day. 'Sure,' I said. From that day there was no trashing and we ran a model park with our protectors keeping guard.

Officially no one under five attended, but once it was known there was a 'nice lady' there, some of the six and seven-year-olds—Sabu and Leroy being two of my favourites—started to bring their little sisters. 'Me Mum says you won't mind if my little sister comes for a while. She's got to do some shopping, Miss, and then visit me dad.' Little sisters, sometimes only nine months old, would arrive in strollers with cigarette lollies in their mouths and one nappy for the day. We developed deep pockets and good networks of support so that milk and bread would appear.

I became cunning at identifying the mothers and inviting them in.

I would see them loitering with intent half a block away with their prams. They would never have given themselves permission to be there, partly because of their mistrust of authority and partly because of their colour. White was still the colour to be. Before long I had a regular group of mothers in a playgroup with their children. A great spin-off was their improved understanding of the expectations of the school system.

Sabu and Leroy were special—West Indian with broad cockney accents, they bounced with enthusiasm and energy and were my self-appointed guardians. In recognition of that affection they would arrive most days with little apples they'd scrumped for me. For 'scrumped' read: stolen. I had to explain that I'd prefer to buy my apples. They were astonished by such stupidity, but eventually agreed to quit scrumping.

Nineteen sixty-six was the year of the World Cup in London, and there were many summer nights when we'd close up, go down to the local pub and watch the soccer. It was a truly happy summer working in the playground and getting to know the mostly immigrant families.

By contrast, on other evenings I turned into the corporate wife of the bright young Aussie working at Cooper Brothers. In one place I was an angel, in the other I heard my career described as quaint. People often asked why I refused to take umbrage at these remarks and the truth is I am not sure. It had something to do with my view of myself as not being available to be patronised. Where I worked was far more real and more likely to be the future, and I considered myself privileged to be part of it. I often found I knew more about parts of London than the people I had dinner with.

The classrooms and staffroom of Gilliatt were a microcosm of London in the sixties. The teachers were upwardly mobile, regardless of their origins. They included the daughters of Welsh coalminers and the wives of middle-ranking public servants. The girls, with their invariably perfect skin, transformed themselves at the school gate as they went to work in the new boutiques in Kensington and the North End Road. English popular music brought us all together. It was a fantastic time to be in London and as I went to work in my black Courrèges boots and my mini skirt, I thought I was swinging too.

When I left Gilliatt in the summer of 1966 I asked Miss Kindred for a reference. She wrote:

> Mrs McCarthy is conscientious, efficient and adaptable and teaches with a zest and enthusiasm which she can also arouse in her pupils of all abilities so that good work and good discipline result. She is generous with her services for extra curricular activities, arranging theatre and other educational visits and helping with games—especially in coaching a rowing crew and accompanying them to regattas, as well as taking a full share of supervision duties in school. I am sorry that Mrs McCarthy has been able to stay with us for a comparatively short time as her contribution to this school has been greatly valued by her colleagues and pupils. She will be an asset in any school.

Oh, to be so professionally and affectionately valued; I wept as I left the school and life in London. Where else could it be so good?

This was also a time when I was separating from my family and growing in confidence as both a corporate wife and a professional woman. My first letters home seem immature and more dependent on my mother's approval than I remember being. However the letters remain, and I don't think I was pretending. In June 1965 I wrote: 'Please hurry and write. I'm getting desperate and can't afford to ring this week. It's horrible not hearing. I get so homesick and irritable ... and I am thinking of you all yesterday with Kerry going away' (to Vietnam). In July 1965 I wrote: 'It's exactly three weeks since my birthday which means three weeks since I've had a word from home. It's too much and this is the second time it's happened. Last time it was a month. For all that I'm meant to be selfish and thoughtless it seems rather unfair ... Charm and Alfred [Gordon's brother and sister] write more to Gordon than you have to me of late.'

It is hard to remember the intensity of the feelings. Yet I knew my emotional well-being had improved and evened out. Gordon was calmer than anyone in my family and I did not miss the emotional seesaw that the relationship with my mother had become since I had finally left home. I was also meeting many other women and seeing different role models.

English women were different from those I had grown up with, and although they may have been asked to leave the dinner table before the port, their opinions and authority were more acknowledged. This was the first time I had seen women with infrastructure. Health systems designed for them like the Flying Squad, which enabled them to birth at home if they chose. It gave them a confidence about their place in the world, unlike many Australian women. I could not think of an Australian equivalent of Lady Antonia Fraser, a woman who wrote historical biographies, had five children and was married to the owner of Harrods. Later, when she left him for Harold Pinter, I mused that her life was charmed.

In mid-1966 Coopers advised that Gordon would be transferred to the Pittsburgh, USA office of the firm. It hardly seemed a fashionable appointment. However, it was the USA and we were curious and excited about living there, although I was apprehensive about finding a job. My first inquiries about teaching opportunities in the public system were depressing as the only responses to my letters came from Arkansas and Tennessee, both a long way from Pittsburgh, and hardly the working environment I saw myself in.

The Pittsburgh appointment confirmed our decision to travel for as long as possible and the firm was very flexible about this. In August we packed up our house, bought our air tickets to the USA and set off for Europe until the money or enthusiasm ran out. Planning this itinerary had been fun, and this time we had upgraded to a Volkswagen station wagon and travelling was more comfortable. We could also afford the occasional *pensione* if the weather was too awful.

For ten weeks we wandered around Europe absorbing the experience, visiting icons and sharing meals with young people like us who were exploring the world. In Florence we found a convent where we ate lunch every day; in Paris we stayed in a Left Bank Hotel, and realised our school French belonged to another country. We visited all the great tourist places and then travelled through East Berlin and Dresden to our favourite city, Prague. In Prague we camped the night in a campsite on the Vltava River. We had a great night at a jazz cellar, where we met the US ambassador and his wife. Taking their advice, we went to hear the Czech Symphony Orchestra play Dvorak and Smetana, and the next night for five shillings we had seats for *Aida* at the Prague Opera House. Dressed in our shorts, complete with our binoculars, we felt at home.

The eclecticism of these experiences imprinted on me forever my eclectic tastes. My self-consciousness about my ignorance of classical music and art began to wane, for here I met people who not only embraced a diverse range of interests, but who were honest about not knowing and learning. I was completely happy with this sustained gypsy existence and dreamt of living like this forever.

But there were some dark clouds. My brother Kerry had been sent to Vietnam on active service and my mother was distressed. From a distance I wrote of doing his bit and how good he would feel after. How wrong could I be?

In a letter to his mother from Patras in October 1966 Gordon wrote a glowing account of our journey through Eastern Europe and the Alps. I added a note: 'Gordon has a beard and Kerry is still surviving Vietnam though a couple of his friends have been killed.' Was I so casual that death was on a par with a beard? I think not, but ...

Inevitably the money ran out and we returned to London for a few days to arrange our move to the USA, where Lyndon Baines Johnson was still President. Despite studying US history in order to teach it, we were ignorant of matters American. Gordon and I flew direct to Pittsburgh and checked into the Pittsburgh Hilton, delighted with the luxury of it. To indulge ourselves, we ordered room service breakfast. It arrived on a silver trolley and we were charged an outrageous amount. We quickly moved into an apartment.

During our first week in Pittsburgh we were taken out to dinner by a couple of partners and their wives. They were hospitable and friendly and we understood we were being checked out. As the corporate wife, I was offered useful wifely advice about where to live and where to buy Gordon's shirts (Brooks Bros); I refrained from saying we had stocked up in the London sales before we left and Gordon would be wearing Bond Street. In retrospect this was extremely wise as no one could care less about Bond Street. In fact we had just met our first examples of 'America is God's own country'.

Sympathy and surprise at our childlessness were expressed, and then one of the wives confided that the school they'd just helped establish had a temporary vacancy in the History department. While teaching was not exactly what the wives of Coopers men did normally, under the circumstances perhaps I could help out. Quick to see an opportunity, I confided in return that I was longing to teach as we weren't planning to have children while in the States. The fact that I had indicated support for parenthood helped.

Next morning, I had a phone call inviting me to report to Fontbonne Academy to meet Sister Baptista, the Mother Superior and Principal of the school. Some hours later in her study she explained that the teaching sister, who was Professor of American History and Problems of Democracy, was too ill to return to work in the foreseeable future. The school was a new school and was facing its university and college accreditation, without which it would not be the school of choice for middle-class Catholics. It had very strong academic aspirations and Sister Baptista was concerned that the accreditation would be jeopardised without a demonstration of competent teaching in all departments. I assured her that I'd studied American History and was competent, offering my references from Miss Colyer and Miss Kindred as evidence.

It was agreed that I would start the following Monday. I was so thrilled to have the job that I didn't raise the question of money. When she discovered that I did not have a green card, she assured me that God would provide and meanwhile she would pay me as a 'charitable deduction'. I was earning the (less than princely) sum of three hundred US dollars a month, but I was happy—I was working.

As I was about to leave the interview she said she would like my skirts to be longer, as I would be the only teacher not in a religious habit. I could see the point: this was not swinging London, but deeply conservative middle America. The skirts had to come down and later that afternoon I was buying a preppy little baby-blue sweater and knee-length plaid skirt, ready for my first day at work at Fontbonne Academy.

Fontbonne Academy was a school founded and funded by the wealthy Catholic community in Pittsburgh. The school was a direct expression of the growing aspirations of Catholics to play a greater role in American society since John F. Kennedy became the first Catholic President. In Pittsburgh, home of the Mellons and Carnegies, the WASP community ranked high and the Catholics low.

Wisely, the founders of Fontbonne worked with the Sisters of Saint Joseph, an intellectual order of French nuns of whom there were two communities in the US. I was the only teacher with a Bachelor's degree. Everyone else had a Master's or a doctorate. They were an extraordinary group of intellectually liberated teaching women. It was an academically selective school, although it didn't broadcast this widely, and it was certainly financially selective. Pretty well everyone's Daddy was vice president of Heinz, US Steel, Alcoa or a partner in a major professional firm.

Fontbonne was a beautifully designed school, the best I have ever worked in, with marvellous modern equipment and light airy classrooms. The contrasts with the dark Victorian buildings of Gilliatt could not have been greater. For the first few months I missed the neediness of Gilliatt. Here the girls seemed to have everything and I wondered how I could be of any value. Every day the school community ate together in the school canteen. The menu always included chilli con carne, pizza, hamburgers and salads. On Fridays we always had fish, until the Pope gave permission for meat to be eaten. Sometimes I would sit in the canteen watching the girls eat, and think of the stodge served up in London schools. Gilliatt girls would have killed for hamburgers. I have often reflected that this was my introduction to the concept of good customer service. It was assumed that to attract pupils to Fontbonne you would have to offer value, and serving food the girls liked, as opposed to serving food that was good for them and they hated, was part of the package. I loathed doing luncheon duty at Gilliatt. Just the smell of the greasy grey food and the treacle tart and custard was enough to cut one's appetite. God knows what families used to cooking with spices thought of it.

In my first week of teaching I had twenty 'hooded accreditors' (nuns) sitting in my classroom as part of the process of determining which colleges would accept Fontbonne graduates. It was an intimidating beginning. Each night I would have to choose between cramming in more information or grabbing more sleep, which always ensured more emotional energy. This is the constant dilemma of teaching.

The school passed its accreditation with flying colours. Sister Baptista was pleased with me and reported that the girls were responding well to my unusual way of looking at the American experience. She wondered if I would like to stay as it seemed my predecessor was still unwell. (The girls told me she was an alcoholic and in a special hospital.) I said I'd adore to stay. I was privately wanting to negotiate some extra money, but I didn't dare ask. I was really grateful for the job and 'Professor of American History' sounded wonderful. Problems of Democracy, my other teaching responsibility, turned out to be a flexible program of civics and sociology where we could discuss almost anything. This was the arena for running mock political campaigns and discussing whether women should work when they became mothers.

To ensure that I would not be an illegal worker, Sister Baptista decided she should apply for a green card for me. 'Leave it to me and the Lord,' she said. 'It will be done.' And one year later I received a three-year green card—the Lord had provided. Regrettably we had by then decided to return to Australia, so I never did become a legal employee.

Teaching American history was fun and helped me understand the closeness of Americans to their heritage. In their four years of high school these students studied four semesters of history, made up of two semesters of US history, one semester of Pennsylvanian history and one semester of world history. It was not surprising that they thought the world began and ended in the USA.

Although my students knew a lot about America, their knowledge was not broadly-based. They were assisted in their thinking by the Department of State, which released to schools—every couple of weeks, on pale blue paper printed in blue ink—the official State message about the current American position on whatever major international incident they thought the students' attention should be drawn to.

The Rhodesian affair was a perfect example of this. I was asked to discuss it with my students using the background paper provided by the State Department. This was a challenge, as from my perspective it was a biased and ill-informed piece. In the interests of truth I approached it in that way and provoked feedback from some parents, who felt the need to advise me of my mistakes if my political interpretations differed from theirs.

However, the Fontbonne community welcomed the girl from Sydney and her husband. Not only was I given major responsibilities in the school, the parents of the school opened their hearts and homes to us in a way the accounting firm never did. We were constantly surprised by the contrast of extraordinary conservatism—expressed by being asked outright if we were Communists—to great courage in taking a political stance about the role of the church in achieving social justice.

Gordon and I became friendly with one of the nuns, Sister Mary Louise, and one night she asked us to the Convent for dinner. 'It's not usual,' she said, 'to have a man for dinner, but Sister Baptista said Mr McCarthy could have special status for the night. To keep him company we have also asked the Bishop's secretary, Jim Quinlan.' We ate a wonderful French meal, complete with French wine from their excellent cellar. It was probably the best meal we had in the US. Did Sister Baptista have another agenda, I have often wondered? For from that night I was encouraged to visit Washington with Jim Quinlan to meet a history teacher at a Catholic college and compare notes. In fact the meeting was about the Washington march against U.S. involvement in Vietnam and how to look after conscientious objectors.

I found this confronting for many reasons, not least of which was that my brother Kerry had been conscripted in the first ballot for Vietnam and was still serving time there. In April 1965 my mother had written to us in London in great distress about this. I had responded: 'I knew Kerry would get called up although I kept saying otherwise. I had an instinct about it. You will miss him but I think it may be the best thing—he's obviously unsettled at present and a couple of years will give him time to make up his mind about the future. So don't be disheartened, Kerry might do very well in the forces.' In March 1966 I had written to my sister Deborah: 'Guess our Mama is still distressed about our Kerry. Every time I think of the National Service men being pushed into active service I experience a rise in blood pressure but despite their Mothers I wonder what would happen if the boys were asked. I'll bet they would volunteer! Anyway there is not a thing we can do except hope that K Ryan returns intact.'

That's what I thought until I started listening to Catholic activists describing it is a wicked and immoral war and asserting it was our Christian duty to end both the American and Australian involvement. Who to believe and who to defend? It was a deeply troubling time and I began to realise that with Kerry in Vietnam his life was at risk and my platitudes were of no value.

After a few weeks of settling in, Sister Baptista called me in for a chat. She said, 'I've noticed that you don't say your prayers. I can understand as an Australian you may not wish to recite the Oath to the Constitution, but why not the prayers?'

'Sister,' I said, 'I'm not a Catholic.'

'Holy Mother of God,' she said, 'with a name like McCarthy and a maiden name of Ryan. How could this be? Why didn't you tell me?'

'Sister,' I said, 'you never asked.'

'Well,' she said, 'I think that makes my next question easier. Our girls need some personal advice about love and marriage. So I thought who could be better than one of our own teachers. You may have the girls for two hours and we'll just close the doors in the gym. We won't listen.'

'Oh no,' I thought.

And so I gave my first sex education lesson. I assumed from the flushed faces of a couple of my teaching colleagues that some discreet listening had occurred through the walls. My moral and social status were so high that the following week Gordon and I were entrusted with the task of being official chaperones for the school prom, to be held at the Pittsburgh Hilton. It was a swanky event, equivalent to university graduation in our country, and it consumed hours of the girls' energy.

The girls of Fontbonne were confident and articulate. They ran mini political campaigns reflecting the politics of the day and each semester had to make a commitment to community work. This was the America of Lyndon Baines Johnson's presidency, and education programs such as Operation Headstart were flourishing in Pittsburgh. These girls had little or no contact with black Americans as Pittsburgh was geographically divided on racial lines, but at least working on these programs aroused their sense of social justice and for me it was a revelation. Operation Headstart had volunteer support from Fontbonne girls and their teachers. This was the place where I observed the reality of systemic discrimination. The IQ testing for school grading had pictures of houses with and without glass in the windows and children were asked to observe what was right or wrong with the house. If they noted that the house had no window panes they scored points. For some children a house without panes was not unusual and so they scored no points and were consigned further down the IQ scale.

Summer vacations invariably involved community experience in places such as Kentucky, where the girls spent time with the Kentucky Hill Folk. To my regret, I declined the invitation to join them. I was too new a wife and too unsure of myself to agree. It remains one of my lost opportunities. As a consolation, Gordon bought me a book on the Hill Folk.

Fontbonne's combination of commitment, vocation, more than adequate resources and strong parental involvement provided the best teaching environment I've worked in. Even though Americans seemed insular in many ways, the lack of self-consciousness in expressing love of country was impressive, as was the ability to be critical when it was thought to be justified.

I had completed one academic year at Fontbonne when we decided to head for home. We were desperate to have a baby, and Gordon wanted some proper work as he had spent half his time in Pittsburgh reading business biographies in the Carnegie/Mellon library, and playing golf.

Sister Baptista encouraged our parental intentions but told me she thought I would always be a teacher. In the reference she handed me she wrote: 'Mrs McCarthy is our loss and will be the gain of anyone who hires her. She is a real teacher in every sense of the word—a dedicated person who inspires youth with a sense of values and who helps each student to self-motivation. She is totally an unspoiled, gracious, and refreshing personality.'

While my professional development was on a roll, I was feeling anxious about pregnancy. I always wanted to be a mother but children were for later, when we were both ready and felt secure about our relationship. I felt very strongly that this was a commitment we should both make. The first years of married life in London were our investment in ourselves, free from the pressures of the status quo. We needed to find our own way. It wasn't until we began to think about returning home in 1967 that we decided it was time to think parenthood and abandon the Pill. I was amazed when after one month off the Pill I had a period. I had imagined that I would be pregnant immediately. After all, I had achieved one pregnancy and had proven fertility.

This sorry state of affairs repeated itself for some months, by which time I was becoming anxious. I wondered if the abortion was a reason. A voice in my head was inclined to suggest, 'You had your chance, you blew it and this is your punishment.'

Of course the counter-voice would have suggested that one unplanned pregnancy in four and half years of unprotected sexual activity was hardly indicative of high fertility, but people longing to achieve or avoid pregnancies are rarely rational and my knowledge of the statistics of successful pregnancy rates was zero.

After I had been off the Pill and was having a seemingly normal cycle I went to a gynaecologist in Pittsburgh who suggested that if I wasn't pregnant within two months I should make an appointment at an infertility clinic. Two months later I was the new patient at Dr Feingold's Infertility Clinic, and was coming to terms with that word, infertility. Infertility is a bad, indeed a shocking, word. It was the opposite of how I saw myself or my future. I had spent years avoiding pregnancy. Was I now to spend years trying to achieve one?

Now that I was wearing this awful label I wanted to get on with it and Dr Feingold was just the no-nonsense man I needed. At the consultation he took a medical history and asked the usual questions about previous pregnancies. True to form I spared him the information about the abortion and told him an elaborate story about a couple of late periods I'd had. He asked that Gordon and I come in together so that Gordon's fertility could be established. We did this, and Gordon was sent off to produce a semen specimen. A day or so later his semen got top marks for density and motility and I was categorised as the one with the problem. I wasn't sure whether to be proud or relieved.

Dr Feingold suggested instant remedial action. 'Young lady,' he said, I cannot see anything wrong with you but in case you have tubal blockage caused by spasm I will bring you in next week for a histo-salpingogram. Then I want you and your husband to have sex every day, more or less at the same time, until you get home to Sydney, and if you're not pregnant by then, put your name on the adoption list.' It clarified the position.

The desire to be pregnant also influenced my decision to forgo the Fontbonne journey to the Kentucky Hill Folk. Instead I joined Gordon on a work assignment at Lake Erie, where we lived in a motel for a month. Nineteen sixty-seven was the year of Montreal Expo and we decided that we would drive through New England, visit Montreal and then drive from coast to coast. It was an amazing six weeks and confirmed to me that America is the best and worst of the world.

However, pregnancy was on our agenda as well as travel, and no matter how demanding the daily schedule, we had intercourse every day. Dr Feingold's words were treated seriously and as we drove into a Howard Johnson Motel, a chain famous then for low room rates and twenty-seven flavours of ice cream, we at least had the comfort of rooms of predictable standard and layout.

The routine changed little when we shipped the car out of San Francisco and caught a plane to Mexico City followed by a bus to

Acapulco. Our diligence continued and as I threw up one morning in Acapulco I dared to hope I was pregnant and it was not from drinking margaritas. When we flew into Sydney from Acapulco in September 1967 I was overwhelmed by three strong feelings. The first was being reminded of the overwhelming beauty of the Harbour and my love of the Australian light, the second was a feeling of nausea which I welcomed, and the third was the ache in my infected ears. For years I had wanted my ears pierced, but my mother told me it was ordinary. My final act of defiance was to have them pierced in Mexico City at the Red Cross Hospital, an unpleasant event. Retribution was two infected ears on my return home. However I had missed a period so my first task in Australia would be to find an obstetrician who would see me immediately, and establish whether I was really pregnant.

CHAPTER FIVE

BACK TO OZ

rriving back in Sydney was both exciting and an anticlimax. All our family came to meet us, and yet in the photograph we look strained and there was an unease from the beginning. We had become accustomed to ourselves and were not sure how we would adjust to life in Sydney and our family networks. We planned to stay with my mother and Geoff at Palm Beach until we had arranged somewhere to live. I was looking forward to getting to know them all again. However, re-establishing our lives in Sydney from Palm Beach was not as easy as we'd hoped. We felt geographically isolated, not surprisingly after living in dense urban areas for three years. Also the close relationship my mother and I had enjoyed for the first sixteen years of my life was changing, as inevitably it should with both of us in new marriages.

Gordon and I quickly found a flat at Kirribilli and moved out. I think my family thought this insulting and somewhat disloyal but, with my usual response to any constraint, imagined or real, I recognised that Gordon and I needed our own space. Also, I was preoccupied with my own hoped-for pregnancy and my first task was to establish that it was real and then find a compatible and competent obstetrician whom I could stay with throughout the pregnancy. Many friends recommended Dr Alan Bradfield who delivered at King George V. I met him with my urine specimen and liked him immediately, as I thought he understood the kind of patient I wanted to be.

When he called with the joyful news that the test was positive I found myself sobbing with relief. He suggested I come in for a checkup the next day. When he took my medical history he asked the appropriate and inevitable question about any previous pregnancies. True to form I lied and said none. I still find it astonishing that I felt the need to lie. Did I not think it an important piece of medical information? Well yes, but the taboos surrounding abortion were stronger and the code was secrecy.

Dr Bradfield asked if I had any views about managing my confinement and I nervously blabbed on about the birthing I'd heard of in Europe and the USA: home births, watching the delivery in mirrors, etc. I told him I wanted to be awake, aware and have my husband with me. He responded, 'You're definitely a candidate for psychoprophylaxis and I suggest that you contact the Childbirth Education Association.' (Psychoprophylaxis is a method for conditioning pregnant women for childbirth through training in labour technique, and controlled breathing.) He asked the receptionist to give me the form, and described the work of the French doctor Ferdinand Lamaze in controlling pain in childbirth. What I found persuasive about this was that women could be more in control of the birth and husbands were encouraged to be actively involved.

Curiously none of the people who recommended Bradfield to me had followed this method and indeed were rather dismissive of it. I became increasingly aware of an attitude commonly expressed in lines like, 'Just wait until it's your turn, you'll be screaming for the gas.' It was almost gleefully punitive and suggested acceptance that 'this is the way things are'. I have never been convinced by that argument and this was not the time to be persuaded.

I was determined to do my best to enjoy the experience of childbirth; after all, this was something I hoped to do three or four times, and I wanted to do it in style and with dignity. Who better to follow than a distinguished French obstetrician. I rang the contact at the CEA, who was warm and friendly, and within a week I was a member of a new club, the mothers-to-be—a group that was, in effect, a lobby group for birthing choices.

I often reflect on how lucky I was to find Alan Bradfield. He was unusual for his time: he questioned existing beliefs and encouraged his patients to believe they were the main event in childbirth and that he was but the wise assistant and manager. This was a radically different view from that held by most obstetricians in Sydney, who saw themselves as the main event in childbirth. 'Trust me,' they would say. 'You won't remember a thing.' Well, I wanted to remember and enjoy the experience and my observations of birthing in Europe and America encouraged me to believe that was possible. Alan Bradfield coached and encouraged me all the way.

Years later I was very honoured to be asked to give the eulogy at Alan Bradfield's funeral. The service was held in St James Church and was well attended by the obstetric and gynaecological community. I told the mourners stories about the availability of this man to his patients to discuss new ideas and issues and his affectionate patience as we found our position on subjects ranging from tubal ligation in my case to circumcision. I wondered as I spoke how many of them understood just how important this man was in empowering women in childbirth.

After a couple of weeks settling into our little red brick flat in Kirribilli, I decided I was not suited to being a full-time wife on a limited income. It was back to the Department of Education and the reality that to the NSW Department of Education the views of Miss Kindred and Sister Baptista didn't matter a toss. The clerk who interviewed me was dismissive of my references and explained that overseas teaching experience did not count in NSW. He said they had standards to protect and could not give credit to anyone who 'just walked in off the street' and claimed experience overseas. His mouth curled as he said that word of disloyalty, 'overseas'. Welcome home, Wendy.

I asked that he clarify my status as I now had six years' teaching experience. He painstakingly explained that one year's seniority was lost for resigning and for each year out of the service a penalty of one year was applied. So I was now the same status as a first-year-out teacher, despite my continuous employment. Few permanent jobs were available and his advice was to take casual work. He promised to try to have me paid as though I'd had three year's experience. Of course he was referring to the three years in NSW.

Beggars can't be choosers, I thought, as I agreed to have my name on the casual list for 1968, but I felt profoundly depressed. I had

developed professionally in those other teaching experiences and I
wanted to contribute to my own country. A few days later I received
notice of my eligibility for employment as a Casual, Graduate Assistant at 4th Year Rate. The rate was $20.84 per day, to be changed
to $4,252 per annum when I became Temporary. At least it was
4th Year. As employment was dependent upon medical fitness, I
advised them that I was pregnant and I suggested I be appointed to
a school that could comfortably manage my departure in April—my
baby was due in the first week of June and the Department required
that pregnant women stop work six weeks before the expected confinement date. On 22nd December I was asked to report to Mosman
High in January 1968.

I then turned my attention to house hunting. We had a $5,000
deposit and Gordon's mother was happy to be our guarantor. I
started at Balmoral and moved around the water's edge to Balmain
when it was clear Balmoral was out of our price range. Ideally we
wanted to be on a ferry service and close to the city so that we would
need only one car. We found the right house at McMahons Point, a
large, four-bedroom Edwardian place overlooking the water at
Berry's Bay. We bought it for $22,000 and moved in on our third
wedding anniversary. I thought how fantastic it was to be pregnant
and have a mortgage.

This was to be our home for the next eleven years. It was a wonderful house with large rooms, a fibro and crinkle glass sunroom
which, when opened up, revealed extensive views over Berry's Bay,
plus decorative plaster ceilings, and newly polished floorboards. On
the down side, the kitchen and bathroom were grotty, and when our
families came to lunch on Christmas Day they were greeted by us
solving the plumbing crisis which had happened an hour before. Fortunately it did not affect the gazpacho.

McMahons Point was a significant choice. Our families thought we
lived in a slum suburb, while conceding that the house had promise.
The Hills Hoist in the front garden, which was on street level, was
not, in 1967, an attractive Aussie icon to be treasured, but an ugly
bit of gear to demolish, and why would you want to display your
washing to the world?

Right: Elsie Mary Ryan (Nana Ryan), my paternal grandmother.

Bottom left: Wendy Elizabeth in her best.

Bottom right: A family picnic in Orange— mother, father and friends.

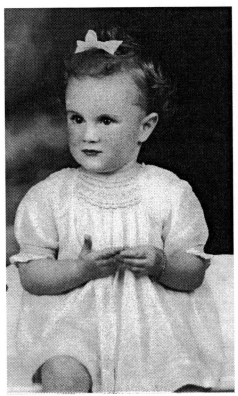

Above: Kerry, me, Deborah and Daddy at the Forbes Show.

Left: A Forbes High schoolgirl.

Right: Marching in support of producing more scientists (complete with fake belly) in Armidale, 1958.

Below: Formally attired for graduation day, 1961.

With Gordon on our wedding day, 18 December, 1964.

'Mrs Gordon McCarthy: US History, Problems of Democracy, World Cultures, History Honor Society, Student Congress, Extemporaneous Speaking', according to the Fontbonne Academy yearbook, 1967.

Gordon and Sophie, 1969.

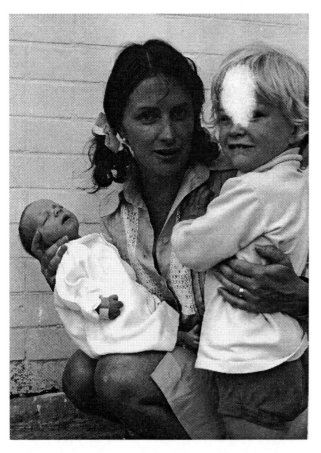

Sam comes home from
hospital and Hamish sticks
close to me, March 1973.

Grown up and trainee feminists marching. *Left to right:* me, Annette Evans, Margaret Winn, Colette Parr, and Sophie McCarthy in front.

The Family Planning education team—Margaret Winn, Colette Parr, me, Virginia Knox and Robert Sobczuk, 1976.

Gail Wilenski (nee Radford), me and June Surtees (nee Williams) at a very early WEL meeting at the McCarthy McMahon's Point kitchen.

Within a week of moving in our neighbours, who were mostly elderly, called in to say hello and suggest we join the Progress Association, which was dedicated to improving the suburb. The President, June Mountjoy, lived around the corner and like many of the neighbours, had lived there for a long time. She told me that she had been a long-time member of the Communist Party and was one of the first Westerners to visit Russia in the early sixties. Her disillusion was now complete and she advised strongly against me joining the party. I wondered if I looked like someone who would join the Communist Party.

McMahons Point was under threat from high-rise development. At the bottom of the peninsula was the Harry Seidler-designed Blues Point Tower, where Gordon had lived when we met. And there were Seidler proposals for similar buildings along the spine of the peninsula. It was zoned industrial, and residential refurbishment was discouraged, as we were to discover when we put in an application to the Council to renovate a year later. It was a great community to live in—a diverse and changing neighbourhood, with corner shops, friendly butchers who delivered your order and an active timber yard and boat building business below us. We loved the energy that comes from such a mix and enjoyed walking around the neighbourhood. It was a place to defend.

Nineteen sixty-eight was a gloriously happy year. Sydney was alive and jumping with the political issues we had been exposed to in Pittsburgh and Washington. We found new friends, renewed old contacts and played at house renovation as we prepared conscientiously for the birth of our first baby.

In late January I joined the staff of Mosman High, my first co-ed school since teaching practice. The English/History master, Don Brown, faced a dilemma in staffing his classes as he was short of teachers. I told him on the first day that I was pregnant and would fit in wherever. He chose to assign me the senior history classes, so I moved back into the system at full speed. My students were a lively group and I enjoyed teaching boys and girls together. Mosman High had some good students and teachers but suffered a poor reputation, partly because it was in an area where many parents aspired to private school education for their children; shades of Cremorne Girls High and North Sydney.

The Childbirth Education Association lived up to expectations and referred me to a physiotherapist in Crows Nest for childbirth preparation. The physio, Poss Beck, was a strong disciple of psycho-prophylaxis and liked to teach patients in pairs. My pair was a charming young blonde woman called Anna Murdoch who also happened to live in McMahons Point and gave me a lift home if I was without the car. We bonded quickly and were both diligent about preparing for our first births. We read endless labour reports, did our exercises and dreamed about our new lives as mothers. We were so self-absorbed that we did not talk about our husbands initially. It was not until she mentioned that Rupert was in publishing that the name Murdoch clicked. Such is the levelling effect of childbirth. Sophie McCarthy and Elisabeth Murdoch were born six weeks apart at the same hospital. The shared experience has kept a fondness between Anna and me over more than thirty years.

I loved the physicality and sensuality of pregnancy. I also loved the science and experience. It was exciting meeting new people who were connected to these momentous changes in my life and with whom you established a level of intimacy as you discussed body changes and expectations. When I had the inevitable moments of blind panic as the birth approached, I overcame them by practising pelvic contractions and of thinking of people I didn't like much who had had babies. I would think 'If they can get it out, so can I'. My biggest shock was realising how ignorant I was about my reproductive system. Human biology was a mystery to me, a legacy of studying physics and chemistry rather than biology for the Leaving Certificate.

My favourite Mosman High story relates to my pregnancy. This was of considerable interest to the class, especially as it was becoming more noticeable and no replacement had been nominated. I kept deferring my departure until one of the boys described his dream about me delivering in the classroom. It was a timely communication of the pupils' concerns—they were making progress with me and were apprehensive about my replacement, especially those doing advanced level history, which would contribute significantly to their university entrance mark. To reduce this anxiety we agreed that after I left they would come to my place one night a week for their first level history work.

For the three weeks between my leaving school and Sophie's birth, they came to McMahons Point on Thursday nights. As arranged, one of the boys rang each week to check whether I was in hospital. When Gordon told him that Sophie had arrived (she was one day old), the boy asked whether they should come the next day. Gordon suggested leaving it for ten days. Two weeks later we recommenced in front of the open fire with Sophie snuffling beside us. They, like me, were enchanted with Sophie and, satisfyingly, they exceeded my highest hopes with their Higher School Certificate results.

CHAPTER SIX

BABIES AND BANNERS

First birth, there can be no experience like it. I cannot find the words that best describe the joy, the sensuality and the power of being female that childbirth confers. To experience the brain and body so perfectly synchronised and the rush of a profound love for a person you have just met is to feel life on a higher plane.

I am amazed at how much I remember thirty years later. I can see us sitting around the dining room table at McMahons Point. It was a Sunday night in May and we had friends to dinner. The fire was burning and it was cosy. I'd cooked moussaka; we drank lots of red wine and finished off with port. The guests stayed late, the last leaving about 1 o'clock, and we joked that this was the last dinner party before motherhood, which was two weeks away. We crashed into bed after deciding to leave cleaning up for the morning.

A couple of hours later Gordon woke me with the news that the bed was wet and the waters must have broken. I was feeling warm and sleepy and disagreed. I wanted to go back to sleep. I was not interested in going to hospital, but he was on the phone and agreeing with the sister in the hospital labour ward, in an extraordinarily disloyal way, that it was time for me to go.

I wondered as we drove across the bridge at 4 a.m. if I'd ever come back. Childbirth suddenly seemed like a long tunnel that would change my life for ever. I suddenly wanted everything to stay the same. It seemed a good idea to call the whole thing off, but as we drove into Camperdown my mood changed to one of anticipation and excitement at the thought that I was going to leave there as a mother.

At King George V's admission desk there were the obligatory

questions about my mother's maiden name. Then suddenly I was on the birth conveyor belt, with first stop the euphemistically named preparation room for the supposedly essential enema and pubic shave. I'd heard that some brave women were challenging these procedures, but on the list of things to argue about they didn't seem as significant as others, so I watched as my labia were reduced to a hairless and childish state, and practised my psychoprophylactic breathing during the enema. I remember the nurse saying the enema was essential so that I didn't 'dirty' the bed. Strange how words stay with you. It hadn't actually occurred to me that dirtying the bed was an issue.

Then into the labour ward, where the lights were bright, the noise distinctive and I didn't hear anyone asking for hot water like they do in the movies. Because my waters had broken I was confined to bed because of the risk of infection. I was there for eighteen hours of contractions, Scrabble, backache and some boredom. When the transition we had read about arrived and I was told to push I understood why it was called labour. It is the hardest work you can ever ask of your body. As I sat up with two nurses supporting my legs (no stirrups for me), Dr Bradfield suggested Gordon go to the foot of the bed so I could aim the baby at his watch face. If I had been told to stand on my head I would have tried, but the face of that watch was the target.

At 9.10 p.m., in the world's most orgasmic rush, a 6lb 5oz baby girl slid out. She was perfect. It was love at first sight and as the three of us cuddled up we named her Sophie, a name meaning dignity and wisdom.

I felt elated that I had managed a drug-free labour and my darling husband had not fulfilled those dire predictions and fainted when he was exposed to my genitalia. Instead he had been my partner and coach in the greatest event of my life. I cannot imagine birthing without him.

As the placenta was delivered I wondered why so many people had counselled us that awake and aware birth was not achievable, and that having one's husband there was not quite nice—'Fancy letting him see you like that.' To have missed sharing this experience was unthinkable.

After Sophie's birth I had no desire to return to teaching. I was utterly and totally in love with my baby daughter. I just wanted to be with her. The strength of it sometimes took my breath away and I marvelled at the social and family approval motherhood bestowed. We were a real family with a baby, a house, a cat, a dog and a mortgage. I was revelling in the image of myself as Gordon's wife and Sophie's mum.

For six months Sophie and I explored the world of our local community at McMahons Point. We got to know our neighbours and the local shopkeepers. We started putting down very strong community roots. Even attending the local baby health centre was an interesting political experience, and it was there that I met Carole Baker and became interested in local government. The most important people in my life at this stage were my neighbours Jack and Dorothy (Pank) Downes, a couple in their sixties who had lived in the house next door for over twenty years. They had three unmarried daughters and adored children.

Sophie and I spent hours there with Pank, who in true Australian tradition was known by her nickname, a reference to those great advocates of women's rights, the Pankhursts. Pank was a wise and intelligent woman who ran a home-based typing business; Jack had driven Commonwealth cars after a life as a pastry-cook and a time in the army. They were de facto grandparents to our children, all of whom adored them. It was a child-rearing situation to dream of and confirmed my view of the value of mixed communities.

During this time I was sharing baby-sitting with my friend Caroline Griffith who had recently returned from England and whose son Andrew was six weeks older. She was studying Law and I was enrolled in a pottery course at Willoughby and we minded each other's children one day a week. This was the model of childcare we continued to use as our families grew.

When Sophie was about six months old I was surprised to find myself thinking about teaching and how it could be managed. Discussions with Gordon produced this pragmatic response, 'Well, of course I expect that you'll go back to work. Why would you waste all that education and skill, and in any event I don't see any reason why one person should provide for an entire household.'

This seemed reasonable and appealed to my sense of justice, if not the image of myself as a kept mother. Discussions with my mother and my mother-in-law were extremely negative. They couldn't imagine why I would want to work and both thought there was a loss of social status involved. Indeed most people thought there was something wrong with me that I was not 'happy' to be at home with my baby, especially after all those years working and travelling.

Well, I was happy, but it wasn't enough for the long haul. And nor was there enough money to pay off a house, run a car and have the lifestyle that we might aspire to without Gordon having to work himself into the ground. And that seemed neither fair nor sensible. This was a partnership and he too was in love with Sophie and wanted to be with her. During this period of decision-making one of my few supporters was Pank, who thought it was for me to decide and gave me a line I have used for years: 'Whatever decision you make will be the right one, if you do your homework first.'

My loyalty, comfort with and commitment to public education led me back to the Department of Education to check out the opportunities. However the system offered only day-to-day casual work. This was not an option for me as I needed some notice to organise childcare. So I started looking for regular part-time work and wrote to all the independent schools within half an hour's travelling. Not one of my letters was answered. I started responding to advertisements, first to one placed by Shore, an Anglican boys' school at North Sydney, which had advertised for a history teacher three days a week. It looked like my job. When I rang for details I was told there were no facilities for a woman. I think they meant lavatories!

An advertisement for a full-time geography teacher at Wenona, an independent secular girl's school at North Sydney, was more fruitful. The Headmistress, Barbara Jackson, called me for an interview, took a close look at my references and asked what I would really like to do if I could choose. I said, 'I'd like to teach three and a half days a week in a concentrated mode. If you could timetable me to teach that way, I'm happy to do school excursions and regular duties but I don't need to spend a lot of my time in the staffroom.' She agreed and I was timetabled for a three and a half day concentrated week, but hired as a full-time geography Mistress on an annual salary of $3,085.

I was ecstatic. I had created a new persona to add to Gordon's wife and Sophie's mum. I immediately set about the task of finding someone to mind Sophie. I already had in mind a mature woman who would offer a contrast to me and complement Pank's role. It was also important that she be a good housekeeper, as that was part of the deal. We found the wonderful Mrs Fox, who spent 1969 being a version of me while I went off to Wenona to be Mrs McCarthy, Geography Mistress.

Wenona was a private comprehensive and secular school whose students revealed a wide range of intellectual ability. It was not the chosen school of the very well-to-do, but was popular because of its reputation as a school that cared for the whole person. It was a good environment to work in, and its Head was determined to make it a school that mattered. I was the Geography Mistress for 1969, and the combination of working and being a wife and mother I found wonderful. Sophie occasionally came on geography excursions and the school was flexible if I needed to bring her to school. She would sleep in her basket in the school staffroom. My Year 5 students joined the McCarthy baby-sitting brigade. Life felt integrated. When I left in December I was already four months pregnant and looking forward to my next baby.

In December 1969 Gordon left Coopers and the accounting profession to work with Gordon Barton at Tjuringa Securities. One of his first assignments was the takeover of Angus and Robertson, the Australian publishing house. Gordon Barton's company IPEC was a potential purchaser of the controlling interest of the British publisher William Collins and there were many late nights while the game was played out. I loved listening in to the saga. IPEC was successful in buying Angus and Robertson and Gordon McCarthy was made Executive Director. At 29, he had been handed a huge responsibility. Angus and Robertson was a complex business incorporating publishing, retailing and printing, but culturally dominated by publishing. When Gordon's appointment was announced, the first criticism was that he was not a book person, not in the industry. 'What would a chartered accountant know about books?' I was often asked. Even admitting to an Economics degree did not help.

I ended my teaching assignment at Wenona and moved increasingly into the politics of my community. There were so many things to do, I was high on it. Gordon and I had become active in the Childbirth Education Association and the local Resident Action group. We supported the fight to save The Rocks by backing Jack Mundey and The Rocks Resident Action group. It was the seminal battle which had to be won to acknowledge and save Sydney's heritage, and our passion knew no bounds. Pasting posters on telegraph poles in the dead of night, writing letters to the papers and continually persuading the more conservative progress associations to take direct action were part of that campaign, while the childbirth activity was directed to both the medical profession and parents-to-be.

CEA was a small and dedicated group of people who believed that education about childbirth increased the choices and safety for women in childbirth. Less medical intervention and more control by women were positives. The use of psychoprophylaxis was seen as a way of achieving this, and the method was taught by a network of key physiotherapists around Australia. Classes were taught at our house and our most famous pupil was Jackie Weaver.

With Gordon's move to Angus and Robertson corporate life was suddenly very engrossing. We needed the evening as well as the days to meet and get to know people. It would have been an unusual week that we didn't host at least one dinner party or weekend lunch. I took great pride in my culinary skills, most of which were derived from Elizabeth David's cookbooks. I worked hard at attending Gordon's social functions even though I resented those after-work cocktail parties, which are anathema to family life. I had seen enough corporate life to know how easy it was to stay in the office and miss the children's bed and dinner time, or 'crash down' as we called it. I made a decision that I was not going to take my marriage for granted, and I would be a visible wife, but it was a struggle.

One night Angus and Robertson was hosting drinks for the publisher Sir William and Lady Collins at 6 p.m. I raged internally when I received the invitation. How does a new mother fight the traffic and the baby-sitting requirements at that hour? The blessed Pank came to the rescue and I went into the city location in my silk separates and white Courrèges boots. When I arrived I couldn't see Gordon and was feeling left out, as a couple of secretaries ignored me. And then I was introduced to Lady Collins who, upon hearing that I was Gordon's wife, made a big fuss about how hard it was to make these anti-social, anti-family events and said that she was flattered I'd come to meet her and Sir William. I could feel my eyes moistening with gratitude and could have hugged her. Such approval could focus me for weeks and probably only women with those experiences can understand the contrasting feelings of social vulnerability and mother power. That anchor has always stayed with me and I have tried hard to ensure I give support to new mothers.

It was through CEA that I first found a public voice. Helen McCarthy (friend, not relative) and I met at CEA and had a lot in common, including being married to McCarthys. We were asked by the magazine *New Idea* if we would agree to an interview about our birth experiences. We shared the same obstetrician and our first children, Sophie and Joshua, were the same age. We were delighted to do it, and I was taken aback when criticised for speaking about such private matters. Such criticism has been a feature of my life since. It is usually prefaced by the line, 'Why do you need to draw attention to yourself and speak publicly about these issues?'

For years I have answered that public discussion and scrutiny are the best ways to change attitudes. In the case of childbirth practices, change would have been far slower if there had been no publicity. The *New Idea* article was driven by the screening of the CEA film *Don't Cry Baby*, a film made to promote psychoprophylaxis. It was screened on Channel 10 and I thought it deeply moving; CEA member Jenny Burton delivered her first baby on screen. The frontal view was very confronting, yet there were many people willing to appear, such was the passion. I would not have volunteered but I loved the film and it was used as a teaching film for childbirth for years.

Our son Hamish Gordon was born on 6 May 1970, three days before Mothers Day. He was the best present. Like many second labours this was much shorter, only 8 hours instead of 18. We had the same hospital team and felt confident as we approached King George V at about 8 in the morning. I was in the labour ward by 9 and he arrived at 5 p.m. We always called him the 9–5 boy. Gordon and I could not believe our luck: a son and a daughter, and while we always said gender didn't matter, I acknowledged a sense of completion and social approval at the birth of a son. The entire community is pleased with you, and it reminds you how much we value male children.

Years later I wrote a piece for the *National Times* on raising sons and reminisced about just how much approval is given to those who produce boys, and by contrast, how much pressure can be placed on women who produce 'only girls'. Within days I was wondering what the next McCarthy baby would be like. I felt like Mother Earth who had just hit her straps.

For the next two years I stayed out of the paid workforce and discovered community activism and feminism. It was a feminism grounded in fertility and reproduction, although I would not have used those words then. That is a later language. Speaking about choices in childbirth gave me confidence about reproductive choice. Abortion was only the next step, although some people found this incomprehensible. How could I be crazy about abortion and childbirth simultaneously? Well, no-one could be crazy about abortion, but you could passionately believe in the right of women to choose when, if and how to birth.

The answer was not complicated. If you supported choice in birth it had to include when or whether to give birth. So when I was asked to attend an Abortion Law Reform meeting on behalf of CEA, I agreed. I didn't know whether I would be motivated enough to go on my own and I was a little apprehensive. But when I arrived and listened to the discussion it was like coming home. These were the issues that mattered for women yet we were powerless. From fertility to feminism was only another short step. For the first time in my life I had the time to read, think and talk about these ideas and I became totally engaged with the idea of making community changes.

I'm constantly asked why I feel the need to go public. People ranging from my mother to my friends say, 'Why do you have to say all that stuff in public, why can't you just treat it as a private matter and get on with it?' There is a suggestion that I am publicity-seeking. Such comments have been made about my speaking out on childbirth education, fathers in labour wards, abortion—all this seemingly private women's business—to my public statements about education philosophies, matters of censorship, public policy on organisations like the ABC. The short answer is being polite and not challenging the status quo doesn't work, and during that period we were discovering the power of narrative and shared experience.

I'm not sure of the evolution; it's probably part of the reason for trying to write my memoirs as honestly as I can. On looking back through old photograph albums, I am reminded of my first public demonstration as a first year student at the University of New England. Why did I agree to dress as a pregnant woman wearing a sign saying 'produce more scientists' and march along the streets of Armidale? It was hardly a feminist statement, but who or what persuaded me? I don't recall the circumstances, but I do remember wanting to do it and feeling good, if apprehensive, as I walked along the streets.

Sometime during the three years Gordon was the Executive Director of Angus and Robertson and I was the corporate and community wife, one of the main book buyers asked me if I would like to read some books. I think he described it as being part of the poison testing for new titles. One of the first he asked me to read was *Sexual Politics* by Kate Millett. He said to me, 'A few people have expressed an interest in this, but quite frankly I think it's the boiler suit brigade. You're clearly not one of those. How about you read it for me and tell me what you think.' I was flattered both to be called intellectual and not to be of the boiler suit brigade, and took the book away. I read it from cover to cover, entranced, went back to him and said, '*Get heaps, it will sell.*' He was aghast; he truly believed I'd come back saying it was hopeless. However, he took my advice and ordered copies, and it sold very well.

Not long afterwards *The Female Eunuch* was published, and Gordon Barton and Angus and Robertson launched the paperback edition at a Writers of The Year dinner at the Argyle Tavern in the Rocks. *Vogue* recorded the event, but the article does not quite capture my feelings of excitement, awe and insecurity. It was my ambivalence about the effect and consequences of the motherhood path. While the book sang a song in my heart, I was treading unknown paths. I was not sure how to be a feminist and a mother, but I knew I wanted to be both.

In May 1972 Beatrice Faust flew to Sydney on a mission to convert local women to the idea of a women's political pressure group. The people invited were contacted through the Abortion Law Reform Association and met at the home of Julia Freebury in Bellevue Hill. Helen McCarthy and I went together, complete with Hamish and Claudia and committed to rigid timetables to collect Sophie and Joshua from pre-school. The others present were postgraduate student Anne Summers, journalist Caroline Graham, Women's Lib activist Mavis Robertson, Joan Evatt, Victoria Green from Canberra, sociologist Liz Fell, Faith Bandler of FCAATSI (Federal Council for the Advancement of Aborigines and Torres Strait Islanders), Helen L'Orange, a local council alderwoman, Helen Berrill, an independent candidate for the federal elections and June Surtees, a teacher. Helen L'Orange has since assured me that Bob Ellis was there. I have no recollection.

Beatrice spoke persuasively of the article written by Gloria Steinem in *New York* magazine for the first edition of *Ms* entitled, 'How women see candidates for the White House'. It was based on a nation-wide survey of candidates' attitudes towards issues women considered important, and American women thought the information influenced the vote. Ten Melbourne women had looked at the questionnaire and developed it for Australia. Would we support it? We were a group of ten or twelve people. It needed national coverage. We would need a control group, a lot of people willing to conduct interviews and a good media campaign. At the end of the session Beatrice looked around the room to see who was enthusiastic and who would co-ordinate it.

Nobody volunteered. Some of those present were only mildly interested and thought the tactics would lead to superficial reforms.

When the moment of truth came—almost by default, as we seemed to have the least to do—it was agreed that Caroline Graham would be the convener and June Surtees and I the deputy conveners. Grand titles for an unknown task, but the idea sounded right and we wanted an answer to the question: How did politicians define women in Australia? As the election was eighteen months away we three did not meet until early June, when we decided to call a public meeting to test interest in the idea. The organisation already had an embryo name, Women's Electoral Lobby or WEL. It was a great name for one-liners such as Get Wel and Get Wel and Truly ...

To our first public meeting, held at the Women's Centre, we asked our own networks of friends and acquaintances who might be interested in redefining where women fitted. Was it wife and mother, or were there other opportunities in Australian society? When we outlined the idea to the forty women who turned up, they loved it. It felt like we could do something, not just be handmaidens to the main events of Australian political life.

Membership and enthusiasm were astonishing. We were on a roll. Within two months we had to move to a larger meeting space to accommodate the number of people who attended, often over a hundred. We discovered a whole new network of women like us. At either the first or second public meeting, sociologist Eva Cox became involved and worked with June Williams and the Melbourne WEL on the questionnaire so that it could be administered and processed more easily. This was an invaluable contribution as it quickly became apparent that the profession of most WEL women was teacher, not sociologist or market researcher.

When, in July 1972, WEL member Anne Conlon decided to run as a Labor candidate, in the by-election in Mosman, we lovingly and enthusiastically offered support—a real woman candidate at last. We held a 'meet the candidates' meeting and this was to become the WEL methodology prior to elections. All candidates were invited to attend a public meeting where they would be asked questions on their attitudes to women and policies that had an impact on women. The meetings were invariably packed out. It was exciting—politics, grassroots style—and revealed some extraordinary attitudes which illustrated how far apart men and women were.

When the questionnaire was completed and collated, we were gobsmacked by the Neanderthal views expressed by so many, but my favourite remains Sir John Cramer's statement: 'A woman must be taught that virginity is the most valuable thing that she possesses.' Those of us who had lost ours years ago wondered about our residual value. Did he mean it?

All this activity was organised out of people's kitchens or sunrooms. I don't recall anybody having an office. The institutionalisation of WEL came later.

My first interview on radio was with with Paul Lynch on 2UE. It was a talkback on a Sunday evening. I remember wearing a green woollen shirt and long black skirt. It was my confident, good luck look for that year. I spent hours getting ready to make sure that I looked good. Yes, I know it was radio, but you never know who will see you. Despite the great external symbols, I had to stop the car and throw up from nerves. I then stopped at a garage and bought some chewing gum in case I smelt of vomit. I got there pretending I was cool, calm and collected.

The interview went well. Paul Lynch wanted to know why a nice young married woman like me would want to be involved in Women's Lib. 'No, Mr Lynch, I'm not a women's liberationist, I'm simply a woman who believes that we should know how politicians think; we want to know how they will vote on women's issues. We are insulted that they have not even thought about these issues.' There was no self doubt, but still denial about Women's Lib. WEL defined its role as reformist, not revolutionary.

In the WEL world it was my job to manage the PR and the media, and eventually that grew into a key role when deciding how we would release the results of the national questionnaire. Within a very short period of time WEL had gone Australia-wide, and the national campaign became the new phrase in my lexicon. I got the PR job (unpaid) because I had done some publicity for CEA and lived near a few journalists at McMahons Point.

We spent hours at meetings, working on ideas that we hoped would become public policy. We endlessly lobbied politicians and even in the early seventies we knew that we had to lobby some of corporate Australia: Nestlé, on infant formula, Drake Personnel on employment practices, Mark Foys on window displays. We could organise a crowd and media coverage in a very short time.

The camaraderie that came from meeting women who felt and thought the same was extraordinarily liberating, breathtaking really. WEL crossed so many defining boundaries of geography, husband's occupation and political allegiance. I've never been braver, happier and more determined than at that time in my life. I'd go to meetings, play mum all day long, deliver press releases around town with the children in the back seat, go to meetings at night, work on policy, and return home many nights exhilarated to snuggle up to Gordon.

He was a wonderful partner to have during that time because of his support and commitment, and I think he found the energy charge that this gave me exciting and seductive. When people said, 'Don't be bold' and 'You'll ruin your marriage', I heard it, but all my evidence pointed the other way and this liberated in me a voice I hadn't known about before. It was and remains a voice that encourages me to new personal challenges.

I wanted to tell other women, 'Don't be sucked in, don't believe what people are telling you. You can be a parent, a mother and a worker too.' If political men really value the family in the way they say they do, let's see the public policy response. The evidence was clear—women's voices were dismissed. Equal pay was but a dream, access to education for women and girls was limited, abortion was illegal and unsafe and contraception not easily available. WEL had plenty to do to remove systemic discrimination against women.

Our family life was changing. In 1972 Gordon quit the Barton empire after a dispute about the future management of the Angus and Robertson group to write a book about takeovers and start his own consulting business. I was keen to have another baby despite the zero population growth messages of Paul Ehrlich and the disapproval of some of my friends, both feminists and others. Nothing would dissuade me.

Partly to distract myself and partly because Gordon was at home writing, I looked for some part-time work. As luck would have it, I found a position as Geography Mistress at Monte St Angelo at North Sydney, where I worked for the rest of that year. It gave me the professional stimulus I needed and seemed to assist my fertility. By the end of the school year, to the joy of the nuns and our family, I was six months' pregnant and looking forward to our new baby.

For three months over summer I did WEL work and went to Balmoral beach every day. On 19 March 1973, two days after Gordon's birthday and a day after my brother Kerry's, Samuel Gordon was born. He arrived upside down. Despite all the prodding and encouragement, he refused to move into the regular birth position—an omen of things to come. A breech delivery with a different medical team was hard. I missed the relaxed, wise and friendly coaching of Alan Bradfield, who was hospitalised following a heart attack.

The replacement obstetrician was anxious. He and the anaesthetist kept encouraging me to have some pethidine to relax. I wasn't feeling tense until then, but their concern was effectively transmitted and I wondered if they knew something about the baby that I didn't. Before entering hospital I had focused on the advice that breeches were best delivered by experienced mothers who knew how to push effectively when instructed. I could do this, but the power of those in charge is strong, and eventually I acceded to their wishes and took my pethidine like a good girl. It was a mistake, and made me feel groggy and less able to respond to instructions.

Sam was born with a low APGAR rating and suspected greenstick fractures in the legs. Fortunately at 8 pounds he was bigger than his brother and sister and his respiratory system seemed sound. However, he was whisked off to the intensive nursery. When he hadn't been brought to me some hours later, I began to worry and went searching for him, despite having been told by the nurses that I was to stay in my bed because I'd taken the wretched pethidine. I went down to the next floor to the intensive care nursery and started creeping around to find my baby. I opened a door and quietly moved in and ran into an equally guilty-looking man, Gordon McCarthy, looking for his son. We found Sam, and after assurances that he would be brought to me soon, I went back to my ward to sleep.

Nobody said our baby was to stay in intensive care. We had to be vigilant to find out what was going on. The news got worse. As well as greenstick fractures, the paediatrician thought he had clicky hips and that a plaster cast would probably be a good idea. I immediately visualised this dear little boy lying in his cot for months and thought, 'No way'. I had just finished reading about babies in Vietnam who stayed in their cots all the time and couldn't move and were seriously under-socialised. Not for my baby.

For the rest of the hospital stay I listened carefully to all the advice, and as soon as I was discharged, I went to my experienced GP, Tom O'Neill, for advice. He recommended double nappies for Sam, certainly not plaster. Whose advice to follow: paediatrician or GP? I stuck with the GP who had six children of his own. Within six months the clicky hips had gone, but for the first five years of his life he had to wear cute red and navy orthopaedic boots. When he wore his first sneakers, I couldn't stop weeping.

For the next six months I continued to fantasise about another baby. I decided I would rely on breastfeeding as a contraceptive, in the hope that it would fail. I loved the baby routine and felt that even three children under five had not overextended me. I was in love with the Earth Mother image of myself. After a year with no sign of a pregnancy, I went back to Alan Bradfield to talk fertility help. We agreed to try some Clomid to stimulate ovulation, but after three months of treatment I suddenly changed my mind. It was time to do other things. I was absolutely sure. I rang Bradfield who had returned to work after his heart attack to say I had decided to have a tubal ligation. It was a strange decision in many ways for someone whose fertility was as erratic as mine. Perhaps it was overkill but I couldn't have my life determined by my menstrual cycle. I had to move on. Gordon was feeling the burden of supporting three children, and while he would have gone along with it, he too felt that we'd reached our parenting limit and should quit while we still had reserves of energy and finance.

One week later I checked in to King George V for a tubal ligation. The admission clerk was not quite so friendly as he had been when checking me in for Sam's birth. He needed additional information which I would not provide. Where was the written proof of my husband's consent for a tubal ligation? I explained that it wasn't necessary, that it wasn't my husband who was being sterilised, it was me. This threw the system into chaos.

They pleaded for Gordon's consent, but I stood my ground and it was finally agreed that I would go to the operating floor and 'doctor' could decide. But my inner voice was saying 'No way, these are my tubes, not doctor's'. As I travelled along the corridor on the trolley, the same anaesthetist who'd insisted on the pethidine at Sam's birth said to me, 'It's very irregular, you know; nobody is ever sterilised here without their husband's consent'. Some years later I found out what a lie that was. My last words before the anaesthetic were, 'Well, I'll go down in history as the first woman to give her own consent.' Waking up some time later I reflected that this was the end of the baby era, but it was my decision and it felt right. To celebrate, I opted to stay overnight and went down to Grace Bros and bought a new Robin Garland bikini which I wore on the balcony of the hospital for the remainder of the day.

Pregnancy and birthing were wonderful experiences, worth every missed period, contraction and push. It was sensual and politicising. It was about where women fit on the continuum, and understanding and sharing the quintessential female experience. I adored it. Moving into motherhood gave me political dimensions, bravery and courage that I could never have imagined. After becoming a mother I was never afraid, except for my children. Where birth is the desired outcome of pregnancy, there can be no experience like it. Where the outcome of pregnancy is termination, it can be tough. Where the outcome of pregnancy is adoption and never being allowed to love and hold your baby, it seemed to me that the pain would be beyond endurance. The options for pregnancy became my consuming interest for the next decade. I wanted to change the world and never doubted that with WEL's support I could.

CHAPTER SEVEN

FAMILY PLANNING

The slogans for International Women's Day said it all: 'Not Just a Day But a Year', 'A Woman's Place is Everywhere', 'It's Great to be a Woman', 'A Woman Needs a Man like a Fish Needs a Bicycle' and, my favourite, 'Women Last Longer'. They reflected the different ways that many women were thinking about their lives and it seemed that anything was possible. Like many others, I was swept along by the energy. It was a good time to be female in Australia.

Gloria Steinem described the seventies as the decade of consciousness raising and it was as true for women in Australia as it was for their sisters in the USA. With it came a new political awareness and a growing and powerful sense of self-esteem. We truly believed we could and would change the world, and sooner rather than later. Everything seemed possible.

The appointment of Elizabeth Reid as the Women's Adviser to the Whitlam government in 1973 was groundbreaking and caused endless media hype and speculation. For the conservative tabloid media, it offered a free kick to trivialise women's issues and she quickly became known as Supergirl. In more thoughtful places it was seen as recognition of the contribution that women could make to government and public policy. For WEL supporters, it was a seat at the table, and we believed the world as we knew it would be transformed.

The first UN World Conference of Women in Mexico in 1975 demonstrated the readiness of women to participate at a political level not witnessed before. Before the conference ended thousands of women took to the streets of Mexico City to demonstrate their commitment to improving the position of women.

I had decided the time had come to distance myself from the daily affairs of WEL, where I was still handling most of the media management. I was already finding being a WEL spokesperson a constraining role. I wanted a broader identity, a proper, paid job and I needed to focus on other areas of my interest and expertise. Education, abortion, birthing and family planning were the obvious areas. Education was both my profession and my passion, and family planning was close to my recent life experience.

By late 1974, as mother of three, I had closed the option of becoming mother of four and I began to think 'what next?' I wondered what was wrong with me. My life was rich and secure with motherhood and wifehood. How could this not be enough? We were a real family complete with Lucy our wise black cat and Alice our Springer spaniel. (Other pets came and went but these two were with us for fifteen years.) I had the Women's Electoral Lobby, the McMahons Point community, new friends and feminism—what was missing?

I wondered about this as I walked the streets of North Sydney during the next Council election when I was a candidate for local government. I was third on the ticket and I loathed every minute of the campaign. Any idea of mine that I would be a suitable candidate for local or any government disappeared during that time: although I was very happy to sell the team and its policies I hated having to sell myself. I was proud of my association with the Resident Action team, full of admiration for Carole Baker's political skills but I couldn't bear the personal exchange. It crowded me and I felt constrained. Don't fence me in.

Relief was in sight though; I wasn't elected. Public office would not be my next career. I began to think about resuming my teaching career which had now been part time for six years. People were encouraging: 'Motherhood and teaching go so well together.' 'Aren't you lucky you can teach part-time, earn some pocket money and still be a full-time mother.' 'Being a teacher means you will be a better mother and can help out at school.' There was the tidy stereotype

again and I resisted it. Yet I loved teaching and I did want to be a
good wife and mother. Why couldn't I find a nice job in a private
school like so many of my peers married to professional men? They
seemed happy but they were not engaged in lusty image-bending feminism which made you examine everything you did, and suggested
you could wipe out any barriers in your path. As summer holidays
approached I settled for motherhood on the beach and feminist activism wherever.

There were other decisions to be made regarding my professional
educational background and that was in the education of my children.
Teachers often have professional dilemmas about the education of
their children, and one issue can be when to intervene and when to
avert one's gaze. My respect for teachers meant that I wanted to
establish a relationship of trust but did not want the teacher to think
that I knew best because of my experience. But choosing the schools,
or rather, the pre-schools, was the challenge.

Our primary school choices were clear. We lived near North
Sydney Demonstration school and were committed to public education so the children would go there. As I was, and still am, a believer
in early childhood education, I wanted our children to attend two
years of pre-school. I imagined that finding one would be easy but it
was not the case. Kindergartens run by the Kindergarten Union were
the most desirable and were booked out. They also organised their
program in very short sessions: three hours a day, a couple of days a
week. If you were lucky your child might be able to attend for two
mornings between nine a.m. and twelve.

It was obvious that kindergarten was not seen as an educational
priority on the North Shore but rather an upmarket form of baby-
sitting. Mothers (and it was never fathers except for those in tragic
circumstances) were seen as rather selfish if they even asked for a full-
time kindergarten placement. That was referred to as childcare for
poor mothers in lesser circumstances. These assumptions and prissy
attitudes enraged me.

On many occasions Carole Baker and I, both ex-teachers, deplored
this lack of choice, and in her position on North Sydney Council
Carole established a groundbreaking family day care service. I had

chosen a small private kindergarten in a church hall at Crows Nest for Sophie, while Carole sent Zoe to Lance Kindergarten at Millers Point. Zoe was happy and Sophie, who was a very gregarious little girl, had spent two weeks being brave and hiding under the piano. A week later I removed Sophie and enrolled her at Lance. The professionalism of the Kindergarten Union management was clearly demonstrated, as Lance was a triumph of good, early childhood education over an unattractive physical environment. It looked like a mini-version of Gilliatt school for Girls in Fulham: dark and Victorian. However, it offered a five-day program, a hot meal and a wonderfully broad range of kids and teachers. We felt at home the minute we walked in the door. Nita McRae, a mother whom I had met through the Resident Action movement, was very pleased to see us and told us that sending our children there was probably the only way of keeping the numbers up and the place open. It was one way North Shore mothers could help inner-city kids get a pre-school education. Lance Kindergarten turned out to be a rich educational experience for all of us and some good political strategies were hatched by the mothers outside the school gates.

So began the long association with Lance, and The Rocks, as a special place in our lives. Sophie went five days a week and often travelled on the ferry with Gordon, much to the initial surprise of the other business passengers. Inevitably the boys followed their sister and there was a McCarthy child at Lance for six years. *Click* to 1996 and it was like old home week at Lance. It was the hundredth anniversary of the Kindergarten Union and Antoinette Wyllie, mother of Daniel and Jacob who were longterm friends of Hamish and Sam and who attended Lance together, is now the Executive Director. She invited me to give the anniversary speech. It felt like the more things changed, the more they stayed the same.

Some time in 1974 I had joined the Family Planning Association of Australia in response to Dorothy Simon's well argued case that we WEL women should be changing the structure that existed there to encourage a feminist understanding in the way they provided service. Family Planning clinics were a classic example. Effective, accessible contraception was a major theme of the feminist agenda and many felt that FPA clinics were far too middle class and selective in their service delivery. The Humanist Society wanted to change the Board and force the Association to be more active in community education and WEL members were asked to join the FPA and vote for a new Board. They did—with the result that WEL gained control of the Association. To my surprise I was elected, albeit on the bottom of the ticket. It was my first Board appointment and I was excited and apprehensive about the task.

As we moved into 1975, International Women's Year, I was getting that wistful and itchy feeling about paid work. I liked being paid for my contribution and I needed some income. I was already engaged in a lot of unpaid work. Unexpectedly I was called by Penny Hume, Carmel Niland's sister-in-law, with whom I had taught at Monte Sant' Angelo. There was a part time position teaching geography at a TAFE on the North Shore. Would I be interested?

I was definitely interested. I had not been in the classroom since Sam was born in March 1973. The timing was perfect: Sophie was at kindergarten and I had a well-organised system of shared childcare for Hamish and Sam with my friends Elsa Atkin and Antoinette Wyllie. I jumped at the opportunity. It was a part-time casual job, about ten hours face-to-face teaching students who, for various reasons, had not made it in their years of compulsory schooling. They were a mixed group, ex-defence force blokes, pregnant schoolgirls, people wanting to change their professional lives, especially women whose parents had not valued education for girls. The ache for second-chance education was inspiring as was the TAFE system's effort to provide it.

Teaching adults was a whole new buzz. My hours gradually crept up till I was regularly teaching eighteen hours a week which was the maximum face-to-face time for permanent staff. I could easily manage that amount of classroom teaching as well as my family and other interests and a whole new career seemed to be available. I could see myself staying at TAFE. It was the most wonderfully flexible system of learning and, unlike the regular education system, could accommodate change—or so I imagined. I liked its quirky nature and I would do anything rather than miss my evening classes. The commitment of those students was too strong to let them down.

So, when a permanent position to teach geography became available I applied confidently.

Some weeks passed and I heard nothing. I went to the senior teacher and asked him when the interviews were being held. He looked rather embarrassed and then said that an appointment had already been made; a nice guy with a young family. I asked why I was not interviewed. Was there a problem with my skills as a teacher? He assured me I was a wonderful teacher but this person was seen as more appropriate and more needy—after all he had young children. Was I missing something, I wondered? Didn't I have young children? I already knew the answer: 'It's different for men'.

I was stunned. I went and talked with one of the female teachers I trusted. She said, 'Well, the truth is, Wendy, you don't go to the pub on Friday night, everyone knows it. You go home to your family and that's not where you get the jobs. Grow up.'

Driving home that afternoon I was awash with tears for the end of my teaching career. I cried because I really loved teaching and wanted to be a great teacher, and I cried for my naivete and raged that I didn't understand how the system worked. I thought that being a good teacher was enough. I did not have the faintest idea what else I could do because I had only ever seen myself as a teacher but I knew I was on the way out. If I was not considered good enough to get a job as a permanent geography teacher I had a problem and I had better take notice.

By the time I had accepted the unpalatable truth, I began to rationalise my position and came to the view that this was an opportunity to change my definition of self. No longer would I make a virtue out of a career that fitted in to family life and assume that this was the sole indicator of my career options. The family would have to adjust. I was going to find the right job for me.

A real issue for me was how to find another job, now that I had faced the fact that I had no future as a teacher. Could I put my theories about change into practice and reinvent myself? I still did not think in terms of having a career, and had only ever visualised myself as a teacher. It was impossible to imagine myself as anything else and I did not know where to start. I held on tightly to my determination to find something else to do. Checking the papers was of little value and I felt very ill-informed about the opportunities available. A couple of attempts to place myself in a different occupation resulted in failure. I was even knocked back for a job as a tour guide on Sydney Harbour. It was further reinforcement that I was hopeless at pushing myself, despite seeming to be good and effective at pushing issues I was committed to.

In a sense the next job found me, thus beginning a pattern that has been repeated ever since. The opportunity grew out of my growing interest in family planning, which brought together my involvement in WEL, the Childbirth Education Association and Abortion Law Reform. These were voluntary commitments, something valuable to be involved in, a place to make a difference. There were no careers in those places for people who were other than doctors, nurses and physiotherapists, so it would not have occurred to me to seek paid work there.

Meanwhile I joined with women's groups who were persistently lobbying for access to family planning services. This was successful and resulted in funding for both women's health centres and family planning, which in a sense reflected the WEL–Women's Liberation nexus. Women's Liberation would take the new ground, the revolutionary position, and WEL would try to reform the existing institution. But both were shifting the paradigms of female sexuality.

The national lobbying campaign had been successful. The Whitlam government promised funding for family planning, but there were strings attached—there had to be a comprehensive federal body. The birth of this body was difficult and bitterly fought, but in 1975 the Australian Federation of Family Planning Associations was incorporated as the national body. Its task was to promote family planning, develop training and education at the national level and participate in the central and regional activities of the International Planned Parenthood Federation. Some feminists saw this as very establishment, and instead pursued the Women's Health Centre option with great success. I stayed with the Family Planning agenda, reflecting my task-oriented approach.

The new Family Planning team set about restructuring the organisation so that it better fulfilled the feminist agenda of broad access to contraception, sex counselling, abortion referral and sterilisation. From 1975 the clinic services became eligible for Medibank rebates. One of the first resolutions was that the consent of a spouse for any procedure carried out in the clinics would not be required. (In reality this meant vasectomies, which were performed at Family Planning clinics.) This was a powerful statement. It made the 1971 feminist demand to take the luxury cosmetic tax off the Pill seem light years ago.

I joined the Board's Education Committee and once the funds were secure we advertised for an Education and Information Officer. We were surprised and disappointed when we did not find the right person and decided to readvertise. I remember saying to Barry Maley, the President, that I couldn't understand why there were so few applicants for such a great job. His response was that I should resign from the Board and apply for it.

Such an action had not occurred to me, but I thought it a great idea and acted immediately on his advice. This time two jobs were advertised: an Education Officer and a Training Officer. My friend Antoinette Wyllie and I decided to apply together, as parts of the job overlapped. Our children and skills were compatible and complementary and we argued that we would support each other, as both jobs required evening work. However, we also were firm that our working day would have to fit in with our childcare. We would be leaving by 5 p.m. each day.

The day after the interview our family plus my youngest sister, Sarah, went to the farm owned by our old Forbes friends, Bruce and Val McDonald, at Manilla in Northern NSW for a holiday. I tried not to think about the job, as I was not confident and of course knew nothing about my competition. As time went by and I heard nothing, I was sure I had missed out. Then Board member and feminist advocate Alison Ziller called to ask when I could start my new position: Media Information and Education Officer for FPA, NSW. The peppercorn trees were singing, I had a new career. Better still, Antoinette was offered the Training Officer position. We were to begin in October 1975.

The immediate domestic issue was the care of the McCarthy children. Sophie was at North Sydney Demonstration School and Hamish was at Lance Kindergarten, but Sam could not be enrolled there until March 1976 when he turned three. It was Pank to the rescue. She had a cousin who had a private kindergarten at Cammeray. After an interview Sam was enrolled to attend five days a week. Sam was a fairly typical third child, sociable and confident and familiar with the educational places attended by his brother and sister. I was relaxed and confident about his ability to settle in quickly. I was so happy and did my usual girlie thing—rushed out to buy some new clothes to wear.

Oh silly me. On his first morning Sam McCarthy screamed the place down and clung to me with the ferocious strength of children who do not want to be parted. I was astonished and shocked; this was the gregarious gypsy of the family, raised in the back seat of the car while I ferried Sophie and Hamish around. He knew and talked to everyone.

Driving over the Harbour Bridge on that first morning I could hear all those voices. They spoke of guilt, neglect, abandonment and emotional scarring when children were forced into care against their will. I wondered if I was doing the wrong thing and should have waited until he was three, which after all was only five months away. I tried to put my head and heart together, and decided to give him three months to settle in.

Sam protested for weeks, except when Gordon took him, when he waved goodbye cheerfully. Day after day I would arrive at work emotionally fraught and turn to Dr Spock or whoever I was reading at the time to find a reassuring paragraph. Just as the partings began to improve, he got chicken pox. In fact the five Wyllie and McCarthy offspring got chicken pox serially. Antoinette and I bonded even more closely as we struggled with temperatures, scabs, tears and our new careers.

These are testing moments for working mothers when it all seems too hard. Then you remember the fun and companionship of sharing responsibility and taking professional pride in your work, and you find another solution. Had we not worked for an organisation which liked children and supported our efforts, we could easily have given up. Earning money was heady, but money was not enough of an incentive because almost all we earned was spent on childcare. But I do remember the watch I bought with my second pay packet. I felt so liberated, that extraordinary feeling of being a full contributor again and the independence associated with earning my own money.

And the job? It was heaven, better than I could have imagined. My head and heart were connected and although I had much to learn about working in an office, I do not remember feeling daunted by the task. The arrival of the divine Collette Parr as my assistant prevented disasters on a large scale. We operated from a grotty little terrace in Chippendale, a place friendly to rats and cockroaches and next door to the main clinic, which fortunately was hostile to rats and cockroaches.

Gradually we built a team of educators, including Virginia Knox, Margaret Winn and some of the Family Planning nurses who wanted to become educators. Culturally, nurses were very different, yet Audrie Wray, a senior nurse, was one of the best educators. The education position had previously been a volunteer position and had been done well, but like most voluntary tasks, it had not been given the recognition it deserved. I had a chance to build from the ground up and could create and define the role. From the beginning I worked with the media, as my experience with WEL as de facto media manager had convinced me that would be the only way I would reach the broader community. In retrospect my media skills were probably my most valuable contribution.

The educational context in NSW was liberal. The Personal Development Program developed by the NSW Department of Education for secondary schools was a world leader, although difficult to promote from within the education system because people were anxious about a conservative backlash. FPA, as a non government organisation, was in a good position to provide school education and train the teachers. Having a trained secondary school teacher (me) at

FPA was a bonus. I was the right person at the right time, able to develop close and trusting relationships with the Department. We were away on an adventure of sex education for everyone, and the requests rolled in to run programs for teachers and pupils.

Over the next three years the FPA Education Unit ran programs in primary and secondary schools, university medical schools, psychiatric hospitals, colleges of advanced education, gaols, hospitals, mothers' groups. It seemed everyone wanted to talk and think about sex in a more public way. And everyone wanted to know more. As the responsible manager, I developed a management strategy which has stood me in good stead since: I would not ask someone to do a job I would not do myself. This was a new and sometimes scary place to be, and there were few models to follow. It did not seem fair to me to put other people at risk if I was not prepared to take the risk myself.

The upside was the extraordinary opportunities I had to teach in a variety of settings. During 1978 I was working in Silverwater Men's Prison, Mulawa Women's Prison and Albion Street Boys Remand Centre on special programs, and simultaneously teaching in the postgraduate Health Education course at Sydney College of Advanced Education. There was always more work with teachers and schools than we could do. Our credibility was always under scrutiny. It was great training for working in teams under pressure.

The buzz around family planning and sex was attractive to creative people, and when approached by film-makers we were keen to cooperate. *Getting it On* by Gilly Coote was the first film I appeared in. Needless to say it was about condoms and we thought it daring and wonderful and held public showings at Family Planning headquarters quite often.

Not long after, Film Australia agreed to make *Growing Up*, a series of six films about adolescent sexuality. Either Delys Sargeant (director of the Social Biology Centre at Melbourne University), or Stefania Siedlecky (adviser to the Commonwealth Government in Family Planning) and I were the advisory panel. The series was made by two young film-makers, Phil Noyce and Jan Sharp, who proceeded to international fame and married each other. The films were aimed at teacher trainees and senior students, and dealt with socialisation patterns among teenagers, unplanned pregnancy and homosexuality. The films won the AFI Silver Award in 1978 for the best documentary and they were successful internationally. Family Planning was pleased to be in a leading role. However, their success resulted in calls for the series to be banned from schools. Only a top level meeting with the Minister for Education prevented this. Commonwealth politicians, including the Minister for Health, Ralph Hunt, Senator Shirley Walters and Senator Peter Baume viewed the films. Senator Walters was shocked, Senator Baume thought they could be a useful educational resource in the right hands. A senior administrator, referring to the films on homosexuality, told Stefania, 'I see no reason for glorifying the aberrant.'

Later I collaborated in the series *Let's Talk About It*, directed at primary shools. It attracted similar comment from the vocal minority opposed to sex education in schools. Typical of the reaction was a petition signed by twenty people and presented to Federal Parliament by Senator Hill of South Australia in 1982. The petitioners considered that the films advocated morally controversial behaviour, demonstrated serious moral and educational deficiencies, and were suitable only for in-service work with experienced teachers. They called for withdrawal of both series from Australian schools, and urged that 'no more funding be made available to Film Australia for production of sex education films in conjunction with the Family Planning Association' and 'an examination of the activities of the Family Planning Association in health and human relations studies in Australian schools be undertaken at an early date'. Such was the community environment. From my point of view it was fantastic to have Australian product after the endless stream of American audiovisual material.

The media was hot for sex education stories and a commercial television network invited an English woman family planning doctor, Dr Elphis Christopher, to be the guest on the high-rating Mike Willesee show. I was invited to be one of the studio guest commentators and enjoyed my three minutes of fame. Next day the phone rang with a request that I meet the editor of the *Sunday Mirror* to discuss an advice column. This was commonly described as the tits and bums newspaper of Australia and many a feminist, including myself, had protested about it.

Would I want to be associated with it? Driven by a mixture of curiosity and a belief that this could open up a whole new area of communication, I agreed to meet editor Gordon McGregor and feature writer Gus d'Brito at the News Ltd building in Surry Hills. It was a short meeting and the offer was to the point. They wanted me to write their sex advice column. The letter supply was constant and they needed ten answers a week. The fee was non-negotiable and the deadlines were immovable. I asked for a day to think it through.

After talking with a few friends and colleagues, I accepted, in spite of their advice. No-one thought it a good idea and there was general support for the sentiment, strongly expressed by one friend, that writing in the *Sunday Mirror* was the ultimate sellout. I was astonished as I thought family planning advice and service were for all of us, and being a reader of the *Sunday Mirror* shouldn't disqualify you. Worse, I thought it was a coup to have an opportunity to reach a wider group of readers and to learn to communicate with them. My feelings of success were quickly squashed by the criticism but this did not stop me from agreeing to write the column and the truth was I loved it. It was a seventies version of email, and the response could be fast—a request for advice could be answered within two weeks. For FPA it was valuable because I could refer readers to our clinics and encourage them to visit.

The big issue was contraception and how to negotiate sex in a relationship. 'Dear Wendy, I've just met this guy and he says if I don't have sex with him he'll go to my girlfriend. What should I do?' It is hard for people to imagine just how inaccessible the Pill was. If your doctor didn't 'like' it, it would not be prescribed. Unplanned and unwanted pregnancies were a huge problem, as the Royal Commission on Human Relationships had convincingly demonstrated in its report to the Commonwealth in 1977.

This was a crazy time, a time of ignorance about sex and contraception and a time of sexual liberation, for the Pill offered contraceptive safety no previous generation had ever had. Family planning agencies were in the fore as the emphasis shifted from pregnancy spacing for married women to fertility control and choice for all. Within the spectrum of the Women's Movement, women's health clinics were seen as far more radical politically than family planning organisations. There was continuing tension between Women's Liberation and the Women's Electoral Lobby, and again I found myself in the reformist rather than the revolutionary space. I did not believe the revolution would happen and was more interested in changing the present environment.

Writing in the *Sunday Mirror* put me outside the pale, and yet on reflection, it was one of the best things I've done. It began a time that I think of as the Dear Wendy era, when I received hundreds of letters through the *Sunday Mirror* and later *Cleo* magazine. Here are three fairly classic examples:

STOP THIS NOW

'My stepfather is 32 and I am 17. I am very fond of him. He doesn't have sex with my mother any more as she doesn't seem to enjoy it. My stepfather often comes into my room in the early morning with an erection. We have now started having sexual intercourse and while I enjoy it I don't feel this ought to go on for my sake and for my mother's sake, and I am afraid of becoming pregnant. Could you tell me what I should do about this without hurting my stepfather's feelings?

I would not believe that your stepfather and mother no longer have sex and even if that were the case, you are under no obligation to act on your mother's behalf. Your stepfather is exploiting you and you should tell him you are not available for exploitation especially when it involves your mother's feelings and relationship.

NOT SO PERFECT

Ten years ago, when I was 23, I got married. We both worked very hard to put a deposit on a house and four years ago had a child. It all sounds so perfect—just what every girl dreams of. Unfortunately, I feel as though I'm going mad. My husband won't allow me to work because he thinks it's my job to look after our child. He also doesn't believe in only children and wants to have another child. I feel dependent, frustrated, angry and unloved. For some time now I've been wondering how I can get out. It seems that the only thing I can do is just walk out, but how can I face it? I feel so guilty—what's wrong with me? My friends act as though this is the perfect life.

As a working woman who is a wife and a parent it would be dishonest of me to pretend that I believe a housebound mother's life is an easy one. Don't feel guilty. Lots of us decide that marriage and parenting are not full-time careers in themselves. The realisation that you are a parent for life can be overwhelming, but it doesn't follow that you can't pursue other roles as well. Try to solve your problems one by one. To begin, try to get help with childcare so that you have some time for yourself. If you cannot afford to pay, perhaps you could arrange to exchange children one day a week with a friend. It's good for the children and wonderful for mothers. Perhaps you could join a playgroup in your area (you can contact the nearest Playgroups Association). Although you cannot leave the child you will meet other mothers and you can be positive that there will be others who are feeling just like you. Once you get that going I think you should have serious discussions with your husband about why he feels so strongly about you staying at home. I think they would have to be very strong reasons to justify you doing so. He must see that you have the right to grow and develop in your own way. I don't mean to make your problems seem easy—I know they are not, but I'm sure you can make it.

I WANT HIM BACK
About six months ago I met a wonderful guy at a party and we really hit it off well. We were going together for a couple of months. He told me that he loved me, and spoke of such

long-term arrangements as marriage. I am only 18, with little experience of guys, and this permanent type of relationship really frightened me. Somehow I thought he was too good for me. Because of this I broke off our relationship and my problem is that I now realise what a fool I was. How can I tell him I want him back without making an idiot of myself? I can't just say 'I want you back', and I'm not even sure that he still feels the way he used to. I am really afraid that he won't want me now but I can't stop thinking that I made a mistake.

If you still care for this guy as much as you say you do, take a risk. Ring him up and ask him if he would like to meet you somewhere for a coffee or a meal. The worst thing that can happen is that he will say no. I do understand that it can be agony wanting to make contact with someone and wishing you knew whether that person wanted to see you. Perhaps, as women, we should try to understand how very difficult it must be for men, who are always expected to initiate such contact. Get in touch with him in a low-key way. Meet him on neutral ground and see how you feel then. It's quite possible that it may be an anti-climax. Don't try to pick up the relationship at the point it ended. Instead consider this a new affair and allow it to develop along those lines.

About a year later I was gently but firmly sacked from the *Sunday Mirror* with the explanation that I was too serious. My replacement was Jeannie Little, who it was thought would make them laugh about their sexual frailties. The editor assured me that laughing was the best response. I did not agree. Some weeks later Pat Dasey, the editor of *Cleo*, rang and asked me to write their agony column. I loved the idea of a glossy magazine with a large readership of young women and accepted immediately. My peer group saw this as more respectable and appropriate.

I found writing these columns a wonderfully grounding experience. Not many have the opportunity to conduct a public conversation with a wide readership. Despite its image as a woman's magazine, *Cleo* was read by men and it was the male letter writers who alerted me to the risks to women of STDs and, later, AIDS from their husbands' homosexual encounters. I had many letters from men imploring me to approve their need for gay liaisons while living within apparently regular heterosexual marriages. This was pre-AIDS and I often wonder how many of those couples are now HIV-positive.

My *Cleo* years were seen by my children as my finest achievement. When the advance copies of the magazine would arrive, the neighbourhood children would read them closely and say admiringly, 'Your Mother doesn't know that, does she?'

We can be absolutely sure that they did not think I *did* it. Knowing was enough.

All this publicity meant that the enemies of Family Planning became more vocal. There were many conservative forces to deal with. Family Planning was a threat to the medical profession, and many doctors were insulted at the suggestion that we would train them in the delivery of contraceptive services. After all, what would we know? Our answer always was that they should listen to what women were saying. 'You are not providing the service they need.' Meanwhile, our clinics were continuously booked out and our phones rang for referrals to friendly doctors who did not patronise their patients and had a proper understanding of the contraceptive choices available.

In country NSW hostility to the FPA was palpable, and usually led by the medical profession. However, it was a war they would not win and my strategy from the beginning was to work with the system and support creative FP doctors like Edith Weisberg, Sian Graham, Sue Hepburn and Sue Craig. They were prepared to offer the leadership and risked their reputations to do so. Twenty years later their work and courage have been vindicated. Indeed, family planning stories are full of unsung heroines like Ruby Rich, Dorothy Simons and Stefania Siedlecky.

The strongest and most active opponents of family planning were Right to Life and the Reverend Fred Nile. I was often in the public spotlight and a visible target. While I was learning that confrontation was not the best tactic with this group at least once I consulted my friend and lawyer Helen Coonan to seek advice and we discussed the advisability of taking legal action. As it happened the threat faded, but I felt reassured knowing the options available to me. I had to develop a thick skin. Since that time the targeting from those groups has persisted. On at least three occasions when I have been appointed to a public body the letters have rolled in describing my wicked ways. Right to Life, the Anglican Mother's club and the Catholic church remain on the Wendy McCarthy case.

A classic demonstration of the conservative corporate memory occurred in 1984 when I accepted an invitation to be the guest speaker at the graduation ceremony of the Catholic College of Education, Sydney. Brother Ambrose Payne's invitation, dated March 21, ended with the statement that 'the College looks forward to welcoming you on the day'. On April 19 Brother Ambrose Payne wrote the following letter:

> Dear Mrs McCarthy,
> It is with deep regret and an acute sense of personal
> embarrassment that I write to withdraw the invitation ...
> Under present College practice the Principal is responsible for
> making invitations to address the Graduation and reports the
> matter to Council ... the Chairman has directed me, on behalf
> of the Council, to write and to indicate that whilst very much
> recognising your own undoubted capacity to speak as a
> Commissioner of the Australian Broadcasting Commission, the
> audience would be extremely hard pressed not to confuse this
> with the other roles, most notably that in relation to Family
> Planning. The College is, in a particular sense, obliged not to
> confuse its public image in areas in which divergent and
> opposed views are held.

As I write this I am reminded yet again of the persistence of those opponents. A friendly mother/daughter article was published about Sophie and me in August 1998 in the magazine section of the *Sydney Morning Herald*. There was a reference to my position as Chancellor of the University of Canberra, which produced a torrent of rage from one reader:

Dear Madam Chancellor, May one inquire to the use and purpose of a picture of you as if there weren't more interesting things to write about and take pictures of? Even Monica Lewinsky is more interesting than some write up about some marxist crap CEO and/Women's Electoral Lobby or some female who is neither an engineer or a tradesman been given Chancellorship of some university. I am not surprised at all that we got a Pauline Hanson and her One Nation. Ready to clean out all you marxist lot squandering all our taxes on the ABC, on those Women's Conferences, with those Family Planning Associations, National Trust and so on to further that ultimate agenda of those Marxist Socialist Internationals of yours.

And on and on it goes, and I wonder, is this public engagement? Does this scrutiny happen to other people or is it just me? Curiously, it has made me mindful and respectful of difference, as well as constantly reminding me of the disapproval outside my circle of approval.

Family Planning and the Women's Movement provided wonderful training in conflict and crisis management. Nothing since has been so hard or so exhilarating. FPA NSW was a turbulent corporate body, and between 1974 and 1985 there were three takeovers of the Board of Directors and a succession of executive officers and educators. An attempted takeover of the FPA by the Right to Life was as dramatic as any corporate raid I've observed since, and there was more at stake than money. It was our attachment to the values FPA could represent that was the bottom line. When we could postulate those values, the agenda could shift in a meaningful and responsive way for women. And it did.

My appointment to the National Women's Advisory Council in 1978 came at the right time for me. It was a stressful time at FPA NSW and the staff were feeling the tensions of a new board. While I looked good from the outside, inside the organisation I was on the outer, seen as having too high a profile and being too big for my boots. I was probably seen as too structured, not collective enough. There were many days when I would turn my car into the last street before the office and begin to feel apprehensive and sick. I hated the conflict and disapproval. A part of me wanted to resign, but the other part said hang in there and go with dignity on your own terms.

When my appointment to NWAC was announced I was told by the FPA Board President, Professor Charles Kerr, that my salary would be docked for the time I was at NWAC meetings. I felt I was being punished rather than supported. I protested that this was unfair, but to no avail. I knew I did my job well and my appointment to NWAC was a public testimony to that and, more importantly, a recognition of Family Planning and WEL. It was too bad if I was out of favour with a group whose ideas I thought were off beam. I was determined to stay, as there was still so much unfinished business at FPA.

In 1978 I applied to attend an International Planned Parenthood conference in Bangkok on adolescent sexuality. After a lot of negotiation it was agreed I could be the Australian representative. I was keen to share my experience and see what our region was doing with adolescents. It was a life-changing experience attending that conference. It was my first visit to Bangkok and I found it a steamy and exciting place. We all stayed in a fairly average hotel, and breakfast was a sea of Asian faces, apart from two women from New Zealand and my colleague, Kay Dunne from Melbourne. I fantasised that this could be a glimpse of my future professional life—an international career.

With our new films on adolescent sexuality, I imagined we would be pacesetters and in a sense we were, but we were also irrelevant. The needs and priorities of adolescents in Thailand, Malaysia and Indonesia were different and I was inspired by the imaginative approaches taken. During this visit we met Mr Mechai Vivavaidya, director of the Thai Family Planning Program which was funded by a United Nations grant. His work in Thailand was already legendary. Visiting his fertility clinics and observing his map of Thailand, which showed the location of the family planning health teams, helped me understand how family planning can be a matter of life and death.

At night we went nightclubbing in the quarter where Mechai had his instantly accessible vasectomy clinic and saw the colourful Mechais being handed out, as condoms were now known as in Thailand. My experience suddenly seemed very limited and Mechai—Anglo Thai, Geelong Grammar, Melbourne Uni, and connected by marriage to the King of Thailand—became the role model. I was on a salutary learning curve.

I returned to Australia, increasingly interested in the national and international politics of Family Planning, and dreaming about working in Asia. Australia was a donor country to the International Planned Parenthood Federation and the contact for all this activity was the national office.

The national Family Planning executive officer's job was unexpectedly advertised in 1978—it was the only other family planning job that mattered. I was excited at the thought that I could become involved. The departing CEO was a retired university administrator who hoped that Family Planning had nothing to do with sex and resisted all attempts to make the connection. He commanded little respect from the state bodies and he responded similarly. Hearing of my 'confidential' application, he strongly advised me to withdraw as it was a dead-end job and I lacked the necessary administrative experience. I took no notice and hoped the election committee was over retirees. I wanted to put energy in the place.

There were few candidates and only two were invited to an interview. The other withdrew at the last minute, but even so I could sense that I would not be automatically appointed. There was a concern that I was too radical, too feminist and too outspoken. Finally I was offered the job for the less than princely salary of $12,000, $4,000 less than I was earning at FPA NSW. Ignoring all professional advice about dropping pay, I accepted, with the proviso that I would stay on the National Women's Advisory Council and could earn other income. This was the best professional decision I ever made because it gave me some independence and was the beginning of my building a portfolio approach to my professional life, although I would not have described it in that way then. My decision was based on instinct and survival.

The Chairman of AFFPA, Professor Colin Wendell-Smith, was a

Quaker and a true internationalist. He was a gentle man, and strategically and politically skilful. We were an unlikely and productive combination. It was a wonderful time for me: there were so many opportunities to spread my wings and yet I had a wise person to counsel me. I also had an organisation whose roles and responsibilities I could lead and grow. Professionally I had two major tasks and they related to money and education. We needed more of both. I worked hard to secure Commonwealth funding for the Family Planning Associations. This was always a tough call, and it was in that context that I first had direct contact with John Howard, the then Treasurer. I had been advised by Department of Health officials that the Family Planning funds would be cut because the Treasurer had decided there was no need for the Commonwealth to be involved in direct funding. I was furious as the Health Minister, Michael McKellar, was supportive and we had argued for years about Commonwealth leadership and national equity. I tried to make an appointment to see Howard, but his staff stonewalled.

At this stage our family had moved from McMahons Point to Longueville and John Howard was my local member so I decided to approach him as a Bennelong constituent. I made an appointment and when I arrived it was obvious that other people had chosen the same route to reach him—Wayne Harrison from the Sydney Theatre Company was in the waiting room at Gladesville. It was a productive meeting. Howard listened carefully as I put my case in the context of unplanned pregnancies and demonstrated the effectiveness of the program. I was impressed that he responded reasonably and courteously and agreed that the Family Planning Commonwealth Program would continue. The Department of Health officials who wanted to bury the program were furious.

The NWAC appointment was my first statutory appointment and the way in which it happened is worth telling—few people would understand how unexpected and casual these approaches can be. Yet these appointments would not be offered without the consent of Cabinet. In many ways it is a salutary tale because it was so normal.

What did I expect? Nothing, because there was no frame of reference. Every appointment since, except one, has happened in a similar way.

One July day in 1978, when I was teaching in a Family Planning training program for nurses, my assistant Collette came to the room to say that I was needed on the phone. It was unusual for her to interrupt me, as the established rule was that I was not to be disturbed while teaching. As we went outside she said, 'There's a man on the phone who says he's the Minister for Home Affairs, and he insists on speaking to you.' My response was, 'Collette, it's perfectly clear that Gordon McCarthy is playing a joke. Whoever heard of a Minister for Home Affairs. However, if he's insistent about speaking to me, it must be important.'

I picked up the phone and said, 'Wendy McCarthy'. The answering voice was definitely not Gordon McCarthy but, 'Bob Ellicott here, Minister for Home Affairs. Have you heard about the National Women's Advisory Council we're establishing? I'd like you to be a member. Would you be interested?'

I said, 'Yes, but what would I have to do?'

He said, 'Well, you'd meet in Canberra and around Australia and you'd be advising the Government on women's issues.'

It sounded like heaven, a public voice, and a channel to government. I tried not to sound too eager, while enthusiastically indicating my consent. 'When is this likely to happen?'

He said, 'Well, I'm not sure, but I'd ask you not to speak to anyone about it and I'll let you know.' It was my first such conversation with a politician. I was very excited and couldn't believe that a Minister would just ring you like a normal person and invite you to do an important national job.

I resumed my teaching program, told no-one except Gordon and waited to hear formally. Not a sound and I began to think it must have been a practical joke when, some weekends later in Broken Hill with Bettina Arndt and Sue Hepburn, running a sex counselling program for doctors and health professionals, I saw a tiny piece in the *Sydney Morning Herald* which said the National Women's Advisory Council had been established. My name was there. I had read it in the *Sydney Morning Herald* so it must be true. Such are the processes of public appointments of those who are outside the loop of political parties.

The combination of working with the National Women's Advisory Council and the Australian Federation of Family Planning Associations meant that I was thinking nationally and meeting Commonwealth public servants who, until that time, had been an alien species with whom I had had no professional or private contact. Indeed I had no understanding of their work or the nature of the political power exercised by them. These were new relationships for me and in a sense my ignorance was useful as I was not afraid to ask advice. There was no script to follow; we made it up as we went.

When I wandered around the corridors of power (Parliament House) I understood why politicians lost the plot. Their lives in Canberra were dysfunctional. It was like being in a boarding school or a prison, where different codes of personal conduct were accepted. Somehow it made them more aggressive about women's affairs and family planning, almost as though they had to prove loyalty to their wives at home. I could understand that but I didn't think it should dictate public policy.

What these two issues had in common was the assumption that they were private rather than professional matters. Our challenge was to place them firmly in the public policy arena, and that required leadership from both ministers and the bureaucracy. Throughout this period my respect for the skills of the bureaucracy grew and my ability to research and present ideas improved.

I also learned to find the opportunities to speak out in a way the bureaucracy could not. Once at a conference I pointed out the double standard that politicians applied to the abortion debate. So often they would take the Right to Life position publicly, while privately they would call me or other people in Family Planning, seeking a referral for a termination of pregnancy for a 'friend'—wife, girlfriend, sister etc. We would always provide that advice confidentially. Yet, as I pointed out, if ever the women who now provided these services decided to blow the whistle, there would be many embarrassed people around. The next day the headlines in *The Australian* newspaper read, 'Woman threatens politicians. Wendy McCarthy to publish lists of MPs who have used abortion services.' I was roundly chastised for this but remained unrepentant. It was the height of hypocrisy to use services you voted against, and then rely on the secrecy which surrounded them to protect you.

Abortion was a constantly difficult issue. The family planning associations were ambivalent in their support of the feminist catchcry 'abortion on demand' for fear of losing their funding. There was pressure on them to become abortion service providers on the grounds that they already ran high quality clinical services and early terminations were straightforward procedures. It was a divisive policy debate at both the state and national level within the FPAs. At the international level it was even more vexed. The International Planned Parenthood Federation (IPPF), of which the Australian Federation of Family Planning Associations (AFFPA) was a sovereign member, brought together many nations which had lobbied for family planning to be a recognised human right. The issue of providing abortion services related to an intellectual debate about whether abortion was a contraceptive method. The semantics of the debate were carefully constructed to enable the array of religious and cultural practices to remain part of IPPF.

Similarly, in Australia the semantics of abortion were continually changing to accommodate the wide spectrum of beliefs and 'the right to choose' became the acceptable phrase. For the FPA the responsibility to provide effective contraceptive education and services was seen as an abortion deterrent. This offered an opportunity to take the moral high ground in the debate.

In 1971 the Reverend Peter Hollingworth said in an interview in the *Age*, 'The churches cannot have it both ways, nor can governments. Either abortions must be made easier or more birth control clinics must be established.' When Preterm opened as an abortion clinic in Sydney in 1974, FPA NSW decided it would refer women there and abandon the idea of becoming a provider, a win all round. Also, lobbying for abortion to be added to the medical benefits schedule was a better use of our energy. This had been achieved in 1974 by the AMA and was not formally challenged until 1979 when

Stephen Lusher put a motion to remove these benefits from Medicare.

As a member of NWAC as well as CEO of AFFPA, the Lusher motion was a tough test for me. It was untenable to belong to a body such as NWAC without persuading its members to advise the government to vote against the motion. As I saw it, if we were to represent the interests of Australian women, it would be unthinkable not to speak out. While I was agonising, the issue was raised by another NWAC member and in a very short space of time we agreed to go public in our unanimous opposition to the Lusher Bill. Beryl Beaurepaire then persuaded Malcolm Fraser to delay the Lusher debate for three weeks on the grounds that debating it in the House on 8 March—International Women's Day—was political suicide. This gave us breathing space to lobby hard against it. The women's movement went into action and the defeat of the Bill demonstrated the extent of the support for NWAC leadership.

It was an important victory for NWAC and for me it was especially poignant. I no longer felt outside the mainstream (was I too feminist?), and as some of my NWAC colleagues joined their state FPAs, I felt reassured that my personal and professional convictions were shared by others. It gave me a new level of confidence with the Canberra bureaucracy, as I felt I had the backing of the government to pursue the family planning agenda which I had never seen as radical, but as sensible public health policy. Without fertility control women had no chance of being independent and playing their chosen role in our society. However, I was not so naïve that I failed to acknowledge the opposing forces, and they persist to this day.

At a quarter to eight in the morning on a grey day in 1979, I arrived at the NSW Teachers' Federation. I was there to launch the book *Living Mistakes* by Kate Inglis, a book about the experiences of relinquishing mothers (mothers who gave up their babies for adoption). As I walked in I was surprised that the room was packed even though adoption had been outed as a political issue over the last couple of years. I'd been asked to launch the book because of my family planning role but this did not seem like the usual family planning audience.

Prior to the launch I'd spoken to the author who told me that she had included her own experience in the book and indicated that I may know some of the other people. In deference to the emotion and craft of the book, I read passages from the book rather than use my own words. As I read the stories I kept making eye contact with women in the audience who signalled to me that they were relinquishing mothers. At first I thought I was imagining it. It was eerie and felt almost voyeuristic. Some were people I'd known for a long time.

I emerged from the launch very emotionally shaken. As I walked towards my office an acquaintance joined me and confided that she was really sorry her sister, whom I knew, couldn't be there, particularly as it had been such a huge thing in her family when she relinquished her first baby. I didn't want to hear this story, least of all from an observer and even a close and friendly one. The news was a surprise to me and reinforced my despair about a society where there were so many secrets about pregnancy. Equally it reaffirmed the value of my work. But there was also a happy ending. Two or three days later I heard from the author that her long-lost daughter had found her. She'd seen the promotion for the book, gone with her own child to a 'meet the author' session and introduced herself saying, 'I think I'm your daughter, and if I am this is your grandchild.'

My appointment to the National Women's Advisory Council placed me firmly in public life and took me into a broader spectrum of women's politics and leadership. I joined an extraordinary group of twelve women, led by Beryl Beaurepaire, who became both a role model and mentor. The appointment of a women's adviser to government by Gough Whitlam had been the ALP response to pressure from women's groups for better access to policy development. The Fraser government made an election commitment in 1975 that it would continue that access through a national women's council, in addition to maintaining the individual Women's Adviser position. In 1978 women's affairs had been moved to the Ministry for Home

Affairs and Bob Ellicott was given the responsibility of creating an appropriate body which would 'provide an effective channel of communication between women in the community and government'.

A threshold decision was that women be appointed for two years in their own right, not as representatives of groups, a classic example of Liberal philosophy. Ellicott wrote in the formal offer of appointment that the twelve part-time members were selected on the basis of 'individual experience and expertise and as far as possible reflect[ed] the diversity of backgrounds and interests among women in Australia'.

It was a clever strategy and because we did not know the process for selection there was no sense of obligation to one's proposer. Lyndsay Connors writing in the *Age* thought the Council 'looked conservative' and identified me as the only feminist. She thought the lack of feminist representation unfair, given that feminists had created the new political consciousness that led to the formation of the Council. Certainly it was by no means a radical group, but it was a group to be respected for its broad base of experience and commitment to women's business.

At our first meeting, which I remember so clearly, Jan Marsh, Quentin Bryce and I sat together. It was the beginning of enduring friendships and it is difficult to think of my life before Quentin, as we have been close friends since that first meeting. We were ably nurtured, bossed and led by Beryl Beaurepaire, who was then Vice President of the Liberal Party's Victorian division. She made it clear from the beginning that this was a lobby group and should not be seen as a creature of government or as window dressing for the Liberal Party.

Her political know-how and skills were a marvel to watch. When she realised that few of us knew the Prime Minister, she arranged for us to meet him at our second gathering. She immediately took charge of the meeting, dispensed with the pleasantries and focused the discussion on improving resources for the Council and its Secretariat.

'No, Malcolm [Fraser], I don't think that's a good idea. I think this would be a better way, don't you?'

'Well, yes, Beryl.' He nods.

She was talking to the Prime Minister and we were watching and learning. He agreed that Minister Ellicott should fix these concerns. Of course, the Minister agreed. Mission accomplished and the pleasantries were resumed. It made a deep impression and inspired us to work harder, despite our sitting fees being at the same rate as those for the Pig Board.

The NWAC agenda was long and in essence reflected the feminist agenda of the Women's Electoral Lobby. Equal pay and maternity leave, access to family planning, the problems faced by migrant women, violence against women, Aboriginal women and girls, family law, isolated women and girls. The research was solid, it had to be if it was to attain credibility and influence government policy and action. When 'Migrant Women Speak' was tabled in Parliament in 1979, it was seen as an important study and many of its recommendations were acted on.

NWAC offered wonderful avenues for networking and fact-finding and NWAC members generously gave of their time and energy. We met in every capital city and many regional places in our efforts to be sure that what we were pushing for with Government was in line with the aspirations of Australian women.

The United Nations had declared the period 1976–1985 the Decade for Women. The Mexico conference had opened the Decade, and a mid-decade conference was planned in Copenhagen so that progress could be monitored. The advice from Kath Taperell, the head of the Office of Women, was that NWAC become involved in the Australian agenda. Beryl accepted this advice, seeing it as an opportunity to broaden the awareness and vision of Australian women. It also might help to divert attention from the tedious and troublesome Victorian group, Women Who Want to be Women (4Ws), led by Babette Francis. This was the Realpolitik in Beryl's home state and was making some politicians nervous. The essential concern of the 4Ws was the status of women in the home and the demand for financial support for homemakers. NWAC was accused of being elitist and out of touch with ordinary women, whoever they were. Petitions arrived in Parliament insisting it be abolished.

It was decided that NWAC would rise above this and prepare for the Copenhagen conference by consulting widely with Australian women through regional and state conferences. Through this process Australian women could identify their problems and solutions and prepare a plan to represent their views in Copenhagen. It was a high-risk strategy because it offered heaven-sent opportunities for the opposing forces, but the chance for women to have their say outweighed those risks and NWAC needed to test its assumptions that its activities enjoyed substantial support in the community.

Meetings were held all around Australia on the central themes of health, education and employment. Every meeting turned hundreds of women away because of lack of space. In Melbourne, as the registrations reached 4,000, the meeting had to be abandoned as there was no hall with sufficient accommodation. For Judith Roberts in South Australia the turbulent meeting at Christies Beach was a gruelling experience and changed her life. Until then she had not understood the passion that women's politics unleashed.

For me the most reinforcing and surprising aspect was that the Council views were so often aligned with mine. Yet when the Council was created I, as a publicly declared feminist, was seen as the odd one out. I had actually never felt that I was an outsider but my feminist experience was noticeable, giving me an ease with the rhetoric of the issues. And I had rehearsed the discourse of fertility, education and employment in my WEL life and, more recently, in my Family Planning existence.

After all the state and regional meetings, the National Conference was held in Canberra in March 1980. There were 120 delegates elected from the state conferences, and more than 100 representatives of women's organisations, members of the media and interested individuals from Australia and abroad were invited to attend as official observers. When opening the conference our Minister, Bob Ellicott, stressed the importance of the conference as a means of providing Government with a statement of the priorities and aspirations of a wide cross-section of Australian women. At least some of us thought that we were having the definitive public conversation about the perception and definition of being female in Australia. This was being resourced and led by a conservative government and the results could not be dismissed as a Labor party plot.

The Council agreed that the conference procedures should be based on consensus in order to foster a spirit of cooperation among the delegates and to highlight, wherever possible, the areas of agreement. I found the preparation and debate exciting. The process was fascinating. We followed UN rules of debate and hours were spent on the semantics. It seemed that every word had multiple meanings. Yet the goal always was to find a common ground, so if we reached an impasse some members would form a drafting group to seek resolution which the plenary could consider later. Reading this later it doesn't sound so innovative, but in the context of 1980 it was.

Beryl chaired the plenary sessions with ease and firmness. In her opening address she said: 'The conference was part of the political process: a way of having the government hearing what women have to say. If all members of the government hear that women are divided, they are likely to conclude that there is no point in taking action and simply dismiss our recommendations. Division and confrontation is not in our interests. A victory for one faction at the expense of another would, so far as our potential to influence government goes, be a loss to us all.' She steered the conference to a high degree of consensus and thus demonstrated effectively that women are united in many common goals and aspirations when we discuss the basics: health, education and employment.

Taking time from my AFFPA job to do this caused some tension but I argued that it was in the interests of the family planning movement generally that I be their advocate there. I finally attended with my Chairman's blessing. I chaired some of the sessions and enjoyed the buzz of activity and the energy put into the debate. I could not have been happier with the results and nor could the Family Planning Associations, for the preamble to the resolutions on health stated:

> Health is a state of physical, mental and social well-being. It is not merely the absence of disease. The main determinants of a state of well-being for women include adequate housing, sanitation, nutrition, health care and welfare provisions and the means of controlling their own fertility. Access to such facilities is a fundamental human right.

The supporting recommendation spoke of education in human sexuality, and concluded: 'All methods of fertility regulation, including abortion, with supporting counselling services, should be offered to women so that they have the right to choose.' One memorable exchange came when Babette Francis was speaking and prefaced her remarks with the statement, 'It is a well established scientific fact that women's brains are smaller than men's'. Evelyn Scott, a tall, substantial and handsome Torres Strait Islander, rose to her feet and said, 'You used to say that about us.'

The draft document which emerged was criticised for being both bland and radical, and of course was somewhere in the middle. Even so, the Ballarat *Courier* editorial wrote of 'militant feminists' 'stacking' the conference and asserted that Ellicott owed it to 'the women who had not burned their brains along with their bras' to take no notice of the outcomes (*Courier*, 17 March 1980). Despite this advice the conference outcomes provided the basis for the Australian document to be taken to Copenhagen. At NWAC we were optimistic that the Australian Draft Plan of Action was a good working document which would enable Australian women to move forward.

The World Conference was run from 14–30 July 1980, and I was delighted to be chosen to attend the non-government forum as a representative of the NGO sector in Australia. (This meant my fare was paid, but I had to find the other expenses myself.) Jan Marsh was joining Beryl, Bob Ellicott and Valerie Fisher in the government delegation. Judith Roberts, another NWAC member, was at the forum with me and the fifteen other women who were assisted to attend.

Babette Francis from the 4Ws managed to organise her attendance as a media representative, although it was hard to believe that the *Toorak Times* would normally cover such an international conference. Fortunately her presence was balanced by Lyndsay Connors from *The Age*, Rosemary Munday from the *Women's Weekly* and Janet Bell from the ABC.

Gordon and I had been to Copenhagen before. My memories were that it was a friendly and accessible city and I was excited to be going. But on this particular arrival I remember feeling a sense of insignificance, especially when observing the colour and energy of the African women at the airport. Perhaps it was the recognition that Australia was small on the world scale and in this company we might not have much to contribute. It was unnerving. The next day we went out to the forum and I decided to hire a bike and travel like the Danes. That was fun and gave me a feeling of adventure and well-being. I felt less like a tourist and more like an independent woman with a purpose.

There were 8,000 women at the forum. It was an overwhelming experience, like a giant women's bazaar, heady just to walk around. Women of the world talking, talking, and talking, and clicking on shared experiences; finding the same issues mattered everywhere, in one form or another.

There were a few Australians staying at the same hotel and we soon found ourselves bonding in the sauna. After a few conference sessions we got smart and shared the daily coverage so we could compare notes at the end of the day. Our media team, other than Babette Francis, were trying to cover the government conference as well as the forum, but as NGO attendees we had almost no contact with our delegates until Beryl, at the suggestion of Judith Roberts, began a series of daily briefings to bring the forum energy and ideas to the government delegation. Very few governments did this; indeed many of their delegations were all male and not much interested in the issues, let alone the NGOs.

Writing about Copenhagen conjures up so many images—the bicycle, the reception at the Australian Consulate, slathering on hair conditioner in the sauna, spending my thirty-ninth birthday on 22 July at the Tivoli gardens, and the optimism of even the most oppressed women. The goddesses were there in strength—some known, others to be revealed. And aspects of women's lives I'd never considered were on the agenda for discussion.

For example, despite my privileged access to family planning literature, I knew almost nothing about female circumcision. It was at that conference that I heard about it. An extraordinarily brave Egyptian doctor, Nawal el Sadawi, spoke out in one of the health sessions about it. I, like many, was deeply disturbed, and while I understood the defence of religious practice, I believed it was a practice to be exposed and ended. Together with Janet Bell from the ABC, we persuaded Dr Sadawi to speak on the record about the practice and it was broadcast back in Australia. It was the beginning of a campaign across the world to end the practice. The conference also changed the terminology and now, nearly twenty years later, female circumcision has become genital mutilation and is a far less acceptable practice.

It was in Copenhagen that I met the famous Betty Friedan. One morning reading the daily sheet of activities I discovered that the 4Ws were running a session on payment for mothers at home. It was billed as an Australian presentation and I was determined to go at the very least to defend national honour. I did not want the rest of the world to think that the majority of Australian women held these views. It so happened that they were put in a slot with a group from England called Wages for Housework, a front for the prostitutes' union. The juxtaposition was wonderful. But my thrill came when I walked into the room and realised that I was sitting two seats away from Betty Friedan. I watched her body language as she listened to Jackie Butler from the 4Ws. There was no need to defend national honour because, with one line, Friedan fixed the whole thing. After listening to the pitch she said with that fantastic gravelly voice, 'Listen, sweetheart, you're only one husband away from welfare.' There was nothing else to say. They were a disregarded group.

Still the 4Ws had a further brush with fame when the time came for our Minister, Bob Ellicott, to sign the UN Convention on the Elimination of all Forms of Discrimination Against Women. When Beryl and the Minister arrived at the ceremony, they were surprised to find Babette Francis and a small group of supporters blocking their entry. They were carrying banners and chanting that signing this would be a betrayal of Australian women. Ellicott was appalled and the future for Women Who Want to be Women was suddenly limited. It was an altogether satisfactory outcome from my point of view.

The Convention was signed but the Australian government refused to ratify it on the grounds that they would not get agreement from the states. Three years later the Hawke government ratified the convention without reference to the states, with the view that it was national policy.

From NWAC's viewpoint, Copenhagen poignantly demonstrated

how much still needed to be done in Australia. Equally it revealed that Australian feminists were able to play a role on the world stage. On July 15 the term of the first Council members expired. I was pleased to be offered a year's extension and a little later I accepted an invitation from the NSW government to be a member of the NSW Women's Advisory Council. It felt like all the bases were covered.

CHAPTER EIGHT

FUTURE DIRECTIONS

The eighties began well for me. In many ways 1980 was a watershed year. I was riding high, doing so many things that I loved, Gordon and the kids were in great shape, we were settled into our new community at Longueville. I felt as though I was flying as executive director of the Australian Federation of Family Planning Associations, writing the *Cleo* column was a buzz, and as a member of the National Women's Advisory Council I had the privilege of travelling Australia listening to and meeting women from every conceivable interest group.

Add to that my increasing understanding of how Canberra worked. I was meeting political activists, politicians and bureaucrats and learning to manage the system to achieve outcomes. It was fun. When NWAC met in Canberra, Quentin, Jan and I would walk the corridors of Parliament House and lobby about the issues we cared about. We were sure that anything we wanted to do could be done almost immediately. We had endless dinners in the Parliament House dining room, persuading anyone who would listen to us of the virtue of our views. Being a feminist whose reputation was based on sex and family planning gave me a certain status with those who were titillated or curious. It also aroused great hostility in those who saw me as the reincarnation of the devil. I saw both as opportunities.

Beryl B (Beaurepaire), our leader, took her responsibilities seriously and was constantly expressing her concern that we didn't get home too late and were not seen in the wrong company, although she never really specified what that was. She worried we would be led astray. The realities were rather different in that we spent hours talking about our children and husbands and giving each other confidence to manage the social disapproval we so often encountered as feminist mothers who wore lipstick and smoked. We also loved staying in hotels and having room service.

When I returned from the Copenhagen conference in 1980 I moved straight back into the family planning agenda with renewed energy. So much of the work I was doing had been validated by that conference. Fertility was one of the fundamental, universal issues and women were united in their struggle to find ways of managing it in a variety of cultural settings. Although I knew of the opposition of Senator Brian Harradine, it made me more determined to keep Australia's consciousness raised so that its aid commitment was linked to family planning progress. AFFPA, as a member of the International Planned Parenthood Association, had a key role to play in our region and that was my responsibility. I could not have imagined that there was any other job I could do that would be so affirming of all my values.

Only two days after my return I received a preposterous telegram. It read:

> YOU ARE INVITED TO JOIN A SELECT GROUP OF NEXT
> GENERATION AUSTRALIAN OPINION LEADERS AT RESIDENTIAL
> CONFERENCE ON FUTURE DIRECTIONS FOR OUR COUNTRY STOP
> DATES AUGUST 10th–14th VENUE LA TROBE UNIVERSITY MAJOR
> SPONSORS THE AGE AND COMMONWEALTH GOVERNMENT STOP
> ORGANISERS AUSTRALIAN FRONTIER STOP EMPHASIS ON GROUP
> DISCUSSION TOWARDS AGREEMENT STOP WE URGE YOU TO
> RESERVE DATES NOW STOP DETAILS AND DOCUMENTS WILL
> FOLLOW FOR INFORMATION CALL . . .

I was very flattered to be thought of as an opinion leader and before I had time to treasure the telegram, documents arrived describing the expected and required commitment. They advised that already agreed participants included Phillip Adams (who didn't come), David Armstrong from the Australian Bicentennial Authority, Senator Gareth Evans, Senator Susan Ryan and Sam Lipski, radio commentator. It was mandatory to stay for the entire four-day program.

This was a big ask when I'd only been back from the Mid-Decade Conference for a few days. I felt apprehensive about asking Gordon to hold the family fort again so quickly, and I was not sure that my AFFPA Chairman would be enthusiastic about me being away from the office for another week and I had no holidays due. Whose approval should I seek first? Why must I always seek male approval and/or permission? I decided Gordon should have the first input and while reluctant emotionally, he agreed. Fortunately Colin Wendell-Smith also thought that this was an opportunity I shouldn't miss.

I have often reflected how lucky I was to have that encouragement and equally how loyal I am to people when they give me room to move. It's something that I have always tried to do as a manager.

I accepted the invitation. First I had to prepare a 500-word statement setting out what I saw as the major problems and challenges facing Australian society in the next fifteen to twenty years. This I found very intimidating. I thought of all the experienced people whose words it would sit beside, and wondered what on earth I would write about. In the end my piece reflected my passion about the shifting definition of being female. In the conference book, the quote next to my picture says: 'By taking over decisions about population size, family size or succession of heirs, women are challenging nationalism ... and challenging the power structure, whether religious or familial.'

On Sunday 10 August I caught the plane to Melbourne. The first person I met was David Armstrong, chief executive of the ABA. We had been at university together, but had seen each other only once since 1961, when I left New England. The plane was full of people attending the Future Directions conference and there was a nice buzz in the cabin as we chatted throughout the trip. He had left academic life and was very fired up about his new appointment. It sounded really wonderful to me. After Copenhagen, I became even more interested in events, and I wondered how I could be involved.

The Future Directions conference was a life-changing event, a heady mixture of carefully planned isolation from the outside world for four days and four nights, and the opportunity to let your mind range over previously unexplored ideas with a group of animated and very different people. You began to believe that these ideas could be reality, rather like the feelings I'd had working in prisons in my family planning programs. Disappointingly, we realised that even in this group we had to confront sexism. On day two some women, including me, decided to call a women's meeting. The announcement caused a flurry so we agreed that anyone (men) could come but they should understand that we women would be managing the agenda. Despite the rumbling, almost everyone came and Susan Ryan, Helen L'Orange and I explained what we thought was missing from the discussions, and how ignorant of and resistant to the basic tenets of the women's movement we found the men. It was as though the last decade had not happened; males kept reverting to type, dominating the conversation and dismissing alternative perspectives. It was an interesting intervention which paid off with better male behaviour and interaction.

Since then I have done it a couple of times in similar impasses, most memorably at a World Health Meeting in Sundsvall in Sweden in 1991. Again, a group of women, including Gertrude Mongela, who was later the UN Coordinator for the Beijing Women's Conference, started talking about their irritation and boredom with the inability of the traditional males to understand either female or indigenous views. So we called a women's meeting and changed the strategies of the conference. It is effective, as those men who get the point monitor and manage the ones who don't. There was no suggestion in either instance that we would form a breakaway group. We simply needed a breakthrough in the proceedings so we could be heard. Sometimes I wonder why I need to do this. Why don't I 'leave well alone' and settle for a quiet life? It would be easier, but it is the labelling and assumptions that enrage me. Everyone has a right to have their point of view respected and to be heard.

Opportunities to build friendships and networks and think outside the box don't often come as well orchestrated and managed as the Future Directions conference and those networks have survived in various forms. This was also my introduction to scenario planning, a technique I have used many times since. Of the 114 participants,

35—including me—were attracted to the Convivial Equity scenario. It reflected a very Australian vision which many of us have since pursued. So often people who attended that conference find themselves in Australian life working on the same issues. Most have provided leadership and added value to Australian society since that time, and at least some of the credit must rest there, for it gave us an extraordinary optimism that we could effect change.

Looking back and realising it was twenty years ago I think how prescient it all was. The five scenarios we developed have all occurred in one form or another. The connection with the Asian region, the growth of high technology, knowledge-based industries, the feminisation of Australia and belief that 'they' would not change the world. We needed to do it ourselves.

Going home I was again chatting to David Armstrong, who asked, 'What are you going to do when you leave Family Planning?' This was a surprising and unusual question as I was enjoying my role at AFFPA. It had not occurred to me that I would leave. He asked if I would be interested in working at the Bicentennial Authority and if so to give him a call as there were a couple of jobs about, such as the NSW manager's job.

I thought about it for a couple of days and became more and more interested in the idea. I loved the thought of the big canvas and pushing the boundaries of the Australian experience. I sent in a résumé and expressed an interest in the position of state manager. He rang a few days later and suggested I call in, as some of the people involved in the job would like to meet me and have a talk. I thought I was going for a background chat, but it was a full-scale interview. I remember I was wearing a black dress with buttons down the front, the two buttons undone at the bottom. I did have black stockings on, but it was not a dress I would have worn to a normal interview situation.

The all-male interview team asked the predictable questions about my work and were clearly disconcerted by the fact that someone with a Family Planning background would consider herself able to manage anything as regular as an office. Where did they think I worked? On the street? It was as though I didn't have a proper job. One said, 'You know there's a lot of travel in this job. How would you manage all those children? One of the reasons my wife doesn't travel much with me is that she hates leaving our children.'

I looked in utter amazement before responding, 'You'll see from my résumé that I've been travelling around Australia, in the Pacific, Southeast Asia and I've just come back from being part of the Australian contingent to the World Conference in Copenhagen for two weeks. There's utterly no indication that being a parent who travels is a problem.'

'No,' he said, 'but there'll be a lot of pressure on you in 1988. You'll have to be at functions every night and out at things every day and working at weekends. And your children will be adolescents and my wife says that they need you more then and you just wouldn't be able to leave them or they'd get into trouble.'

'Well,' I said, 'I don't think that's a problem and I'll face that when it comes. My husband counts as a parent, we share bringing them up.' This was clearly a more threatening statement. I left knowing that job was not to be mine.

The interviewers contacted my two referees, David Moore, Chairman of the NSW Anti-Discrimination Board, and Dame Beryl Beaurepaire, Convener of the National Women's Advisory Council. Both were quizzed about my ability to do the job because of 'all those children'. I hasten to remind you, dear reader, that I have only three children. I had never thought of them as a problem. Perhaps they were a convenient excuse, but the interview became a case study of the sexist interview. Why did I not complain, I wonder.

I discovered that the successful candidate was a male with a scouting background. His career for the Bicentennial Authority was short. It's a phenomenon I've observed over many years, this inclination to recruit from the establishment, either corporations like AMP or services sectors such as the defence forces. It's something about craving a sense of traditional order, a good officer who supports the status quo. Choosing someone like me is seen as risky. Perhaps it's the fear of change or the idea that those who are different are not easy to control. I do recall the appointment in the early seventies of Major General Peter Young as the CEO of Family Planning. What could he know about family planning, I wondered? Yet the International Planned Parenthood movement placed a great reliance on people from the defence forces. It's a pattern that repeats itself and it keeps women and other people who are different out of a whole range of activities and responsibilities.

So I continued working in Family Planning, despite a new restlessness. A couple of times I applied for other jobs to test my marketability, but rarely did I see a position I was interested in. I remember at one stage being persuaded to apply for a job as a Deputy Director of TAFE and my experience as a teacher, my membership of the Higher Education Board and Education Commission seemed appropriate. However, I was unsuccessful. While disappointed in the short term, I could see my working life was developing in a particular way so that I had a core job and other appointments. A pattern was emerging, I liked to be doing three or four tasks simultaneously. It's been a feature of my working life. I like to be someone's wife, someone's mother, an executive, and a non-executive director simultaneously. The Future Directions conference had been an opportunity to clarify and acknowledge my energy and ambition.

CHAPTER NINE

BLACK FRIDAY

I'm not given to prayer or superstition, although I acknowledge that in moments of crisis I might retreat to the language and comfort of the High Anglican litanies that I learnt to love as an adolescent. I have walked under ladders without consequence and I owned a black cat for nearly two decades. But Friday, February 13th, 1981 was a day to test all the reserves of prayer and superstition, and since that day I am inclined to stay in bed when Fridays and the thirteenth day of the month coincide.

Friday the 13th of February, 1981, is the touchstone day for our family. We were never the same again and when trying to understand the family memories, I often return to this day to make sense of it all.

We had a gorgeous summer holiday, which included a week in January on a houseboat on NSW's Myall Lakes with John and Carmel Niland and their children, Adam and Joshua. We caught eel, swam, took endless photographs and talked for hours. We looked and were the personification of a happy young Aussie family. Gordon by now had moved from being a corporate consultant to joining one of his clients as an investor and then managing director. Wolseley Castle was primarily a manufacturer and supplier of powder detergents and other domestic cleaning products to Australian supermarkets. It competed with the might of Unilever and Colgate and a few other Australian-owned companies for its share of the market. I was a busy working mother and delighted that my children were happy and well adjusted, despite the predictions of those who said that working mothers damage children.

But there was some discord. Gordon was slightly short-tempered and was sweating a lot at nights. Being intolerant of illness, we'd dismissed the idea that there was a problem and put it down to too much sun and not enough fish.

The children returned to school. There were questions raised about Sophie's subjects and behaviour and the headmistress had suggested that I visit her for a talk. We agreed to meet on 13 February and joked that it was Black Friday. I hoped the news of our daughter was not too bad. 'No, no,' she said, 'it's fine. Come in time to have a cup of tea in the morning.' I liked the Headmistress, Barbara Jackson, and had enjoyed working with her when I'd taught at Wenona.

So we agreed that I would come straight from the airport to the school. I was flying in from Young that morning about ten, after a speaking engagement at the View Club at nearby Temora. As a member of NWAC I received many invitations to speak to country groups who were hugely interested and curious about women's issues, especially after the Mid-Decade Conference in Copenhagen. I made an enormous effort to attend these rural functions. That's where my roots were and I felt that I owed it to people to be available and explain the things I was involved in and to share some of the aspirations and policies of the Council. And of course they were always fun.

On this occasion over a pleasant dinner I renewed contact with Sue Tout, the girl who'd been my only classmate at Garema Public School. We swapped stories about our families and friends and I spoke to the group for my supper. When we returned to the comfortable homestead of my host there were more surprises, as he parked his car next to what seemed a very small plane. He casually mentioned that we would fly to Temora in the morning so that I could have a good look at the country. I have a horror of small planes. It is one of my real fears, and I know that at least part of it stems from the fact that when I was in second year high school at Forbes, four of my classmates were killed in a small plane at an air show. My memories of standing on the streets of Forbes with those four coffins being carried by are vivid.

I went to bed feeling anxious and assured my hosts that I didn't want to inconvenience them, I was perfectly happy to be taken to the airport by car. Not at all, they said, 'the view is glorious from the plane'. I woke up feeling scared. To no avail. The hostess waved her husband and me goodbye, and they laughed about it being Friday the 13th. When I could bear to look, I conceded they were glorious views. My host made a skilful landing and I walked across to the regular commercial plane, due to depart for Sydney.

As I recall, the Sydney plane was a 12-seater with no toilets and no in-flight service. I sat down next to a Catholic priest and we started talking. He had been staying with family after a long illness, and spent some time confiding in me about his fear of flying. He then began throwing up and convulsing. I was sure he was having a heart attack, but with no flight attendants, nurses or doctors on board there was little we could do other than make him as comfortable as possible. As his seating companion the task appeared to be mine. The pilot radioed ahead, and was advised to keep flying to Sydney where they'd have an ambulance waiting.

The half-dozen people on the flight were strained, white-faced and feeling ill, both from the nauseous smell of the vomit and from the anxiety about our newly acquired friend, the priest. It seemed that I was the person who would help, so I stayed with him as we touched down with preferential landing rights and were met by the ambulance with people from St Vincent's Hospital.

My legs were turning to jelly and I made an instant decision that after visiting Sophie's school principal I would take the day off. I rang my office to say this was a bad luck day for me and a very bad luck day for the Catholic priest. My assistant's immediate response was, 'Of course, that's because he sat next to a family planner.' Be that as it may, I made my way to Wenona at North Sydney. We had our talk about Sophie, the meaning of life and the future of Wenona, and I went home to Longueville.

I'd just finished making lunch for myself and was preparing to go to sleep in order to erase most of the dramas of the morning when Gordon walked in to say that he'd been out to lunch, felt really sick with pains in his abdomen and chest, and thought perhaps he should go to bed. I was convinced he was having a heart attack, so I made him lie down and called our North Sydney GP, Dr Lele, who arrived about an hour later.

Dr Lele examined Gordon, and said, 'I think this is not good news. You've got a very inflated spleen and I'm not sure quite what that means. It's now late Friday afternoon, take things very quietly for the weekend and I'll arrange an appointment at North Shore Hospital with the Professor of Surgery on Monday. As you have a few friends in Longueville who are surgeons, I suggest you call one of them to have a look at you.'

By 5 p.m. Bob Perrett, one of our surgeon friends, had arrived, examined Gordon and pronounced that things were very black indeed. His spleen was enormous, the sweating he'd been having suggested a problem with his immune system and he should take things quietly over the weekend before he started what would be a battery of blood tests and investigations.

As a family planner, I had an extensive network of medical practitioners who would offer honest advice, and I sat on the phone seeking advice and possible diagnoses. We were in shock for most of the weekend. The word cancer was floating around, and a gut tumour had to be high on the possible list. On Monday we visited the Professor of Surgery at Royal North Shore who referred Gordon for a CAT scan and blood tests and repeated the new mantra, 'This is a bad story, but we can't offer you a diagnosis yet.' The hospital CAT scan machine was broken and the alternative machine had a four-week waiting list. I found a machine at the North Side Clinic through my friends the Sextons and Tuesday became CAT scan and blood test day. With a growing sense of unreality, we tried to put one foot in front of the other and keep life as normal as possible for the children. On the Wednesday we agreed we would both go to work, as it would help pass the time. We were on automatic pilot on a moving footway: I had a Higher Education Board Meeting scheduled and Gordon wanted to check in to his office. We would be better diverted by returning to gainful employment rather than sitting around wondering in a powerless sort of way what the verdict would be. I was tearful as I kissed Gordon goodbye and we headed off to work.

At 5 p.m. I was called out of my Higher Education Board Meeting to take a call from our GP, Dr Lele. He spoke very calmly and said the diagnosis was quite conclusive, Gordon had chronic myeloid leukaemia. His white blood cell count was extremely high and the prognosis was grim. Leukaemia sounded like a death sentence and my knowledge of it produced images of small, dying children, not grown-up men. Perhaps he had made a mistake. Could the blood test and CAT scan really show that so clearly?

Dr Lele insisted I did not tell Gordon. His rationale was that Gordon would become angry and dismissive with whoever told him, and it was best that I was not the messenger. That was his task. I was to go home as usual, feed and bath children and sometime after 8.30 p.m. he would arrive to give Gordon the results.

I was a little unsure but agreed to follow his advice. By then I'd have done anything I was told. I returned to my meeting and for a few minutes was fine, numb really, but when someone kindly inquired if I was all right I started sobbing and shaking. The sixteen men who were my colleagues on the Higher Education Board were astounded, and probably distressed. After a few uncomfortable moments while I blurted out the story, they moved into crisis management. One of them would drive me home as I was in no state to drive. Another would follow and collect the driver. We had arrangements in place if Gordon arrived unexpectedly and started asking questions about my inability to drive myself home.

I arrived home safely, played mother provider and cleared the top floor of the house of children. At 8.45 Dr Lele arrived and we sat down to hear his news. Gordon listened carefully, albeit with a sense of disbelief, and asked, 'How long do I have?' Our doctor thought at least six weeks. That didn't seem a very long time, but as he was leaving he kept repeating that we should plan for the worst and hope for the best. Responses to treatment were variable and, while the odds were not promising, Gordon had become a case study of one. We went to bed that night emotionally exhausted, out of words, and just curled up together. My brain went into overload as I started planning the funeral.

In the next few days we found our way to Dr Jim Isbister at Royal North Shore Hospital. We had been told that while significant improvements in the treatment of leukaemia in children had been made, there had been little progress made with adults, and there were only two examples in the local case studies of people who'd survived more than ten years. At this stage ten years was sounding a remarkably long period of time, compared with six weeks. Within days Gordon dismissed the six-week sentence as ridiculous.

When I began writing this chapter, I remembered that Gordon kept a diary while in hospital. He gave it to me when he came out, but I could not bear to read it. So that Gordon's voice can be part of this, which is really his story, I have now read it. Here is an extract:

> Unless you have any prior knowledge of blood cancers all of them sound like one word, leukaemia. The mind is not able to comprehend the differences between acutes and chronics, lymphoblastic and myeloblastic, granularcytic and lymphocytic—they all end with the same crunch, leukaemia. The prognosis offered by the haematology specialists at North Shore was guardedly optimistic or professionally hedged, whichever way you cared to read it. They couldn't really tell you. What caused it? Can't be sure. Is there any treatment? Yes, but the results are unpredictable. Can I go back to work? Yes, but you may feel sick from the treatment and have less energy than before.
>
> My immediate reaction to the diagnosis was to go home to Longueville, close the curtains against the summer sun and play Shostakovich symphonies at full volume. For almost two days I considered the likely causes of the disease, the possible effects and the time I may have left. I read as many books as I could borrow from medical friends but most were uniformly obtuse and positively unhelpful. A common note on my complaint was to the effect that a cure was unknown and death could be expected within a few years. Removal of the spleen, which usually became diseased, was standard procedure. I resolved not to consult medical dictionaries and encylopaedias again.

By Friday 20 February, Gordon was on his way to hospital for an undefined stay, with a bag packed with new pyjamas. Lane Cove

Primary School's swimming carnival was on. It was a horrid grey and rainy day and when we dropped the boys at the pool and said, 'Good luck', tears were streaming down Gordon's face. He said, 'I hope I'll be back here to see you swim later on today, or next week when you get into the District finals.' Both the boys were good swimmers and we worried that all this distraction would interfere with their performance.

Sophie was coming with us to the hospital. I felt ghastly about leaving the boys with no family, but our darling Mrs Downes, their surrogate grandmother who had moved to Lane Cove, was there with her lunch box for the day. She would be cheering them on and making sure they were warm.

At the hospital a couple of the doctors suggested that Sophie should wait outside. Fortunately James Isbister supported my view that it was better to have her there, knowing what was going on, than sitting wondering about it. Gordon was to be put on a cell separator to separate his red and white blood cells and remove his excessive white cells. This was the standard procedure for a very enlarged spleen. Attached to the machine, Gordon looked smaller.

Sophie and I got through the worst parts by being mesmerised by the technology. The centrifuge machine takes the blood through a catheter in one arm and spins it round until the red, white cells and other components separate. The unwanted whites are bagged off and the rest is returned through another catheter into the other arm. In a few hours Gordon's white cell count dropped from 450,000 to less than 20,000, normal being 7,000. Victory. We might avoid surgical removal of the spleen.

We'd packed the bags and put in his new pyjamas assuming that he would be staying there indefinitely, but there were more surprises when Jim Isbister said, 'I think he's better cared for at home. We're giving him some heavy doses of chemotherapy. You're so close to the hospital you can take him home and if there is a problem, it's a quick journey back.' Amazingly, at the end of the day we were there to pick up the boys with their swimming ribbons, and all went home together.

It was a tough couple of weeks; we diligently set about planning for death while assuming life. All our affairs were revised in an orderly manner so that if I was suddenly to be the sole parent and provider in this family, I would be well informed. Gordon's care for us was well reflected in the arrangements that he'd made. I would be able to manage. We talked through with the children what all this might mean and then decided to take each day as it came and assume that the best would happen. Gordon was absolutely determined he was not going to die just yet and emotionally, if not intellectually, I believed him.

From 1981 until 1988 our family lived with leukaemia. We learned when Gordon needed medication—he'd be cranky and irritable and easily stressed. We respected that he did not have the energy he had previously exhibited, but that wasn't so bad—moderate for him was energetic for others.

His legs would ache and he could no longer play tennis and golf. He was delighted—he had a perfect excuse never to come to a cocktail party or anywhere he had to stand for long periods of time. He needed an extraordinary amount of sleep, and he began changing his lifestyle by taking off Wednesdays and going to our farm at Berrima. This was our lifeline to present and past realities: three hundred and sixty acres with a river frontage on the Wingecarribee River, where we bred Red Poll cattle and scratched about in the dirt.

We had to find new life rhythms throughout these years. We had a regular relationship with Royal North Shore Hospital, where Gordon attended the blood collection clinic. He had oral chemotherapy in variable doses, roughly alternate weeks. We already spent most weekends with our children down in the bush and we lessened the expectations of each other's attendance at business-related social functions. We would aim for a working life each and a family life together. We would not bother with a social life—the cocktail scene would not miss us. This was not hard for us as we liked our family better than most of the social life that was on offer.

I kept up my work at Family Planning and my involvement with the Higher Education Board, the Education Commission and the National Women's Advisory Council. It became important for me to have another focus in my life. That was my way of coping. For

Gordon, coping was spending more time in the country and otherwise getting on with the jobs that he wanted to complete. I often smile when I recall how differently we approached this. I suggested talking to a grief counsellor—Gordon was thunderstruck and said he would just go to the bush more, but if I needed such a person, go ahead. I decided against it.

His business strategy was to build a state-of-the-art factory and expand the detergent business. To do this he needed to check out what was happening in the rest of the world, so our first venture out after the diagnosis was a trip through the USA and Germany, looking at chemical plants, trying to decide what would be the best plant for Wolseley Castle. The timing of the trip was difficult as his mother was dying at this time and we made a decision that we would not tell her that he was ill. How do you tell your mother that you have received a terminal sentence? It was too hard. We visited her in May to say goodbye. She died a week after we left and by agreement we did not come home for the funeral. That was painful as we both loved her.

There was no question at that stage of a bone marrow transplant because the odds were not good enough. People too often died as a result of the procedure. Gordon kept a close eye on the research and on the probabilities. He worked it out like my brother worked out the racing guide.

After he passed the six-week milestone and was still alive, Gordon did as Dr Lele predicted. He was dismissive of Dr Lele's skills—after all, he was only a GP. How would he know anything about leukaemia? (This changed later.) The Royal North Shore Hospital doctors were given credit and he followed their counsel carefully. Even a moderate smoking habit was out, stress was out, and sleep was in. Who knows how much effect it had? Our only frame of reference was Michael Daly, the ABC science reporter who was diagnosed with leukaemia at the same time as Gordon. They were both being treated at Royal North Shore. A friend brought us together for dinner so we could talk about it. Michael the scientist refused to give up smoking and drinking or change his lifestyle. Gordon declared that he would work with the doctors to survive, and if that meant some lifestyle changes, so be it. Michael died a week after our dinner. We were shattered that it could happen so quickly, and even more scared that it would happen to us. We hoped being good and moderate would be rewarded.

As a family under stress, we had to make some decisions about what we would do if Gordon was not around. The first one was to decide where Hamish would go to secondary school in 1983. I was concerned that if Gordon didn't make it, our sons would grow up with no male role models. There were no male grandparents around and my only brother lived in the country and was never likely to be close to Sydney. Gordon's only brother also lived in the country. It would not bother me now, but it bothered me at the time that our sons would be raised almost entirely by women and in some ways that might disadvantage them because they would be disconnected from the world of men, a world they needed to know because it was a world they would inhabit.

Also there was simply not enough human energy to cope with three children, a job and an ill husband. I checked out a couple of schools and went back to Knox Grammar where I'd run some successful Family Planning programs in the mid-seventies. The Headmaster, Dr Ian Paterson, assured me that Hamish would be carefully cared for as a Monday to Friday boarder. It seemed like a good solution and in 1983, Hamish started at Knox as a weekly boarder and Sam was booked in for Year Seven three years later. Sophie stayed at Wenona as a day girl. With the boys boarding, our lives were even more focused on bringing the family together at the weekend and during the school holidays. Looking back, I think that reinforced our family bonds.

Chronic illnesses are difficult to handle for both families and friends. Some friends disappeared overnight. One whom I met some years later greeted me by saying, 'Hello, how nice to see you. Sorry we haven't been in touch. Is Gordon still alive? What happened to him?' Others are scared and think the illness is contagious. The ones you end up loving the most are the ones who are there for the good and the bad times.

In October 1984 the new factory was completed and opened by

Senator John Button. The McCarthy family was scrubbed up and full of pride as the helicopter landed with Senator Button and his adviser Phillip Clark. Ken and Yasuko Myer had joined us for the day we had been anticipating for two years. My attendance was very risky as the acting Chairman of the Bicentennial Authority where I was working at the time had advised me that I could not have this day off because the Prime Minister, Bob Hawke, was coming to visit the staff of the Authority. I explained that as a partner in the Wolseley venture I was not intending to miss the opening of the factory as I'd invited Senator Button who was, after all, the Leader of the Senate to do the honours. I said that I'd call the Prime Minister's office and explain it was a longstanding appointment and offer my apologies.

I was advised by John Utz, the acting chairman of the ABA, and two Cabinet Ministers that this was the end of my public life. The Prime Minister was the Prime Minister and I had to be there. I refused. I thought my marriage was more likely to be a longer relationship than my employment with the Bicentennial Authority. Against all the advice I attended the Wolseley Castle opening and returned to the ABA office at 4 p.m. The sky did not fall in but sometime later when I met Bob Hawke face to face, his first line to me was, 'Oh, you're the woman who prefers her husband to me.' I said, 'Yes, it's true.'

The new Wolseley Castle plant was an impressive modern computer-controlled building, and would relieve Gordon of some day-to-day responsibility. Gordon decided that he would spend more time in the country and reduce his working life to four days. He was considering selling or floating the business, and when made a good offer by Clyde Industries, he accepted. The sale liberated him from the daily responsibility of running a business, paid out our mortgage, renovated Longueville, and enabled him to buy some more property and to develop his cattle breeding business. In 1986 he took up residence at our farm at Berrima and became a full-time cattle breeder. I was deeply offended when asked if this move meant we were divorced. Why couldn't people accept our survival mechanism?

By 1988 Gordon was becoming weary of the chemotherapy, the fatigue and general lack of well-being. At the same time, after seven years of managing, there was a false sense of security that this pattern could continue. He had to listen to the medical science which told him that each year 25 per cent of chronic leukaemics convert to acutes.

In Gordon's words:

> Suddenly the entire picture had changed. The major business obligations had gone and I was free of personal debt for the first time in thirty years. The children were now five years older and over the possible trauma of losing their father. Wendy was on the Board of the ABC and a General Manager of the Australian Bicentennial Authority, and quite secure in her own life at the same time as sharing mine. I decided to reverse my normal life and spend four or five days a week with the cattle and weekends in Sydney or in the country with the family.
>
> After a fishing trip to north-western Australia in August 1986, I became a resident cattle breeder at Berrima, determined to build the Red Poll stud to the top in Australia. This seemed entirely possible when we made a clean sweep of all championship ribbons in the breed at the Sydney Show in 1987. It was almost possible to forget about the Myleran and the blood tests in the idyllic surroundings of the Southern Highlands.

The bone marrow transplant option needed to be re-examined. His brother and sister offered to be donors, and his brother's tissue type seemed to be a good match. Gordon, at 48, was seen as on the margin of acceptability for a transplant because of his age, and there was a strong feeling that we were running out of time. In his favour was his good general health, his donor brother's good health, and the professionalism of the medical team at Royal North Shore in whom we had great faith. He decided he would prepare for the operation. Gordon's major Bicentennial gift would be a bone marrow transplant in late 1988.

Sometimes I felt I had a thousand balls in the air, and if they ever came down in the wrong sequence, we would all disappear. It was easier and harder when Gordon moved to the country in 1986 as I had one less person to think of day to day. Yet there is a loneliness that arrives when you lose your daily companion and there is no one there to share the day's stories and events. In 1983 I had accepted an appointment as Deputy Chair of the ABC and was surprised and offended when a friend suggested I should stay home and look after my sick husband. When I look back on those years I remember productive and domestic years of adolescent children, school activities, early nights and sitting at the dining room table writing three books on sex and family planning. It was in many ways a nurturing time and a time when we learned the wonderful skill of living one day at a time.

Gordon's diary records:

> Today is Tuesday November 22, 1988—twenty-five years after the day they killed JFK. I've been riding the Honda around the cattle for the last time for at least a month, checking final details with my dependable manager who will cope easily in my absence. The old news reports of that day 25 years ago in Dallas continue to draw old memories from my mind.
> Tomorrow I'm due at Royal North Shore Hospital for a bone marrow transplant and an early meeting with the psychiatrist.

On 23rd November 1988, Gordon was admitted to Royal North Shore Hospital for a bone marrow transplant. We were greeted at the reception area of Ward 12D and immediately sent off to Radiotherapy for initial planning. This means that various radiotherapy specialists consult the X-rays and CAT scans and decide how best to blast the leukaemic cells in the spleen and then the entire body. It was decided he would have two doses in the spleen, and, over three days, six doses of total body irradiation. We were both very quiet as the assistants drew coloured lines all over him.

The cleaners were still sterilising his room, so we went to the coffee shop for our last meal together and talked about the children and nothing, in the way people who have been together for twenty-five years can.

And then to Ward 12D where Gordon would be isolated and barrier-nursed three or four weeks. I couldn't take any more and I left glad of the need to be in Canberra at 6 p.m. to open the new Australian Science Museum, a major Bicentennial gift, on behalf of Jim Kirk. Next morning I was agitated, knowing Gordon was starting radiotherapy. When I reach the hospital I was amazed that he looked fine, had ridden the exercise bike and was typing.

Two days later it was a different story; the massive doses of chemo had begun and the nausea seemed to overwhelm him. A few special friends and family were allowed in after agreeing to being gowned, masked and booted. By November 29 the immune system had been destroyed, his brother Alfred was in the ward next door ready to be the donor, and it was all systems go. I wanted to stay the night because there was one final king hit of cyclosporin to be dripped into him and I could see he was fading. The body cramps were excruciatingly painful but he wanted me to go and come back for the transplant tomorrow.

Back to Gordon's diary:

> The protocol for today says BM harvest and infusion and cyclosporin. This is D Day in the ultimate. My brother's bone marrow attempting to take root in my body which will attempt to repel invaders if I have a skerrick of my own immune system left surviving. All that RT, all the chemo has been designed to kill my leukaemic cells and also eliminate my immune system to avoid it rejecting the graft. Quite a day for both Alfred, who goes into theatre for two hours at 9.30 a.m., and for me waiting to see I get some marrow to replace what I no longer have in operating order. And then we wait days and weeks to see the new marrow growing in my body—we hope.
>
> Amazingly, although I think about the crazy position I'm in there's no apprehension as I type. I have total confidence in the people who planned and are implementing this transplant. I mentally prepared myself for it almost a year ago and it's like being on a moving belt way waiting for the next inevitable step in the process. You can't get off and you can't go back

even if the chemo and the cramps bring on times you wish you could crawl back into the womb. I've done a whole 10km on the bike to try and break up the cramp problem before tonight. It may make it worse but I need the exercise to push air through my lungs and blood through my heart and body. It's the only real exercise I'll get for the next three weeks and I have to push the kilometres to keep the body functioning and to get all the chemical garbage they pour into me every day travelling through the system and out again ... as fast as possible. My own formula for the next three weeks will be exercise, food, water and writing plus ABC FM—I can survive well on that mix.

Mid-morning Dr Chris Arthur arrives through the door of 12D9 with two ordinary looking blood bags full of the creamy red goodies straight from Alfred. Because we have similar tissue types and similar blood types there was no need to strain any of Alfred's blood components off at all ... I get the lot: marrow, reds, whites, platelets, etc. In a short time the first bag is hooked up on a drip, they give me some anti-allergy phenergan and steroids in the drip and away we go. In less than an hour the first bag is gone and the second is hooked up. Wendy and Sophie are there when I come out of a doze to find all the marrow plus has been dripped in through the catheter. I have my life-creating potential marrow back again after a new week of body racking therapy. The deed is done. Time alone now will tell us the result. We soon hear Alfred is out of the anaesthetic after his two-hour general where they sucked the marrow out of his pelvis and sternum via largish needles and syringes. What an amazingly simple procedure but what a lot of technical, chemical and human back-up to make the transplant work and make sure I don't expire from something simple like a common cold. The lowest point of my white cell count will not be recorded for a few days after the transplant as my old cells are still dying and the new ones have not yet grafted. So there is a crossover point.

On December 1 Alfred's bone marrow was harvested under a general anaesthetic and with the doctor I walked into Gordon's ward and watched as he hooked up those two bags of warm marrow and started dripping it into Gordon. It all seemed so simple. Within three hours he had turned from grey to pink and then we waited to see if his body would accept the marrow and graft. Gordon was as high as a kite and convinced he was cured. He sat up and wrote a long letter to the *Sydney Morning Herald* about capital gains tax, insisting that I post it on the way home. I checked that Alfred was OK and left for home, exhausted.

On December 20 Gordon came home weighing 70 kilograms and looking like something out of Belsen, but with an immune system that could just tolerate being out of hospital. He was desperate to be home for Christmas and he was, but the family photographs of Christmas 1988 are not a pretty sight: a totally hairless man, all bony and grey, sitting at the Christmas table, glad to be there, even grateful, but exhausted and irritable.

Here is Gordon's diary entry of his last day in hospital:

> As a token of protest I have not ordered any hospital meals today . . . one because the better my tastebuds get the worse the hospital food tastes, and two because I won't be here after midday. My final meal is Rob's [Robyn Sexton] apple crumble plus bread and apricot jam plus juice and tea. Luke takes out my shoulder skin biopsy stitch and I'm all ready to go. The packing-up after four weeks in here is a slight anti-climax. To the nursing staff it's a normal event. To me, it's the beginning of the next stage. I ride a final 5km to take the score to 600km in 27 days. I'm ready to go.
>
> Wendy arrives at about midday and Elaine helps with the carrying. After two trips we are loaded and ready to go . . . then we are gone. We drive to Longueville which is all strangely green compared to four weeks ago when everything was so dry and burnt. The arrival home is like returning from an overseas holiday—no real changes that are obvious except for the colour of the grass. We unload, have lunch and then

unpack. It is not one of the great homecomings of my life. Rather the last piece being placed in a four-week jigsaw puzzle where you knew somehow it was only a matter of time before all the pieces were fitted into place. The humidity is a shock after the air conditioning of the hospital but I become accustomed to it during the afternoon. I read, have a sleep during the afternoon and then at dusk go for a walk with Sophie and the dog down Mary Street to the Longueville wharf. On a humid evening looking back to the City this is a view you know will always be worth preserving. The water, the boats, the trees and houses of Woolwich and Northwood surrounded by the evening sunset. This is a good place to start one's second life.

For the children this was a tough time, especially the boys who found it harder to express their feelings. They were twenty, eighteen and fifteen and frankly sick of it all, and although never unsupportive, they found it hard to manage. I understood and accepted that and knew they had to find their way of coping, so I largely let them go but it wasn't a top month for mothering.

Amazingly, Gordon was back on the farm within four weeks. Although told not to have any contact with animals while his immune system was low, he undoubtedly had his hand up a cow delivering a calf some weeks later.

I was and am extraordinarily proud of the way Gordon managed this. He stands as a reminder that you can survive cancer, but it's a salutary experience for a family. It's a bit like alcoholism at one level—if you've got an alcoholic in the family, everyone carries the repercussions. If someone in the family has cancer, it's always there. You join a club you didn't want to belong to. I lived for years with Gordon's funeral planned in my head; every time there was a crisis I replayed the plan and prepared myself for the inevitable. It was an enormous relief to let that imagery go.

But there is a life post-leukaemia; within a year Gordon was leading an active and full life. By 1996 he was technically cured.

CHAPTER TEN

EIGHT YEARS WITH AUNTY

One Sunday night in 1983 I had answered the telephone at Longueville, and the caller identified himself as Senator John Button. He said by way of introduction that a lot of people had suggested that I would be an effective and suitable ABC Board member. Would I be interested in accepting such an appointment if it was offered? At that very moment there was a piercing scream as Sam fell over the only one-bar radiator we've ever owned. I retrieved him and returned shakily to the telephone.

I no longer assumed when I got a phone call saying it was a minister that it was a joke, but this was pretty far-fetched. After all, the ABC was *the* Board. Had I read the Dix Report, he asked. I had to confess that I had not but I'd certainly read the coverage in the papers and understood its general thrust. Would I be interested? My brain was rushing with reasons why I couldn't do it. As my mouth was poised to say no, I took a very deep breath and said, 'Yes, I would be very interested.'

'Please don't mention this conversation to anyone,' he said, 'but you come well recommended and I think you can assume that we'll be making you an offer.' I got off the phone astonished. Had I really said yes? What on earth would I know or be able to contribute? What were the necessary qualifications? How would I stack up? Immediately I began rationalising.

Well, I knew what it feels like on both sides of the microphone. I was, at that stage, doing a radio chat at nine every morning on 2KY with John Singleton and Mungo MacCallum, where we spoke of the political events of the day. On Tuesday mornings for an hour and a half I was doing an interactive sex/human relationships advice column on air with John Singleton. I had met the non-ABC audience.

2KY taught one to be a truly flexible broadcaster. Where else would you be offering personal advice on an issue of some importance to the listener, say unplanned pregnancy, when we would switch to the race results for the Dapto Dogs? Minutes later we would return to continue the advice, and John would interrupt to read the ads. People had to be determined in order to stay with us, but somehow people loved the normality of the program.

I loved radio and I loved doing that job, but did this equip me to be an ABC Board member? Hardly. I thought of other reasons I might have been invited. I had been an unsuccessful applicant for the job of director of education at the ABC quite recently, and had endured a humiliating and patronising interview. It could not have been that I impressed anyone there. I'd been on the *Coming Out* show, talking about women's issues, and was often a commentator on women's issues. None of these seemed to be convincing reasons. Why would I be asked to be on the Board?

No doubt many other people would ask the same question. I decided there was little point in agonising about my competency. Others must have seen some potential, and the fact was I had been asked and had accepted. I spoke of this to no-one except Gordon, who looked rather surprised.

A few days later I was called by the head of the Department of Communications, Bob Lansdowne, who asked me if I'd be willing to be considered as chairman or deputy. 'Of course,' I said. His response was, 'Well, you'll certainly be on the Board and it's now a matter of whether you'll be chairman or deputy.'

I found myself saying yes, while my head was spinning and thinking, 'Wendy, how can you say this, what do you know, how would you do it?' And the other part of me was saying, 'Jump in feet first. If you jump in and steady yourself, you'll be able to do it.' The next day I had a phone call from a friendly National Party MP telling me I would definitely be on the board and with the blessing of the Coalition. Some time later Bob Lansdowne called me to say, 'Congratulations, you are the deputy chair of the Australian Broadcasting Corporation, and Kenneth Myer is the chairman.'

Launching the Aussat satellite turns out to be women's business! *Left to right*: Geoffrey Whitehead (Managing Director, ABC), Graham Goswinckel (Managing Director, Aussat), Michael Duffy (Minister for Communications), me (Deputy Chair, ABC) and David Hoare (Chairman, OTC).

Managing men at the Bicentennial Authority. *Left to right*: Matthew Eton, Gary Martin, Des Walsh and Brian Sweeney.

Left: With Sophie at Government House, Canberra, on receiving the Order of Australia in 1989.

Below: Opening the Wendy McCarthy Childcare Centre at the ABC with Hamish McCarthy, Hazel Hawke and two pupils, 1991.

Above: A typical National Trust event—an exhibition opening at the S.H. Ervin Gallery, this time with Leonard Teale, 1991.

Below: With His Royal Highness Prince Charles at the opening of the Merchant's House, 1995.

Brother Kerry, just months before his death in 1994.

The McCarthys at the beach, Christmas 1996.

A 'Women for Wik' meeting, taken at Anne Deveson's house. *Left to right*: Anne Deveson, Lynn Spender, Rosie Scott, Caroline Jones, Rachel Ward, Jean Carter, Jane Campion, Win Childs, Julie Nimmo, me and Paula Dewes. *Photograph courtesy Robert Pearce/Sydney Morning Herald.*

Right: With Quentin Bryce at a 1997 University of Canberra graduation where Quentin gave the occasional address.

Below: Beryl Beaurepaire and Quentin Bryce—two important women in my life—at the twenty-year reunion of the National Women's Advisory Council at Parliament House, 1998.

The more things change, the more they stay the same. Sophie's wedding day on our thirty-fifth wedding anniversary, 18 December, 1999.

It felt like being in a documentary without a script. But nothing beats being invited, and I loved that thrill of being chosen. It was affirmation of being a good girl.

So here I was, forty-one years old, feminist, change agent, wife, mother, executive director of Family Planning Australia, member NSW Education Commission, member NSW Higher Education Board, *Cleo* columnist and deputy chair of the ABC. I had never ever dreamt of, coveted or lobbied for this position. I would not have had enough imagination to think of being there. It was right out of the blue. I could barely breathe as I alternated between the fantastic excitement stimulated by the chance to do something with an organisation I adored, and an abject terror that I'd be right out of my depth and would not be able to contribute at all.

The Dix Report (1981) into the ABC had been accepted by both political parties prior to the 1983 election. As a result the ABC would be restructured as a corporation and have a new charter. Membership of the first board of the new post-Dix corporation would be approved across party lines. To me that mattered enormously. I did not want to be there feeling that I owed a political party any favours. Again, my resistance to being fenced in was evident. As a member of the NSW Education Commission I had established a good working relationship with the Labor Government. Similarly, I had built a relationship with the Federal Coalition Government, both as a member of the National Women's Advisory Council and as the CEO of Family Planning. I had no axes to grind with either side of politics, and I was quite sure by then that I was not interested in joining either party.

The day before the ABC appointment became public, Ken Myer called me to introduce himself. It was the first of many hundred of conversations we would have. I remembered his charming, warm voice over the telephone, 'I'm Ken Myer, the new chairman, I understand you are to be my deputy. I don't know much about you but we need to get to know each other quickly and I want to bring all the new board members together immediately for a board meeting.' The day the appointment was made public was for me like being engaged: flowers, telegrams and endless good wishes for the future.

We did not legally become the Board until the Commission ceased to exist, which was some three or four weeks later. There was a protocol issue about the relationship between the new Corporation and the existing Commission, led by Professor Leonie Kramer. Also most of the Commissioners were said to be bitterly disappointed not to be on the new Board. In deference to those feelings, we decided that rather than meet initially in the ABC buildings, we'd meet at Telecom House, Sydney, while they completed their term as Commissioners.

It was a difficult changeover time. There was no formal contact between the existing Commission and the newly appointed Board. Media speculation ensured that any chances we might have of listening to the corporate memories of the past Commissioners was not possible, although I'm sure Ken Myer would have had some contact with Professor Leonie Kramer.

When the new Board members met informally for the first time on 23rd May 1983 there were crowds of photographers and journalists outside. Little did I understand that this was an omen of times to come—our business would always be conducted in the public spotlight. However there was enormous goodwill towards this Board and it would have been hard not to feel optimistic.

I was looking forward to meeting my new colleagues on the Board. I was delighted to be again sitting on a Board with Jan Marsh, my colleague from the NWAC days. I was also intrigued to meet Sister Veronica Brady, a West Australian nun about whom I'd heard a great deal. Bob Raymond's career in television was well known and I thought him a sensible choice. Neville Bonner was a household name as the first Aboriginal Senator. Dick Boyer and Ken Myer were the two people totally unknown to me. There was a lot of adrenalin and excitement about.

The first meeting was remarkable. Ken took the chair, and called in the four ABC union representatives (from the Australian Journalists Association, the Staff Union, the Senior Executives Association and the Musicians Union) to ask if they wanted to have a seat on the Board as the Act permitted. He advised them that should that be the case, they should appoint an interim representative immediately. They protested that they needed time for proper process. In an amazing show of mastery he said, 'No, you want a person on the Board, you nominate someone today, or else there's no spot. I'm the Chairman of the Board and that's the way it's going to be. I think the staff should be represented on the Board but there is no time to waste and I'm not prepared to wait. We've got important work to do, I want someone now. You can go through proper process and have an election that can be sorted out within the next six months, but I want someone now.'

Tony Bond was given the nod and it was agreed by the end of the day that he would be the staff representative. It was a classic introduction to the swift Ken Myer decision-making style. I doubt that he consulted anyone else on the Board about this, but he certainly consulted me. In a phone call he said, 'As an article of faith, I think there should be a staff-elected director. I don't think we should be sitting down and making decisions as a non-executive Board without the managing director and a staff-elected director on the Board.'

I had about two minutes to respond and I agreed. It was hardly a thought-out position, but the combination of the Myer authority and the support of the unions prevailed. However, it was quite a leap for me, as in my professional experience in not-for-profit organisations staff-elected directors were not a reality, and most executive directors were not voting board members.

The ABC Board worked hard from day one. Our chairman believed that there was no time to waste and we set about making sense of the Corporation. There was a feeling of energy and commitment to the task we had been given, and the public response was fantastic. Ken and I went on television one Sunday evening to talk of our vision for the ABC and seemed to engage even the most sceptical of the journalists. I had bought a red suit as my ABC signature, to be sure I didn't fade into the greyness of the suited males. I was pleased it worked on television as well.

Ken and I approached the world differently and it was a difference I enjoyed and learned from. I remember in our familiarisation period Ken asked me to visit the ABC sites and meet as many people as possible. I felt uncomfortable, as though I was the lady of the manor patronising people. It reminded me of *Are You Being Served*, with its gentleman walking through the store. Ken was in his element. One day in Melbourne we visited the wardrobe department and the women told me how much they appreciated our visit. No ABC director had ever been there and 'Mr Myer' was especially welcome as they knew he would understand about wardrobe coming from that 'nice' store.

This reversed my thinking—I stopped considering my feelings and thought about theirs. Ken's view was that I had to get over my self-conscious attitudes—people had a right to talk to the non-executive directors, they had a right to be listened to, and if non-executive directors couldn't cope with that they shouldn't be there.

He transformed my view about the role of a non-executive director. I'd never thought about it in any professional way. I had performed those roles instinctively up until then and in most of the organisations I'd been involved in, being a non-executive director meant you didn't trust the management and you tried to manage by default. Ken Myer had the art of the non-executive director defined in quite a precise way. He wanted management and staff to have a voice, he wanted partnerships, but we directors had to have the confidence to let the managers manage. He was also adamant that we were not there to design or deliver programs, and he rigorously and quite properly maintained that position.

The ABC we inherited and whose governance we were responsible for was an unhappy place with a dysfunctional management and an old-fashioned view of the world. Its mimicry of the BBC reflected the worst of the cultural cringe and when it spoke of its achievements it was invariably speaking of the past. It was tired and suffering from political bashing and endless inquiries, all of which wore away at its self-esteem. For about ten years it had failed to recruit young people, so there were few new and fresh ideas and energy pushing the system. The entire senior management seemed to have their titles prefaced by the word *acting*. Nobody seemed to have a sense of ownership of their job.

The people who were best off were people like Robyn Williams of the *Science Show*, who ran discreet parts of the empire and just got on with it. Robyn was a great favourite of the Chairman's, not only because of the success of the Science Unit, but because Ken loved the pursuit of science and technology and Robyn's entrepreneurial approach.

These were years of trying to build a new ABC, of meetings that went on for two and three days while we tried to understand the ABC culture. This process was not assisted by ABC management who resisted all efforts to engage with us. Ken offered all Board members an opportunity to present a vision for the ABC. In August 1984 the Board and management held a two-day meeting to agree on some future directions. The result was the ABC's first corporate plan and was largely directed by members of the Board's secretariat, a group created to assist the Board.

Every director had some particular passion in addition to his or her general skills. Dick Boyer was deeply committed to writing a philosophy for the ABC as he felt the Act and Charter were philosophically deficient. Ken was impatient with that approach, but agreed that Dick should be commissioned to produce a document and was pleased when it was completed. The publication, *The Role of a National Broadcaster in Contemporary Australia*, spelt out the national broadcasting commitment to expanding the range and experience of being Australian and recognised the ABC's pivotal role in that task.

Ken was impatient for outcomes and he often found the Board meetings irritating, for they seemed to produce few. I had a much higher tolerance and regard for process, and would try to keep him bouyant, as did other Board members like Tony Bond. At every Board meeting in Sydney, Ken and I would walk around Hyde Park at lunchtime and sometimes visit David Jones department store. He adored retailing, it was in his blood. While he taught me a lot about being a non-executive director, he also legitimised my passion for shopping. We'd wander around David Jones' ground floor for twenty minutes' retail therapy and switch off from the ABC. When it was time to return to the meeting, the clouds would have lifted from his brow.

By the end of the first year of our life as a new Corporation there was pressure on us to show that we had made a difference. This was difficult, although I think we still had the confidence of the staff and the public. But no organisation as broadly based as that can change quickly, and although we were an interventionist Board, we all recognised that the Board alone could not change the organisation.

Sixteen years later, what memories remain strong? It seems there is no pattern, but apparently disconnected incidents stand out in that first year. The Board's first collective task was the search for a new managing director. Ken was fond of saying there are few things a Board can do, but hiring the chief executive is one of them and we must get that right. He insisted that we use an executive search firm to recruit the new managing director. This was heresy in 1983 in the public sector, and outside the experience of the other directors.

'The price doesn't matter,' he said. 'We want the best and we want the best in the world and only a specialist international firm can locate such a person. Broadcasting is part of a global communications revolution and we must look for the best person in the world, who may or may not be an Australian.' This doesn't sound so unusual now, but it was big thinking then. I don't think anyone really argued against this, although probably some of us had some concerns that maybe an Australian would understand the culture better. We, or certainly I, buried those anxieties for fear of appearing insular.

When the time came to interview the candidates, the security was elaborate. Every journalist in Australia was ringing up trying to find out the short list, and writing pages on their guesses. Probably Ken and I were the only two Board members who knew of all the candidates who had expressed an interest. Certainly some withdrew when they understood that the entire Board would be interviewing.

We interviewed six candidates. Geoffrey Whitehead from New Zealand was by far the best prepared for the interview. He had thought carefully about the job and the structure of the organisation and had a vision that we could live with and we believed he could implement. The personal responses to him were rather detached. He was not a warm person and I think that was to his advantage as there was a feeling that he was professional and would get on with the task. At the end of the day he was in front, but there was not unanimity. At least two Board members expressed their reservation about his lack of understanding of industrial matters, and others worried that he would find it hard to make the necessary cultural shifts.

It was agreed that we would not appoint until we reached a unanimous position, as the appointee would need all the support we could provide. Eventually we put aside some of our doubts because we felt that Geoffrey Whitehead was the only candidate with skills in broadcasting and broadcasting-management in an international environment. He had work experience in the UK and New Zealand. He was also a clean-skin who owed no political favours and no internal broadcasting favours. He could belong to the Board. Following a second interview with Geoffrey the next day, it was a unanimous decision.

I phoned the Minister, Michael Duffy, as the media announcement was being released. His response was Geoffrey who? I explained. 'Well,' he said, 'that is a surprise. I can only wish you the best of luck and hope you've got the right person for the job.' Michael Duffy was the most impeccable Minister in terms of propriety.

We then appointed Stuart Revill as the deputy MD, on the grounds that he was a wise head who'd been around the organisation for years and had a good knowledge of the corporate culture. He had also run the London office and had a good network of international contacts. Other appointments followed, with Geoffrey playing a role in all of them and Board members making sure that they were actively involved in all the senior management appointments. Jeanne Ercole from the World Bank, Gerry Moriarty from Television New Zealand, Richard Thomas from the BBC and TV New Zealand and Malcolm Long from ABC Radio were recruited to the new executive team. It was as international and as broadly based as possible.

We gave a total and utter commitment to Geoffrey and were very much led by Ken who insisted the Board's job was to support the chief executive and his team, determine broad policy and let the managers manage. We followed him faithfully.

The first real challenge to Board harmony came in May 1984, over the *Four Corners* dispute in Papua New Guinea. This began while Geoffrey Whitehead was away on leave and Stuart Revill was acting managing director. Allan Hogan, a reporter from *Four Corners*, had

filmed an interview with the leader of the OPM independence movement in Irian Jaya. When the PNG government found out, it
approached the Australian High Commissioner in Port Moresby, and
several days later the ABC.

The PNG Government's complaint was that 'a visiting ABC television crew held a meeting with self-styled OPM leaders directly contrary to directions by the Government'. Such conduct, it said, was in
direct contravention of PNG's security interests. It requested an explanation and sought assurances there would be no repetition and that
the film would not be broadcast. There was also a threat that the
ABC correspondent in PNG, Sean Dorney, might be expelled.

Stuart Revill assured the PNG government that the film would not
be used. As Tom Molomby wrote in his book, *Is there a moderate
on the roof?*: 'When word of that got out, which did not take long,
the balloon went up.' For two weeks or so the issue became a *cause
célèbre*. The media generally reacted with condemnation that the ABC
would cave in to such a request.

It so happened that the ABC Board was meeting in Melbourne to
meet the local ABC people and attend a dinner hosted by Ken to
introduce Geoffrey to the luminaries of the city. By Thursday the issue
was hot. Resolutions of protest were coming in from staff around the
country insisting that the ABC Board reverse the ban decision. By the
time we sat down to discuss the matter on the Thursday afternoon,
the atmosphere was electric.

Tom Molomby, Bob Raymond and I were already on the public
record expressing strong opinions against the suppression of the interview. Unusually for him, just before the board meeting Ken Myer
offered the view to the enterprising Julie Flynn of 2GB that 'we are
not dealing with a simple domestic Australian issue—a lot of people
in Australia live in an unreal world. In most countries where I travel
in Asia the media is totally controlled by the governments. What I'm
saying to you is that if you want to get into those countries—whether
you like it or not—you've got to follow the rules set by those governments.' This really stirred up everyone.

When we sat down to consider the issue, Stuart Revill outlined
what had occurred and the reasons for his decision. He referred

to various documents that most Board members had not seen. Bob Raymond began the discussion by reading a statement he had prepared, which said that he considered this an issue that went to the heart of the ABC's political independence and, as Directors, we were the final guardians of that independence. As we went around the table there were some surprises. Dick Boyer, Bob Raymond, Tom Molomby, Veronica Brady and myself voted to run the interview, all on the grounds of the independence of the ABC. Jan Marsh, Neville Bonner, Geoffrey Whitehead and Ken Myer voted to support the management decision to suppress it. So the vote was 5/4. As the meeting broke up Geoffrey Whitehead walked out the door muttering that 'Tomorrow you'll see whether you have a managing director.'

The next morning the mood had changed, and we were advised that Whitehead and Revill had offered their resignations. Ken Myer said that if they went, he would go too, and despite the fact that we had all agreed on confidentiality, Geoffrey Whitehead told us that other executives would withdraw their services if Whitehead was no longer the managing director. Before leaving the meeting and battering through a wall of media we agreed to hold a special crisis meeting in Sydney to settle things.

The majority on the Board held firm. We were not persuaded by the argument that if we don't back the management, even if we think they've made an error of judgement, there will be revolution. It was Ken's first defeat on a critical issue and it was a bitter blow. Our relationship suffered a little on this and I realised few people challenged Ken. The special meeting, in a Kings Cross hotel, was a quiet event where we expressed confidence in the management. Geoffrey Whitehead and Stuart Revill then withdrew their resignations, but we never quite regained that early trust and camaraderie. I was already developing the view that the ABC was at its best when in a state of convivial anarchy.

Another memory is my appearance in a *Hypothetical* on Channel 9, run by Geoffrey Robertson. It was on the subject of broadcasting. Along the way I was asked about the practice of issuing D notices.

(A D notice is a security ban placed on broadcasting information.)
Would I defy a D notice? I said, yes, I would if I thought it was in
the public's interest. It was an honest answer but it caused a furore.
The suggestion was that I was an unreliable, even risky, Board
member. I truly thought that those were the principles that people
knew I stood for and that was the reason I was on the Board. I could
not understand why people thought I should change. Did they hope
I would disappear into a white car, now I was a director?

On another occasion I spoke to the Melbourne Law Communications Association and described the 'the old ABC management as
ossified, insufficiently oriented towards product and lacking diversity'. The Senior Officers' Association promptly banned me from
being a member of the top level appointments committee. This was
a curious group of people, like many coalitions of self-interest in the
ABC. No doubt it began with lofty ideals, but at this stage I thought
it exactly as I was quoted as describing it. I could see no sign of its
members embracing change.

The Senior Officers' Association had approximately fifty members,
of whom two were women—one was a market researcher and the
other one the legal counsel. As neither of these positions was a line
management position (responsible for broadcasting), effectively there
were no women in management. Neither of these women was supportive of the idea of affirmative action for women and minority
groups in the ABC. Geoffrey Whitehead telephoned me with the news
the SOA had passed a resolution insisting that I be called to account
for my comments, asserting that these comments made me an unfit
person to sit on any interviewing committee. Frankly, I was quite
relaxed about them boycotting anything I was a member of, because
it meant that I wouldn't have to hire them. On the other hand, I did
recognise that there were many competent SOA members, if not many
brave ones. This was a gentlemen's club. The statements of support
for the status quo from the two women members were what saddened
me. However, I agreed to attend their meeting.

Walking in to the SOA meeting the threatening atmosphere was
palpable. I sat at the back of the room for a couple of minutes before
I was called up, conscious of the extraordinary hostility focused on

me by the senior management. It was scary. But I had an inner calm and confidence that they had to change, or they and the organisation would go down together. A public broadcaster which failed to reflect the changes that had occurred in the community it served was in trouble. Perhaps, in hindsight, I'm sounding more confident than I was.

I stood up and spoke about my vision and made it quite clear that I did have biases and prejudices in favour of the non-SOA people getting a chance to be interviewed for jobs, but that did not mean members of the SOA would be at a disadvantage. In fact, I did not see any reason for membership to be an issue. We were not running a club. I cared more about the ABC than about the SOA, and I would always want the best person for the job. The in-house paper *Scan* recorded that I offered an unreserved apology. It's not quite as I remember it. I don't know that they ever rescinded the resolution, but I kept on interviewing and they kept on applying for jobs. Some of them even got them.

Conservatism was not the prerogative of the SOA alone. The unions had also arranged their work practices to keep the ABC a fortress. Ken and I discovered at approximately the same time that the ABC was still recording on film, despite having video cameras available which had been used in the Commonwealth Games in 1982. Management and the unions had failed to reach an agreement about their use. It drove us to distraction that electronic cameras were in storage gathering dust and becoming obsolete. ABC cameramen were shooting on film which had to be processed while the commercial stations were using videotape which could go straight to air. The commercials were thrashing us. We decided to bring the issue to a head.

We talked to our Minister, Michael Duffy and Ralph Willis, Minister for Industrial Relations. I was told to pull my head in by a couple of very senior bureaucrats. We talked to our unions and still made no progress. Ken and I went for one of our strolls in Hyde Park and he said, 'I'm not having that equipment sitting there unused at public expense.' I felt as manic about it as he did, especially as I could see the commercial television stations being able to get the news to air so much faster and without the apparent loss of quality that our people were telling us would happen. It seemed that the rest of the world had moved to video, and it was hard to see why the ABC wouldn't. Finally Michael Duffy called a peak meeting of the key players, and I heard that the thought of the Board, not the unions, turning the screen black helped focus people's thinking. Thanks to the leadership of Duffy and Willis, settlement was reached. It reminded me of being with the nuns in Pittsburgh who ate fish on Fridays until the Pope said they could eat meat, and then they ate meat from that Friday on. It seemed that the ABC went straight onto video camera, with barely a backward look at film, apart from high quality drama and documentary work. I wondered what all the angst had been about.

In July 1984 *Look & Listen* was launched, a magazine published as a joint venture between the ABC and an independent company. It described itself as more than a program guide, and in the first edition I wrote the following piece about my twelve months as a director.

The First Year
It doesn't seem like a year—well, not really. It's reminiscent of the experience of motherhood; I waited 26 years—and immediately I became one I couldn't remember life without children.

The arrival of an ABC directorship was rather more of a surprise than my first pregnancy and when the pressure is on I can at least console myself that, unlike the children, the directorship can be returned. However the ABC and I have bonded very quickly; the toys and artifacts of ABC directors have joined those already in my place; at last count they included a VCR, a telephone answering service, two floor-to-ceiling bookshelves full of paper and a constant stream of cardboard cartons on their way to the shredder.

The soft swishy thud of heavy duty envelopes at the front door every evening is part of the daily ritual. It's rather like a security symbol and reminds me that paper and policy have their place in ABC affairs. I must not assume that evenings are just for programmes: That was my life before June 30, 1983.

Accepting a position on a public board is always a risk. Being a non-executive director of the ABC has a higher risk component than other directorships I've held because of the high visibility of the corporation. Everyone is an expert on the ABC and more than ready to send you chapter and verse on every issue. Motherhood statements and advice are available everywhere.

The Board appointed in June, 1983 is a most disparate group of individuals. Their common features include intellectual curiosity and successful careers. In practice this means everything is questioned, nothing is accepted at face value. This can be disconcerting, irritating and probably tedious for senior management who may have seen boards come and go. So what is different? Can this board claim any special considerations, are the differences real or cosmetic?

The legislative changes made in the establishment of the corporation should not be underestimated. Although in some ways a deficient Act—for example, the clauses on investment and borrowing are restrictive; there is a belief that the removal of the ABC from the control of the Public Service Board will ultimately be seen as of great significance to the operation of the corporation. In symbolic terms the legislative changes herald a new opportunity for an independent broadcasting authority. The ways in which the Board interprets and defines the new Act will influence broadcasting in this country for many years.

The group dynamics involved in moulding a corporate policy group or board out of such a group of individuals and under a new Act are complex. The background music was confusing—high approval and expectations from the wider community and unprintable descriptions from some inside the ABC community. Moreover, of all the Board members, only Jan Marsh and I knew each other and had worked together.

To a professional human relationship educator like myself, the possibilities for failure were enormous.

It was with this background that we met formally for the first time on June 23—sight unseen, task not clearly understood and only one established interpersonal relationship.

Our first act was to include an interim staff member as a Board member and to record our view that the Board should always include a staff-elected director. The ease of that decision was a good omen, the first meeting's chemistry was marvellous. Clearly this Board was to be a working board willing to be accountable and take risks. The collective view that the ABC had lost its centrality in our national life and that there were signs it was sinking into apathy and demoralisation bound us to a commitment that the ABC must become again the leader of broadcasting in Australia. It is this single goal which dominates the strategy of the Board.

However, boards can handle only so many concerns at one time. In our first year we've moulded ourselves into a corporate entity. We've increased our numbers midway through the year to include the managing director, Geoffrey Whitehead, and Tom Molomby, the staff-elected director. Both of these appointments are significant in the composition of the Board. The skills and talents have been invaluable in the establishment of priorities, particularly because of their experience at the cutting edge of broadcasting. Probably the most important priority decision was our acceptance of the fact that we have to make some sacrifices now for a healthy future for the ABC. We cannot afford to be diverted by the multiple bushfires whose resolution becomes *de facto* policy.

The major restructuring of the organisation has been an important part of the strategy. We've ignored the advice of the chairman of Bendix, William Agee, who described most corporate planning as belonging to the school of 'Get me through the next election of the next board meeting' in favour of the long-term approach. Although all ABC directors except the chairman and managing director have three-year appointments and a short-term expedient approach may induce a warm inner glow, we're settling for a better future and some long-term strategic planning.

To encourage people to believe that the best leaders are facilitators and not order givers may be the contribution of non-executive directors, who are very involved in the affairs of the corporation, but conscious of the fine line between non-executive status and public accountability. If that could be achieved it would be in line with sound, successful management practice theory throughout the world and would equip the ABC to face the next 20 years more nearly in charge of its destiny.

Certainly anyone whose public and community life began, as mine did, in the Women's Movement, understands that conventional bureaucracies can no longer solve corporate problems. Networks offer horizontal links where information is the equaliser. Networking between Board members and ABC staff offers increased opportunities for accelerated learning, for both directors and staff. Indeed one of the most interesting aspects of the life of this Board has been the willingness of staff to develop working relationships with Board members.

This presupposes equality between the directors and staff (quite rightly, I believe) and it breaks down the distance and alienation many people expressed in their relationship to Broadcast House, the management centre of the corporation. The view rightly or wrongly that Broadcast House (derisively known as the Sydney Broadcasting Corporation) was a long way removed from the cutting edge rationalises and excuses much ABC activity. Such perceptions and the decisions and attitudes they influence have to change.

Setting an agenda for change and announcing it publicly involves a high degree of risk because it raises high expectations from the community and accentuates failure. However, it is unreasonable to expect staff to be more adventurous and risk-taking if boards don't do the same. The bottom line for both remains responsibility and accountability.

So at the end of the year what have we achieved? Can the shopping list be checked or should I return to my first analogy about parenting and say that the results can only be measured by the consumers/victims/children? The answer, fortunately, is yes and no.

We've made hard decisions on organisational structure which in some cases only implement updated ten-year-old recommendations. Here are some examples:

- We've appointed an impressive managing director and a Board Secretariat.
- Budget priorities have been established which insist on spending capital funds on accommodation and equipment despite softer trade-offs.
- We've made competitive, well-researched bids for our share of the satellite action.
- We've learned the subtleties between 'Yes, Minister' and 'No, Minister' and found ourselves comfortable with both responses—undoubtedly helped by the calibre of our minister.
- We're involved in *Look & Listen*—a notable achievement.

More subtly, there's a confidence and intimacy that has developed in the Board—a strength and commitment that is invigorating because of a belief in the existence of an independent national broadcasting authority.

Without this we may not have weathered the PNG crisis, which found us arbitrating between dearly held principles—i.e. the responsibility of boards to support management and the responsibility of the ABC Board in particular to maintain and assert the independence of the ABC. We needed all our mutual respect and trust to manage that.

It's more work and more commitment that anyone could have imagined. It's also been fun. Keep looking and listening. There may even be changes in the air waves.

I thought long and hard about what my individual contribution might be to the ABC Board. My advocacy had to match my commitment to women. That was a known when I was appointed and I could not abandon that. In any event it was part of my persona. Women were not visible in the senior echelons of the ABC. The evidence was unequivocal—only two out of fifty members of the Senior Officers' Association were women. There were few women's voices on air. It's hard now for people to remember that, but trust me such was the case.

I thought about how we might assist the process, and early in our term Jan Marsh, Veronica Brady and I discussed how we might manage this at the Board and policy level. Our first success was to pass a Board resolution stating that all new ABC buildings would have childcare facilities. This produced smirks and later active opposition from within the ABC and the government, and comments were made such as 'that won't be a problem as there are no new buildings planned'. Little did they know that the chairman and I were determined to rationalise ABC properties, and at the very least to consolidate the twenty-eight locations housing the ABC in Sydney. We were determined the Corporation would have a home of its own, equipped to broadcast into the twenty-first century. It doesn't seem so radical now, but it was in 1983. The ABC got a community-based childcare centre set up through the efforts of the Women's Co-operative Broadcasting Unit, but the facilities were frequently under threat.

We three also succeeded in pushing through a second resolution which was that no interviewing committee would be considered formally convened unless it included a woman member. This produced further outrage from the SOA. However, there were endless anecdotes that the recruitment and promotion process disadvantaged women. Many women who wanted to work in the ABC were recruited as secretaries or personal assistants, and it was almost impossible to switch into the professional streams. They needed some breakthrough strategies and the Board had to provide that leadership.

Whenever I think about this time I retrieve one of my classic ABC memories. It goes like this: I walk to the lift in the Elizabeth Street building. Two guys nod, they don't know who I am. I am longing to introduce myself, but I'm still feeling a little shy and worried that people will think I am seeking recognition or, as my kids would say, am 'up myself'. I've been a director for about five days. I realise they are talking about the new ABC Board.

'It's amazing,' one said to the other. ' I've just heard about the new Board. It's a Labor dream. The new members include a cycling nun [Brady], a radical feminist [McCarthy], a trade unionist [Marsh], a black [Bonner] and a retailing Jew [Myer]. Can you believe it? The only decent one is Bob Raymond.'

I was deeply shocked. I didn't say a word or even lift my head, but I filed it away. Whenever challenged about the need to change the ABC culture, I only had to think of that conversation to refocus my energy.

It was a tough and exhilarating time of my life. I resigned from the Higher Education Board and the Education Commission to concentrate on the ABC, Family Planning and the family. There was no time or energy for anything else. Gordon's health was variable. He needed a lot of sleep so I organised family life around an early dinner and when they had all gone to bed or to their rooms to do homework (usually by 8pm) I would read my papers, watch ABC TV or write books on sex education. It was wonderful to legitimise my love of television. We watched wall-to-wall ABC and the children were incredibly impressed when the ABC provided superior audio visual equipment, including a VCR (our first).

At the end of 1984 I resigned from both my Family Planning job and my *Cleo* column to become General Manager of the Australian Bicentennial Authority. It was a big switch and marked the end of a decade of community education. In a sense I was reinventing myself. I felt that the ABC and the ABA fitted together well, in that both were in pursuit of what it means to be Australian, and I wanted some synergies in my professional life. Generally the combination worked well.

Other people, however, had different views. One morning I woke up to find a nightmare headline across the front page of the *Sydney Morning Herald*, 'McCarthy double dipping', or words to that effect. The story 'exposed' the fact that I was paid by both the ABA and the ABC. As far as I was concerned the story was in the public domain already and it could hardly have been news.

For a seemingly endless period in 1985 the Bicentennial Authority was in big political trouble and I, in my combined ABC/ABA role, was under constant attack. On 21 May 1985 Senator Peter Rae from Tasmania spoke at the Senate Estimates Committee about the ABC and particularly the *Four Corners* program, where outstanding litigation between the then Premier Neville Wran and the ABC had been settled. He then began on me, quoting from a letter written by Clyde Cameron, a retired ALP Member of Parliament: 'Isn't something going to be done about Wendy McCarthy being permitted to draw a salary from the Australian Bicentennial Authority while at the same time being paid a stipend as Deputy Chairman of the Corporation.' Senator Rae continued: 'The question which a number of other people have raised is: Is it reasonable that someone who appears to be receiving a Remuneration Tribunal Allowance of $13,564 per annum, as Deputy Chairman of the ABC, should also receive payment as a full-time member of the Australian Bicentennial Authority?'

Senator Grimes (Tasmania), Minister for Community Services, responded on behalf of the Government: 'Wendy McCarthy did get a stipend. When Ms McCarthy, who I must admit seems to have raised great interest among Opposition members, was to be employed by that Authority, she raised the matter of that remuneration with the Authority. As I understand it, the Authority raised it with the Public Service Board. In the light of what Senator Peter Rae has said, I wonder what is the difference between someone who is employed in a private, legally limited company, who receives a similar stipend from the ABC, and Ms McCarthy. Is it just that the Opposition has a hang-up about Ms McCarthy?'

Hansard records from this session detailed questioning about my magazine contributions, my role in hiring Geoffrey Whitehead and a claim that my books on sex education were sold in ABC bookshops (untrue). In fact, I had taken legal advice before accepting the ABA position and was quite sure of my ground. I immediately rang Michael Duffy and asked what on earth was going on. It had always been clear that when I accepted the Bicentennial Authority job it was in the full knowledge of government. I checked with both my lawyer and the Attorney General that an appointment to a statutory authority was not in conflict with my management tasks at the ABA, which had an unusual structure as it had been constituted as a company rather than a regular statutory authority. I saw no conflict of interest or I would not have taken the Bicentennial Authority job. So to have this revisited on the front pages of the media some time later was both humiliating and enraging.

Duffy's response was that 'the Silver Bodgie says you can't do both'. I said, 'Well, if I have to choose between these two positions, I'll stick with the ABC because it's a more important organisation than the ABA. That's my decision.'

'No, Wendy, you don't understand. The Prime Minister wants you to stay at the ABC but you can't be paid for it.' I refused to accept that proposition and asked him to convey the message to the Prime Minister, with whom I'd had no contact. In fact I had not actually met Bob Hawke at this stage.

He rang back to tell me that under no circumstances was I to consider leaving the Bicentennial Authority. It had been through too much trauma and I was the most stable and reliable person there, apart from Jim Kirk. The Prime Minister would accept the advice of the Attorney General's department and I could continue in both positions. I was very happy and pleased that I had stood my ground.

The years between 1983 and 1986 at the ABC were volatile and confronting. This was in part due to the extraordinary energy and vision of the chairman. It was a restless energy, focused on his commitment that the ABC should be both more Australian and more international. He was a man for whom the term 'adding value' must have been invented. He was constantly persuading people to widen their vision and was frustrated when they responded in a negative or pedestrian way.

The end was painful and unexpected. On 30th April 1986 we were at a Board meeting in Elizabeth Street and our chairman was a troubled man. As we started what was clearly going to be a tense Board meeting, I was sitting in my usual position next to him, and I could feel the tension increasing. A couple of times he muttered to me and I kicked him under the table, the code to keep cool. He

was in a rage because Tom Molomby was asking questions which
he believed reflected on his chairmanship. This was the persistent
hangover of the Whitehead/Molomby dispute, on which Justice
Beaumont had ruled on in the previous November.

The dispute concerned access to papers covering a range of issues.
Geoffrey Whitehead had refused to give Tom copies of advice he
had provided to the Chair and Deputy Chair, and it had developed
into a legal battle with Tom taking Geoffrey to court for access.
Tom had always made it quite clear to me that he was supremely
confident of his position and I respected his advice. However our
barristers urged us on and assured us that Whitehead would win,
and winning and supporting the managing director became the issue,
shades of the *Four Corners* dispute. Ken and I spent hours trying to
persuade Tom to drop the charges and Geoffrey to change his operating mode. It was to no avail. The case continued in court and the
judge ruled in favour of Molomby. The ABC Board had to pay costs.
Molomby was vindicated, Whitehead was in trouble and Ken was
deeply upset.

The matter had been a painful and unresolved issue at subsequent
Board meetings and cast a shadow over the Board, despite the chairman trying to move on. As this meeting progressed Tom kept asking
questions and suddenly, with a look of white rage, the chairman
slipped his chair back, stood up and said, 'I don't have to sit here
and listen to this' and walked out.

I went onto automatic pilot. I didn't look up or acknowledge the
departure, just acted as though it hadn't happened and proceeded
with the business of the day. I couldn't really think what else to do
and I knew I had to get the temperature down. The managing director
left the meeting, presumably to try and locate and/or placate the
chairman, but I knew in my heart that Ken meant it. He had had a
gutful and he would not be back.

I felt incredibly sad that it had come to this. The beginning had
been so wonderful. I have thought about this so often. This was a
job that Ken Myer wanted but had to be persuaded to do. He
adored the whole business of communications and was in love with
the technology and the ideology of public broadcasting. He wanted

to be a broker between the Japanese public broadcaster NHK and the ABC, and he had the networks to achieve this. Walking out that door must have been one of the hardest things he ever did.

That night, after the meeting finished, Geoffrey and I visited Ken and Yasuko and I took a bunch of flowers for him. He was a man who adored receiving flowers, but even that did not assuage the pain. We talked for a while, but he was adamant it was over. It's one of the few things he'd done in his life where he'd failed to get the result he wanted. He loved many people at the ABC, but he just couldn't take any more of the frustrating process.

After Ken's departure I continued to act in the role of chairman, something I'd done frequently in those first years. When the chairman was overseas, the deputy was in the chair. Invariably it seemed there would be crises when he was away. I learnt to ring Tokyo and other parts of the world with ease to speak with him. Although he may not have been acting in the job his mind was never off it, and Ken-and-Yasuko dinner parties to share the newest adventures remain a strong memory of those first two years.

During the period when I was acting chair, Michael Duffy and I had various conversations about the ideal ABC chair and Board. We did not discuss names but generic attributes. The Government felt it had taken a huge risk with Ken Myer and they were constantly surprised and often outraged by his obsession with technology, his outspokenness and of course his independence—the very things that made him in many ways so ideal for the job. They were also by this stage dismissive of Geoffrey Whitehead, and they blamed Ken Myer for his appointment and for what they saw as an unrealistic view of the ABC about its place in the world.

Of course this is not a new story. Governments who appoint ABC Boards fall out of love with them very quickly. It's the nature of the task and the relationship. When Duffy rang me to say that Cabinet had decided to appoint David Hill as the new Chairman and his appointment would be announced within a day, I was surprised. My limited knowledge of Hill suggested he would be risky because he was young, without experience as a non-executive director and with a big job as CEO of NSW State Rail. But I wanted to be out of the caretaker position. It's not an easy role, and I had a lot going on at the Bicentennial Authority.

I visited David at his office at State Rail. He was charming, intelligent and quick to start talking about all the things he'd do. I liked him immediately because I always respond warmly to people with passion and energy. I was confident that we could work well together. As I was leaving he commented that even Graham Richardson, who'd argued strongly against my appointment, felt that I was okay these days. I think he meant it as a compliment.

Within a very short period of time David became critical of Geoffrey Whitehead, to whom I was still loyal. In fact David was dismissive of much of the management, referring to Radio National as bomb-throwers. There were many early signs that he would exceed a chairman's brief. He wanted change and immediate outcomes, objectives we all shared. I thought he wanted to manage the organisation and was not able to let the managers get on with their job.

Some Board members were quickly restless with his style of corporate governance, so interventionist and so different from Ken, yet most of us could see he had passion and flair and a wonderful analytical mind which went to the heart of the matter. The comparisons between David and Geoffrey were stark. Geoffrey was increasingly trapped in that terrible zone of isolation that happens when trust and communication disintegrate between the managers, the CEO and the chairman.

My observation was that Geoffrey's private life was suffering because of the job, and this placed extra pressure on him. Whatever the dream had been about running the ABC, it had turned sour. I was torn between feelings of despair and responsibility about Geoffrey. I was coming to the view that the Board would have to act when David said to me, 'He has to go. He no longer has the confidence of the staff and the external stakeholders.' While I initially protested he should have more time, I was sure in my heart it was over. The terrible tragedy for Geoffrey was that he failed to engage the hearts and minds of the organisation. In interview he presented as a confident man who knew a lot about broadcasting and management selection. Now he was battered, defensive and isolated in a volatile and political environment. The miracle is that he achieved as much as he did. Geoffrey's contributions were the media split, the rethinking of jobs and systems, the opening up of the ABC, increasing Australian content, and paying attention to the indigenous community's needs. He initiated much of the basic structural change.

After discussions with the Board, David and I were given the task of telling Geoffrey that the time had come for him to depart. It was a truly hideous moment for me. He had counted me until that moment as someone he could rely on, and I felt unable to give him any warning that the axe was about to fall.

After many hours of negotiation, Geoffrey's departure was organised. I went home feeling sick and thought how bizarre that one's professional life descended to a discussion about a Ford Telstar. It was a sad and ignominious ending to a great experiment.

Solving this problem created another. Who could be the next managing director? How could we go about selecting someone? To me it was obvious that David Hill could do the job with great flair. Without consulting him, I raised the matter with the other directors. We agreed that we knew where most of the talent was in Australia. It was only three years since we had interviewed and headhunted around the world. Most of us thought we should find an Australian to do the job. The cultural hostility had worked against Geoffrey. We were committed to the strategic direction we had taken so we needed somebody who would be prepared to come in and manage that approach.

I was given the task of sounding out David's interest. This I did in a series of phone calls to him in various parts of the world while he was travelling. He did not want to have an interview with the Board because he felt they had seen him in action and if they said no at the end of an interview it would be impossible for him to be chairman. I agreed with that. So after a great deal of discussion within the Board, we offered and he accepted the position of managing director.

I rang Michael Duffy to tell him we needed yet another chairman. His response was an atypical silence. I asked that for his next appointment he looked for wisdom and experience in the chair. He offered the position to Bob Somervaille, who was experienced in the communications portfolio, having chaired OTC and Telecom. It was a good choice. He came with a wise legal head and many years of experience dealing with government, corporations and legal practice.

David, Bob and I worked together very closely as a team. We talked about things together and separately and seemed to complement each other's skills, despite our different ways of looking at issues. David hated Board meetings, like many CEOs. He always sat next to me and was only energetic when he was giving his report and when someone brought the ratings in. I'd watch his brain ratcheting around, making sense of the information. The day was lit up if it was good news and went black if it was bad. It's true he occasionally read Phantom comics, but that was just to provoke Tom Molomby.

David's tenure was a creative time at the ABC. He was pushing back the barriers, questioning, analysing and looking for the money in every 'hollow log', as he'd done so well for Neville Wran some years before. If the Labor Government thought they'd got a pussycat because he was a protege of Wran's, they were mistaken. He argued on behalf of the ABC with almost every minister in Canberra. Bob suggested it might be a good idea if I started talking to ministers as well as him so they'd understand that David's impetuousness was cushioned by our more cautious behaviour.

When the ABC funds were threatened yet again and we ran the 'eight cents a day' campaign, people finally did understand that David put the ABC first. The government hated the campaign, especially Gareth Evans, who was by then Communications Minister. He and David could insult each other in the most elegant ways.

Life with David at the helm of the ABC was often high-risk, but the Australian content went up, comedy came back, and there was an energy and sense of engagement back in the place. Much of the tedious work had been done by Geoffrey: the creative task now was to implement and to win the hearts and minds of the organisation and the Australian community. In the first couple of years David could do no wrong and, despite the spats here and there with the staff, the Board generally felt that their decision to appoint him without advertising the job had been more than vindicated. I remain of that view.

One night we had Kim Beazley, who had become the new Minister, for dinner at our relatively new premises—Broadcast House, William Street, Kings Cross. It was an uncomfortable dinner with a tension I could not explain. I reminded the Minister during the dinner that there were appointments to the ABC Board due some months later, in May, and I'd certainly like the opportunity of discussing with him how they might best be filled. He agreed we should meet and in the first instance I met with his adviser, Helen O'Neil, who had been in charge of the Board Secretariat for some time and whose judgement I respected. We talked about the general composition of the Board and criteria that could be used to find suitable people. I stressed that early advice was both courteous and time saving.

It was arranged that a month or so before my term expired, I would meet Kim Beazley. I went to Parliament House and told him that I was interested in becoming the Chair, but I was not interested in continuing as Deputy Chair. He expressed surprise on the grounds that people would kill for this job. I agreed that that was the case, but pointed out that I'd been in the same position for eight years. Clearly this was news to him. I explained that I was not inclined to be seen as someone's deputy or number two for the rest of my life. He told me that he was considering another person and myself and there wasn't much between us and a decision would be made soon. That of course meant that he was not really considering me and had already made his decision. He asked me if I had any other people to nominate. I suggested Lyndsay Connors would be a good appointment. He asked me who she was and how to contact her.

Well, history records that Mark Armstrong, not Wendy McCarthy, became the chairman of the ABC and that Lyndsay, a dear friend and colleague, became the Deputy. I was happy about that. The Minister rang me to say that I would not be the chair, at least 24 hours after various journalists had advised me of the new chairman's name. I was more upset by that offhandedness than I was about not getting the job. I had a good weep and, despite professing a wish to be on my own, was delighted when Geraldine Doogue arrived with a bottle of champagne. It was time to move on.

The timing was perfect—I was about to go on an overseas trip and I was out of the country within a couple of days.

On my return invitations were out to the opening of the Myer/McCarthy dream, the Ultimo, Sydney, headquarters of the ABC. I attended as the previous deputy chair and thought it a fitting way to close that chapter of my life. I wouldn't have changed it for anything—an opportunity to be part of Australia's most important cultural institution is a privilege and it was great fun.

There are tiny, tangible reminders of the McCarthy era. Tucked away in the Ultimo building is one that matters to me. It is the Wendy McCarthy childcare centre. It is to me a metaphor for my directorship, a reminder that change, good public policy and determination can win out. The organisation that brings Australians *Playschool* and *Kindergarten of the Air* has finally come to terms with the presence of children in its corporate life. Less tangible but as real is the growth of the women's network which began as Network 99.

Eight years at the ABC gave me a new view of the world and a new set of skills. I got over my self-consciousness about being musically ignorant and fell in love with the Sydney Symphony Orchestra. That affair continues. I was confident about my ability to be an effective non-executive director of a large and complex organisation. I could see the value of being a specialist generalist.

I could also understand for the first time that the community saw me as one of theirs. When people heard that I may not be reappointed, I received many letters asking that I stay. One probably older man, unknown to me, wrote:

> Dear Ms McCarthy,
>   Allow me to inform you that I view your proposed resignation with some apprehension. Under the circumstances it [the ABC] needs an individual with gumption to remain. Resigning is the easy option.
>   Like Pilate, washing your hands of the whole affair achieves nothing for the common people, of whom I am one. This government needs someone to stand up to them, so they may not ride roughshod over any organisation.

Please pardon my bluntness. In a nutshell we need you. Do not play into their hands by resigning. It's precisely what they want. Stay on and colloquially speaking, give them heaps.

When Stuart Revill wrote on my departure that I had a special skill in clarifying confusion, I was touched that someone would value that. Somehow it made the departure acceptable.

CHAPTER ELEVEN

THE CELEBRATION OF A NATION—1988

After the Future Directions Conference I kept in touch with David Armstrong, whom I did not hold responsible in any way for my failure to secure the NSW Bicentennial Authority job. His wife, Virginia Henderson, invited me to propose a toast at his 40th birthday in 1981 at Len Evans' cellar in Bulletin Place and I was delighted to do so. I thought his approach to the celebrations was innovative and thoughtful. He saw it as an opportunity to change the social agenda in Australia. His chairman, John Reid, whom I'd known for some time, was very supportive and so, seemingly, was most of the Board. In 1983 I rang a few people including David seeking office space for AFFPA. He offered us some of the Bicentennial Authority's surplus space in Sydney's The Rocks with a promise that it would be available for two or three years. It was good value for us as we were a small, flexible organisation in need of a good address and neighbours.

I loved working in The Rocks. After all those years with my children at Lance Kindergarten, it was good to be back there. I was based there when my appointment as ABC Deputy Chair was announced and it was where Michael Kirby launched my book on sex education.

In 1984 David asked if I'd like to have breakfast with him at the nearby Regent Hotel. He spoke of the concerns expressed to him by various people that the Bicentennial Authority was not seen to be reaching out to the community effectively. Nor was it seen to be reflecting the composition of the community—of course he meant women, blacks and migrants. He wanted to recruit someone at a senior level and he asked if I was still interested. I was clearly a very different candidate in 1984 from the one than I had been in 1980. Also, this was an invitation to apply for a senior job in the national office, as opposed to the State office.

I had already indicated to Derek Llewellyn-Jones, my then Chairman at AFFPA, my intention not to stay after the end of 1984. He advised me not to resign until I had another position. I knew that the conventional wisdom is to move from one position to another, but I'm always so involved with what I'm doing that I needed to distance myself formally in order to free my head and look for new possibilities. As it happened, within a week of me telling Derek that I would be leaving, the Bicentennial conversations began.

I'd come to the end of Family Planning. I'd had a great run and done and said everything that I could say about it. I was restless for change, and even the ABC appointment did not satisfy the need to get my teeth into a new task. I had just finished writing and/or editing three books on sex education and felt talked and written out. The only real area of interest to me was to work overseas in aid and development. With three children and a husband with leukaemia that simply wasn't on. Instead, I encouraged and promoted my Family Planning colleagues, Margaret Winn and Coral Knight-Lloyd, to pursue that direction which they did with great finesse.

I decided to throw my hat in the ring for the job of general manager with the Bicentennial Authority. There was no job description at that stage, but the task was to position the Authority effectively in the Australian community. It was a community-based communications challenge and I felt confident that I could do it: I had great national networks as a result of my NWAC, AFFPA and ABC involvements. This time I did not assume I was going for a chat, and put on my tailored suit. It was a proper interview and I did my homework. I was interviewed by David Armstrong, Robert Maher, Rick Bloore and Bill Fairbanks, who made up the executive team.

Two days later they called me back and offered me the job. I was euphoric and decided to have a three-month work-free break. I attended my last Family Planning meeting in October 1984 and arranged to start the Bicentennial job in February, once I'd settled Sam into secondary school.

It felt like a whole new era of life opening up. I loved the idea that this job had to be created from zero. No-one had done it before and the possibilities seemed endless. Better still, I had a proper professional salary, superannuation for the first time and a company car. After the not-for-profit sector, the quasi-public sector looked good.

Predictably, some of my friends and acquaintances thought this was a sellout: 'You're not leaving family planning to go and celebrate a white wank! How could you?' The most serious criticism I faced was that 1988 was likely to fabricate fantasies about Australian life and history and by being there I would perpetuate that process. If my pragmatic view that 1988 was going to happen anyway and the only way to influence it was by being inside the system was sustainable, I had to make sure that I did not waste the opportunity.

I made a shaky start in my new career in February 1985, as I had decided as part of reinventing myself to have a new hairstyle which included streaks. Unfortunately the streaks came out green, so I had to defer the starting day until they were repaired. I wondered if this ever happened to men.

Within a couple of days of being there I was aware from the sniff and feel of the place that things were not as they seemed from the outside. In the time since my recruitment interview, a team of consultants had worked with the managers and reorganised the structure. When I asked what it was that I was meant to do and what my budget was, David said, 'Oh, we'll think of a title, Community Relations, or something like that. We don't have a budget yet. We will think about that later.' Alarm bells were ringing in my brain.

By the end of the first week I could see that my first task was to find a proper role for myself. I had that ghastly sinking feeling that actually I'd been hired as a bit of token window dressing. This was a huge shock. I truly believed I'd been hired because I was a competent person who happened to be female, but who had a strong track record over fifteen years of policy development and social and cultural change management in education, women's issues, reproductive health and media. I felt demeaned by the suspicion that I had been hired as a token. To be hired other than on merit was insulting.

One of the first people I met was Gaye Hart, who had been working as a consultant and had now been employed as a director of the Community Program. The nomenclature of the place was bizarre. Directors were of lesser rank than general managers, who reported directly to the chief executive. There were some major territorial decisions to make. Gaye and I seemed to have remarkably similar expectations about our roles, with the main differential being that I would be more involved with media relations. What the hell was the difference between Community Relations and the Community Program, I asked? No-one had considered this. I thought seriously about leaving before the end of the first week, and fantasised about being a full-time mother. It was just that it was hard to visualise that role with three children in secondary school.

I wondered how I could have made such an error of judgement. When I first visited the Authority, it seemed to be a complex, serious and exciting organisation. I had been working in the same building for eighteen months and thought it had the resonance of the Convivial Equity scenario of the Future Directions conference. David's vision had been compelling and my interview with John Reid, the Chairman, reassuring. It didn't feel like that now I was here. There was a sense of smugness and superiority, as though everyone in there was right and the people outside were stupid for not understanding and trusting what they were doing.

At the end of the first week David assigned me my first major responsibility, the management and coordination of the state and territory offices. He explained that it was the national game that mattered, but we had to put up with these meetings and it would be a good idea for me to organise and manage them. What's more, they were meeting in Melbourne the next day and he'd like me to get on the plane immediately and go down and meet them with a view to working out some sort of game plan about how we might work together in the future.

Remember that I'd just moved from running an organisation which was modelled on Australian Federation, with a fine balance between the eight state and territory members and the national office. The national Family Planning office barely existed in its own right. It was the sum of the parts and member states allocated and/or agreed to the work agenda. It was not possible to run it successfully without the members having confidence in the leadership and believing that they got value out of their membership.

To hear the patronising tones the ABA general managers adopted when speaking about the states was something of a surprise. The Melbourne meeting the next day was a fiasco, distinguished by little resolution, few shared understandings and an excessive amount of expensive food. Lunch was the major event and was followed by dinner in an expensive restaurant. At the end of it we retired to the Windsor Hotel (we stayed only at the Windsor), where another round of drinks was ordered. I was already beginning to have that rather wimpy feel that I was God's police, because I didn't want to keep on partying.

It was a classic example of mixed expectations. The group quite unreasonably expected a program laid out for them to implement. There were no clear lines of accountability and no sense of leadership or direction. They had little interest in changing the social agenda and as a group were very conservative and suspicious of centrally controlled programs. They were committed to organising celebratory events of a fairly traditional kind. They did not want to discuss Aborigines, ethnics or women, and saw themselves, not unreasonably given their backgrounds and age, as reinforcing the status quo. It was apparent that if David was going to make the Authority any kind of change agent, he would have a tough job getting support from this group.

A common view held by senior management was that life at the Authority was first class all the way, with big rewards at the end of the period. I remembered this with an identifiable *click* as I read a newspaper report of the appointment of people to the SOCOG executive who had to be paid an extraordinary amount of money to compensate them for breaking their careers mid-stream. I wondered why being appointed to SOCOG (or the ABA senior executive team) meant you were changing careers mid-stream, and why anyone today assumed they should have a linear career.

I'm sensitive to emotional and corporate ambience, and believe that when you walk into a place you can tell if it's got a good feel about it. The Authority did not feel good. There was already a culture in the minds of the employees that they were different, they weren't the public sector and they should be able to work independently. The establishment of the Authority as a company registered in the ACT was cited as proof of the intent of the Fraser government that the Authority was no ordinary statutory body like, for example, the ABC. I thought this was a very naïve view, but I kept quiet because I seemed to be the only one who thought this way. The others all believed that they'd been given reassurances and affirmation of this decision, and that it was really not the business of the Commonwealth public servants to ask questions or keep insisting on knowing about the program. It would be unveiled in due course, when the Authority was ready.

The election of the Hawke government in 1983 and the shift of Bicentennial responsibility to the office of Prime Minister and Cabinet, a change welcomed by the Authority, brought with it a much tougher bureaucratic regime. The Department of Prime Minister and Cabinet considered the ABA a maverick, and was determined to bring it to heel. This was offensive to John Reid and put pressure on the senior executives at a time when they were patently unready to deliver anything more than well-researched intentions.

Within a couple of weeks of joining the Authority, I had phone calls from a range of people around Australia expressing pleasure that I was there and saying that it would be up to me to 'get the place moving'. I was surprised to receive these calls. As the newest recruit with an unspecified job and a title that was currently meaningless, it seemed a little unfair to assume that I would know what action if any was required to 'get the place moving'.

Phillip Adams and Ranald MacDonald both called to say that they were concerned about David's stewardship and thought he should be counselled to lift his game. Some time later I went to a breakfast with some friends and was told by a bureaucrat from Prime Minister and Cabinet that I had political enemies in the senior executive team, and that Robert Maher had strongly opposed my appointment. I expressed some surprise, as he was on the interviewing committee and had given me no indication that he was other than supportive. On the other hand, I had been observing that as the political pressure was stepped up, Robert did not want to involve me in what was going on. This was not all bad as far as I was concerned, as I did not want to buy into old battles. However, I resented being excluded from decisions whose consequences I may have to manage. I was not there to take orders from above.

My relationship with David Armstrong remained positive during this time, as we tried to define an effective role for me. We agreed that I would be general manager, Community Relations, and some time later this became Communications, with a wider brief. I was to look after the media relations, internal newsletters and information and public affairs, and coordinate the affairs of the states and territories in a corporate sense. It still felt as though we were inventing on the run, but a structure was beginning to emerge. The general manager for Marketing was clearly threatened by my presence and clarifying our roles and responsibilities proved vexatious, especially as the Board was putting pressure on him to deliver a marketing program of some certainty. When he left in 1985, Catharine Retter, who had joined the Authority in May 1985 as Marketing Services manager, became director of Marketing, responsible to me.

In the process of establishing a serious communication division, I ran headlong into an existing plan, drawn up by consultants and agreed to by the other general managers, for each division to have its own media staff. I thought this lunacy and said so very loudly. This delivered a new raft of hostile people. Meanwhile, I was being phoned by my contacts in the media saying that my honeymoon period would soon be over, and slagging the Authority would be fair game. They described it as an arrogant organisation with no sense of accountability to the public who paid for it, and complained about the lack of information in the public domain. Reports from Canberra about the growing political disenchantment with the ABA management were being leaked to the media. As I write this in 1999, and read daily of the Olympic sagas, there is a strong sense of déjà vu.

I advised David that we needed a couple more people in Communications. Ainslie de Vos, a competent and charming journalist, had started the same day as me but was reporting to someone else. I needed more back-up. Ironically, David suggested that we recruit Di Buckley, who had worked with Ranald MacDonald and been involved in organising the 150th anniversary celebrations in Victoria. I thought that such an appropriate set of recently practised skills would be a good idea and went to Melbourne to meet Di, whom I found impressive. She was a good strategic thinker, a good writer and had good media contacts. I offered her the job. It was probably one of the best appointments I made and fortunately just at the right time, because we then went into political freefall and I needed her political savvy and strategic thinking.

The Bicentennial Authority Board was falling apart, and inevitably became increasingly dissatisfied with its management. Gone was the non-partisan approach—it divided on straight party-political lines and became outraged over Prime Minister Bob Hawke's attitude to it. The resignation of Ranald MacDonald from the ABA board in July, citing 'an acknowledgement of a difference in approach', put the cat right among the pigeons. The chairman was working assiduously at trying to keep the thing together, but the 'please explain' from the Prime Minister's Department was soon in the public domain and the media had a field day.

There were varying views about what drove Ranald. My own view was that he was driven by his sense of public duty and outrage. He accused the Authority of waste, overstaffing and an inappropriate style of management. He cited the first-class trips to secure the participation of the tall ships, which he saw as a waste of public money. This had destroyed any confidence he had in David's ability to lead the organisation effectively. He did not want to be a director defending an organisation which had attracted so much hostility for what he thought was indefensible behaviour.

The crises forced the organisation to accept that it was lacking public credibility. When crisis management becomes more important than program design and planning, organisations are in danger. I was asked to put together a plan to manage public opinion. Di Buckley and I presented a strategic plan to the Board, which we thought impressive at the time, but on rereading today looks pretty basic.

David was under pressure from everywhere and everyone. Although he had surrounded himself with people of his own choosing, he was increasingly isolated and alienated both within and outside the organisation. Like many CEOs in similar positions, he delegated many of his management responsibilities to his deputy, Robert Maher. This meant he had more time to represent the Authority publicly, which meant he travelled more, another cause for criticism. There was also growing disenchantment with the performance of the general manager of Marketing, a painstakingly conscientious person with a strong marketing background, but like many people who make the transfer from the private to the public sector, he was finding the processes of public management very stressful.

When the Board met on 15 and 16 August 1985, John Reid was summoned to Canberra by PM Hawke, who put strongly to him that 'the best interests of the ABA would be served by the termination of the services of Dr Armstrong'. All reports are that he argued against this course and he did not raise the matter when he returned to the Board meeting. However, by 22 August David Armstrong had resigned, and damage control was the top priority both inside and outside the Authority.

With seemingly breathtaking speed we had lost a chief executive. Only a few days later the General Manager Marketing left. The terms of the settlement with David were to remain confidential, and John Reid said to me, 'Only two people know the terms of this settlement. Better that you don't know, as you will have to manage the press and can honestly say you do not know. There is no need for anyone else to know.'

I'd been around the ABC long enough to know there's no such thing as a secret in public life, and I counselled whoever would listen that David would be better to be up-front about the terms. But to no avail.

The departure of David was high farce. There was a press

conference called so that the Chairman could announce it while David exited through the garage and out the back door, and went to the north coast to get away from the media. Di Buckley and I rehearsed the Chairman before he went into the media conference.

In those days when we called a media conference, the cream of the Canberra press gallery came. On this occasion Peter Bowers and Richard Carleton, two formidable members, were attending. There were a couple of ambiguous questions but our rehearsed chairman was cool.

Within two weeks the media was running with the story of the Golden Handshake, despite the details being unknown. On 13 September I was with John Reid outside the Senate, where he was to be asked to disclose the terms of David Armstrong's settlement. As we stood in the corridors of Parliament House, I said to him, 'If I am to handle the media, I think the time has come when I need to know.' He handed me a copy of the document which I could see was political dynamite, although probably not unreasonable from David's point of view.

That weekend I was driving back from the farm and I called in to a Shell garage to get some petrol. As I handed the card over, the guy said to me, 'You're from the Bicentennial Authority. I thought you lot would be doing it with the Golden Fleece.' How quickly the Golden Handshake had moved into the vernacular. We now had 'rip off' added to our reputation. The task for the communications division was to claw back public confidence, and the odds were against it until people engaged with the event.

Things got a lot worse before they got better. By 26 September the Prime Minister had sought and received John Reid's resignation. John Utz, a member of the ABA Board, was announced as interim chairman. The staff was deeply shocked and loyalties were fragmenting. Morale was at an all-time low. When speaking about the 1985 horror stretch, Desmond Kennard, director of the travelling exhibition, said, 'You'd get up, read the morning paper, listen to the news and then go to work wondering if you still had a job.'

The internal dynamics of the Bicentennial Authority were

distressing. I hadn't been involved in such tough internal politics since Family Planning NSW in 1978. I often thought of that period with affection now. How well that experience had trained me to manage internal warfare. Somehow the stakes seemed much higher in Family Planning than they were in the Bicentennial Authority. I was also in the position of having a prestigious role in the Australian community as deputy chair of the ABC. I knew that if I had to leave the Bicentennial Authority because of the dramas, I still had the ABC to care about and be involved in while I found another position. Every day I thought how lucky I was to have children and a husband to escape to each night. They were so nurturing and insistent on attention that the day was washed away. On reflection, this gave me a great deal of personal security.

For me, the Bicentennial celebrations offered two challenges: an opportunity to explore what being Australian means, and a management task of daunting scale. There turned out to be plenty of thrills along the way.

In mid-November 1985 Jim Kirk was appointed Chairman of the Authority by Bob Hawke. I'd not met him, but had heard him speak on affirmative action when he was the executive chairman of Esso, and had been impressed by the way in which he understood and embraced it. Esso was the Australian pacesetter in the private sector in the seventies. So I was looking forward to meeting him, and was pleased that the government had chosen an external person with no baggage.

He was a tough taskmaster, and his first action was to bring all the managers together and review the organisation. We prepared budgets, and were asked to justify all proposed expenditure and every individual program. He encouraged peer-group feedback throughout the process, which continued for some days. At the end of the session, decisions were made about which program would stay and which would go. There was a lot of room to talk with Jim on the way through, but once the decision was made you were wasting your time trying to change it. Jim made it very clear that we had our opportunities to make our comments, and then we had to toe the party line. I respected that. At the end of the sessions he announced that he would be changing the role of chairman to executive chairman, so our acting chief executive, Robert Maher, was returned to his previous position as deputy and the responsibilities for program management were reallocated.

Depending on your perspective, I came out of these sessions as a winner, as did Gaye Hart. Since my arrival at the Authority with a vague portfolio, I had moved from community relations to communications, to taking over the marketing and licensing tasks. And now I was given the responsibility for the tall ships and the travelling exhibition, the two big-ticket items. I was excited by the responsibility.

Gaye Hart, who had been a program director, became the general manager, Programs with responsibility for the arts, Aboriginal, education and community-based programs. Bill Fairbanks remained in charge of finance and administration and Robert Maher had no portfolio, but would work with Jim and take the overseeing approach.

As part of the damage control, and before I could get the advertising program off the ground, I started writing again. In December 1985 the following piece appeared in the *Women's Weekly*:

> When I told my friends and colleagues that I was going to
> work for the Australian Bicentennial Authority, their reactions
> varied from astonishment to utter disbelief. 'You must be mad.
> Who cares about a 200-year anniversary of European
> settlement? What has Australia got to celebrate anyway?' they
> asked.
>
> People kept stressing to me that Australians were not a
> people who showed their feelings, who would be able to
> express a sense of national pride. When I said that my task
> was to get 16 million Australians involved in 1988, people
> shook their heads and said, 'It can't be done.'
>
> Perhaps the sheer size of the task was one of the reasons
> I took the job. It was, and remains, an enormous challenge,
> irresistible because of that. But more importantly, I took the

job because I think it's worth doing. The possibility of setting aside a year in the life of a nation for people to look back at yesterday and look forward to tomorrow is a rare opportunity.

The timing seemed right and I wanted to be part of the proceedings.

In 1972 when I became excited by, and involved in, women's issues, the crucial issue always was defining the role of women in Australian society. The Women's Electoral Lobby helped by taking women's issues into the political arena, and during the Decade of Women, the process has been accelerated and developed.

I've had many opportunities to be involved in the movement of social change, or, more simply, finding out where one fits in the scheme of things. In my case, I was particularly interested in where women could be.

In many senses, it's logical for me to look now at what all Australians feel about who they are and where they fit in their country.

My years spent in Family Planning, talking to women, men and adolescents about important and intimate aspect of their lives, and my experience at the ABC (as deputy chair of the ABC), have convinced me even more that Australians, regardless of their heritage, are looking for a definition and understanding of what it is to be Australian.

Being Australian is not only the flavour of the month in the US, it's also high on the agenda here. We do have a sense of national pride.

Knowing who you are, where you come from and what your values are will lead you to a national identity.

So here I am, general manager, Communications and Community Programmes of the Australian Bicentennial Authority, and I'd like you to know that I'm optimistic. I believe that all Australians are coming to the party. It's a BYOI party— that is 'Bring Your Own Ideas'—and it lasts not for a day but a year. So there will be hundreds of opportunities to find the event or celebration that will suit you.

Although you bring your own ideas, the Commonwealth
Government has agreed to be the major sponsor. It has
committed $166 million for a national programme of events
and activities, which works out at around $10 a head. The
corporate sector, State/Territory and local governments are all
making their contributions on top of that.

It's going to be a big party. You might choose to run in the
round-Australia relay, watch the vintage-and-veteran car rally,
sing in the Big Top at the Australian Bicentennial Exhibition,
watch the military tattoo or the air show. Or have you
thought about hot air ballooning across Australia or writing
your local history?

At least contact your local Bicentennial Community
committee and find out about the plans in your area.

If you want to watch it on the telly or hear it on the radio,
we can arrange that. Or better still, you can. Ring your local
radio station and check their bicentennial coverage.

The year 1988 will be fun. We'll all be there, warts and all:
the knockers, the tall poppies, the sad, the happy, the
historians, the politicians, the entrepreneurs, the community
leaders, the do-gooders, the people who hate the do-gooders—
but it will be a great party.

And, most importantly, it will be remembered as the year
which helped us work out who we are and what we are today
—a time to be proud of our yesterdays, and optimistic about
our country's future.

I was preparing a major advertising campaign and it had been agreed
by Jim Kirk and the ABA Board that $10.5 million would be spent
on a motivational and awareness program. In May 1986 my enemies
came out again. Ron Casey on Radio 2KY became hysterical:

Well, I noticed in the latest edition of the *Bulletin* that our
Bicentenary Authority, headed up by Jim Kirk, is about, are
you ready for it, to spend $10.5 million in advertising to boost
public awareness of the Bicentenary. Just imagine that, an

advertising campaign to tell us that we're going to have a
Bicentenary celebration in 1988, 10.5 million bucks. Imagine
what that could do with hospitals, with so many things in our
community today.

And that brings me to another festering sore that I've tried
to eradicate but I just can't get out of my system, and that is
the very high-profile Ms Wendy McCarthy. Now, Ms Wendy
McCarthy is the general manager for Communications and
Marketing with the Australian Bicentenary Authority.

Now you'd think if they're going to spend $10.5 million to
market and communicate with the public, that that would be a
full-time job. Well, it ain't. Wendy McCarthy is the deputy
chairperson, but I'd call her chairman, of the ABC.

Now, the ABC has just had Myer resign, walk out in a huff,
and he's gone back to Japan to eat some rice. And Wendy
McCarthy is now the acting chairman, Wendy—chairman, of
the ABC. And the ABC isn't exactly travelling well. And here
we've got Wendy, boss of the ABC at this stage, boss of
Marketing and Communications for the Bicentenary Authority,
and she's also a very happy housewife who keeps the family
clothed and fed. Strike me lucky.

I wouldn't say exactly the ABC is a raging success. And I
wouldn't say the Bicentenary Authority is a raging success.
And Wendy McCarthy has her finger in both pies.

Those comments just made me even more determined that the advertising program would be a success. And, some months later, shooting
the spectacular commercial The Celebration of a Nation at Uluru, I
had no doubt that I was right. For this commercial I invited a hundred
prominent Australians, from all walks of life, to donate their time
speaking out for Australia and its Bicentennial celebrations. After
extended negotiations with park rangers and tribal elders, it was
agreed that we could shoot the commercial there. Uluru (Ayers Rock)
was chosen because the market research kept telling us that it was
one of the top five icons in Australia and politically, it was neutral.
Minding a hundred large egos with extraordinary energy was great

fun, and the commercial showed the joy of the people who had participated.

Managing big events and having access to a large cheque book made my Family Planning days seem a long way away. But in 1986 I was reminded of the centrality of family planning issues in the lives of all families. Sophie was in first year Arts at ANU in Canberra and occasionally she and her friends visited us at the farm at Berrima for the weekend. Sometime towards the end of 1986 she rang to check that Gordon and I would be at the farm for the weekend as she and her boyfriend would like to join us. It was a fairly normal request but I felt uneasy as there was a tension in her voice and there was an edge from the minute they arrived. Knowing how in love she was I wondered if the relationship was fading. I observed closely but could see no sign that it was faltering—if anything it seemed more intense.

After dinner, when Gordon was in bed, she asked if I would like to go for a walk outside. By the time we had reached the first gum tree she was crying and I instinctively knew before she told me that she was pregnant. As we talked it became clear that one of the big issues for her was the feeling that she'd somehow let me down because of my role in the Family Planning Association. Meanwhile I was thinking on two tracks. One part of my brain was saying, if it is hard for her, imagine how hard it is for others; and the other was thinking how wonderful it was that there were so many people who were available to guide her decision and provide whatever service she required.

Some years later, when abortion legislation was under threat, she told the story to camera as part of a program made to inform the public debate. I felt extraordinarily proud of her. This is what she said:

> I had a termination when I was 18. It was my first year of
> university. It was my first sexual experience. We weren't using
> contraception very effectively I suppose and I became
> pregnant. I was completely devastated. I was embarrassed and
> humiliated really, shocked that I was even capable of being a
> mother. I cried for about a week and didn't tell a single soul

except my partner, obviously. Finally we decided to tell my parents and he told his—they were fantastic and very supportive. I'd never considered the possibility of continuing with the pregnancy and I knew that a termination was an option to me and that it was a safe and reliable procedure. I knew I would be in the best of hands.

I went to Sydney to have the termination just with my mother and I really don't remember much about the whole day. I was in shock and denial, I suppose. I went to the clinic at Surry Hills and there were a lot of demonstrators out the front who mobbed me as we walked in but I think I was on autopilot. I don't really remember crying or feeling much pain.

I didn't tell anyone for about three and a half years. It was a big secret for me. Although I thought it was OK and I knew other people did it as well, it was just something that took me a while to tell other people. I went to work at a family planning clinic and I used to see young women coming in who were sixteen, seventeen, eighteen-years-old who looked at me with that glazed expression and couldn't make eye contact. I thought, 'That is exactly how I was', and it made me feel more committed to working in the clinic.

The more things change, the more they stay the same.

After the Kirk management review we knew exactly what money we had to spend and were committed to getting on top of our tasks. A travelling exhibition was always central to the planning and thinking, because it recognised the size and nature of the Australian continent and the contribution of non-urban Australians to national development. The exhibition was based on a concept that had been tried in America, of a moving road train taking the celebratory story to the American people. Daryl Jackson, the well-known Melbourne architect, had won the design competition for an 'exciting travelling exhibition venue to encapsulate the spirit of the Bicentenary and be moved across Australia by road and perhaps rail'. This one did not seem to be working, and at the conclusion of the review a threshold decision had to be made regarding the Australian Bicentennial exhibition. It was should we proceed, or write off the money already spent?

The exhibition was a romantic vision but the logistics were staggering. To realise the Jackson design meant the exhibition had to be custom-built from the ground up. Existing circus pantechnicons were not suitable. Rather than adapting what existed, everything had to be designed and fabricated. If the construction was vexatious, the intellectual philosophy, theme and content were even more so. When Dr Peter Emmett, the curator, developed six themes for the display-modules anxieties eased about the viability of the project, and a sponsorship of $6 million from BHP made the proposal viable. However, the new Chairman was terrified that we could not deliver, and the exhibition was put under exacting scrutiny. Finally the Board meeting in February 1986 gave it the green light. To Desmond Kennard, who had left a museum life to run this exhibition, the issues were extraordinarily difficult. He came with one set of criteria, was forced to conform to another, and now he was under pressure to deliver in a different way. The exhibition was probably not exactly as he wanted it, but he had a loyalty and commitment to the project.

Again, it was the operating style of the ABA management that aggravated so many potential stakeholders. For example, truck manufacturers were offended that we wanted custom built pantechnicons for the exhibition. It reflected adversely on their stock and their ability to win a contract. Similarly, ABC Concert Music, the biggest music entrepreneur in the world, was rejected in favour of the West Australian Festival to recruit and manage visiting orchestras, yet ABC Concerts had been touring orchestras and performers for fifty years and doing it well. When we went on the search for sail-training vessels to participate in the Tall Ships Race, we paid scant attention to the RAN and Foreign Affairs, at least in their view. It was as though we wanted to reinvent the world and all previous expertise was disregarded. Exactly as I see many SOCOG people doing today.

In the marketing area a new typeface had been designed for the Bicentennial Authority, and so it went on. So many of the years of initial planning had been spent in exploring these sorts of options and I guess we do have to remember the timing was the eighties, and there was more money around and nobody discouraged the Authority in the early days from proceeding in that way. But by 1986 it looked like an extravagant, naïve and rather foolish way to proceed.

Buying a fight with Foreign Affairs by visiting another nation to negotiate a tall ship was dumb. There was barely a minister in Cabinet who didn't berate me at any given opportunity about the way the Authority cocked its snoot at Foreign Affairs. Similarly, the ABC would be telling me that the overseas orchestra people were ringing them up saying, 'Who are these people, should we trust them? Why aren't we travelling with you?' These were real undercurrents and tensions in the Authority which I was aware of and Jim Kirk understood very quickly. The staff didn't want to use the conventional channels and thought they could do it better their own way. They sometimes forgot it was public money and if the public could not see the vision, it was unlikely to be shared.

It was decided that the exhibition would have a dress rehearsal in Ballarat in late 1987 after a training course at a nearby army base. The public response was at best lukewarm and I was apprehensive about its preparedness.

On New Year's Day in 1988 the exhibition was formally opened in Albury. It was a classic event in the Dimboola tradition. Prime Minister Hawke and his wife, Hazel, were there to perform the honours, as was the Chairman of BHP, Sir James Baulderstone and his wife. The weather was dark and threatening, thunder was crackling, the Prime Minister's plane was late and the children were beginning to fidget. The rain started bucketing down, the water swirling on the ground. In the performance space there were some little girls dressed as swans and cygnets and I was transfixed as the little feathers on the girls were slowly dripping and floating down their bodies while they bravely tried to continue with their show. A perfect Aussie scene.

The initial response to the exhibition was worrying. The crowds were way below estimates and far too small. People got a technology buzz from the interactive computers, people who loved trucks adored the Kenworths and the film in the big top was a knock-out, but there was a sense of confusion, perhaps a slight emptiness, when people left. They weren't quite sure what they'd been seeing. The arguments about signage for explanation surfaced again. (Curators thought we did not need them and we should let people respond without direction.) The chairman told me, 'There will be signs, Wendy.' And there were, without any apparent aesthetic loss and perhaps some increased understanding. Still, they were Daryl Jackson-designed; we did not scrimp.

At that stage there was a very small public relations component to the exhibition and although I was the general manager responsible I had tried to avoid putting too much pressure on Desmond, who thought less public relations were required as the exhibition would sell itself. The Australian Bicentennial Exhibition staff were an uneasy and diverse group of people. I had argued that we needed a couple of media people full-time, but the funding was tight and the exhibition management wasn't very enthusiastic, so it had not happened. When I carefully looked at the coverage in Ballarat and Albury and watched the reactions of the visitors, I knew we were in trouble and we needed a community awareness program.

By the time it got to Adelaide, in pre-fringe Festival time and searing heat, and settled into its poor location, it was almost in the dog category. Volunteers were harder to get, the promised local performers were not available, and the attendance numbers were shocking. I persuaded Ron Miller from the central communications group to go on the road for the rest of the year and run the public relations and community program. I believed the exhibition had no chance of survival unless it had an aggressive marketing campaign so that people had some idea of what to expect.

After Kalgoorlie the next stop was Perth where the Queen and Prince Philip would be attending. We needed some drastic surgery and Jim told me to get on the road and stay there until it was working. I took my mother with me, and flew to Perth to prepare for the Royal opening.

Somehow the changes worked and the exhibition team got it all together so that Perth was a success. On the day the Queen and the Duke were there I was sitting behind them in the big top, watching the film *Celebration*. I noticed that the Queeen's private secretary,

Robert Fellowes, was very moved. I asked him, 'What is it that affected you so?' I vividly remember the answer: 'I saw Bradman batting.'

It was my first insight into the awe and reverence that men have for Sir Donald Bradman. His batting makes grown men cry. Later in the year ABC Radio Sport, as its major Bicentennial contribution, released the series *Bradman—The Don Declares*. It was a documentary series of eight one-hour programs produced in conjunction with the ABA and featured Norman May as the interviewer. It was described by Alan Marks as a story which demands the full attention of all Australians. Jim Kirk, as Chairman of the ABA, and Bob Somervaille, as Chairman of the ABC, had a private lunch with Sir Donald to celebrate the release of the tapes and told me meeting the Don was one of the biggest moments of their lives. I felt really happy and not a little mystified by such men's business.

By March/April the exhibition was bedding down and on its way to being successful. A great deal of the credit must go to the people on my team, Ron Miller, Robbie Lloyd and Sarah Gardiner, who just consistently backed each other up and worked around the clock to ensure it got good coverage. The strategy was always to encourage the local population to be a part of it. It was probably never quite what people hoped it would be, but it represented a shift in the way we portrayed and thought about the Australian identity. It assembled objects and images, and left them to speak for themselves. For the million-odd visitors, it was an exhibition of its time and will not be easily forgotten.

The counterpoint to the exhibition was the tall ships event. This event had been a great success for the American Bicentenary and David Armstrong and Robert Maher were keen on it from the beginning. It celebrated the diversity of our relationships with other nations and reflected our multiculturalism. It recognised the unique nature of Australia as an island continent and our relationship with the sea. It was also a way of celebrating the great sea adventures of the world. The Parade of Sail, a feature of a tall ships event, was a spectacular sight. In Sydney Harbour it had the ability to provide the magic that stays in people's imaginations, the aspiration of every event organiser.

Its enduring legacy was sail training, an adventure and character-building opportunity for young people. The announcement that the British would be offering us a sail-training vessel as their Bicentennial gift confirmed the Authority's intention to proceed with the event. On every indication it was a good event, yet it created conflict and division throughout the Authority because of the persistent request of the First Fleet re-enactment proponents, especially Jonathan King, to have their event funded. Theirs was a proposal to re-enact the voyage of the First Fleet to Australia from Plymouth. Their supporters saw the tall ships event as meaningless, and people who joined the Bicentennial Authority were approached to support funding for the First Fleet re-enactment rather than the tall ships on the grounds that the only appropriate event to celebrate European settlement was a re-creation of the First Fleet arrival on Australia Day.

The First Fleet re-enactment people fought a very tough fight to get their idea up, and they had supporters within the Authority who consistently leaked information to them. Wherever possible, they used media opportunities to criticise the Authority and its negotiations with other countries. They were ably assisted by the conservative think-tanks around Australia, who were arguing for more involvement of the British and more recognition of our Anglo connections.

David Armstrong was adamant that this was an inappropriate event to celebrate in Australia in 1988. The Bicentennial celebrations should be more than a celebration of the arrival of Europeans, and a First Fleet re-enactment would be provocative to Aboriginal Australians. It was a view I completely agreed with.

I found them irritating and distracting while I recognised the skill of their persistence as they manouevred their vessels into a potentially nationally embarrassing position in the UK, and thus secured funds from both the NSW and national offices of the Authority. Jim Kirk wrote to Board members asking for their support for a grant of $500,000 and said, 'It is impossible to forecast just what would happen if the First Fleet is not helped through the May crisis. Nor can you say with any certainty what effect it will have in the overall Bicentennial celebrations.' Some Bicentennial staff found this grant galling because of their loyalty to the tall ships event and their belief that this was an inappropriate event and likely to be very commercial. Their worst fears were justified when they saw the leading First Fleet vessel sailing into the harbour with a Coca-Cola logo on it.

However, for the 2.6 million spectators on the waters and shores of Sydney Harbour, the internal politics of the event were unknown and irrelevant. It was a day no-one who witnessed it will ever forget and the flags of twenty-one nations were flying. For Rear Admiral Roth Swan who managed the tall ships event and his small team of workers, it was a triumph.

On the night of January 25 I had taken a room in the hotel opposite our office in The Rocks. Gordon and I had been to the Tall Ships' Captains Ball and returned to the hotel to find Sophie and Sam asleep in the room and a message from Hamish saying he would be there early in the morning. I desperately wanted all of us to be together on the day and wished Hamish was there. We went to bed as I anxiously checked the sky for rain. At about 5.30 a.m. I woke to the noise of a soft but regular sound. My instant interpretation was 'It's raining', and I rushed to the window. It was not rain but the sounds of Aussie feet in sneakers and thongs coming to the party. It was my moment to weep with relief. Everyone had decided to be there.

It's difficult from the outside to appreciate the intensity of the experience of planning for a major national event. This is project management with a high risk. We absolutely have to deliver on the day. There are simply no options, regardless of the significant logistical difficulties. The Bicentennial legacy is staging public events, which we now do so well in Australia.

Probably too little consideration was given to the political tensions between the states. Western Australia, South Australia and Victoria had all celebrated their sesquicentenaries during the 1980s, and were not as enthusiastic about the Bicentenary. New South Wales saw itself as the showpiece and the natural theatre for the celebrations, a cause of great resentment in other states. In retrospect it was probably a wonderful decision that Expo went to Queensland rather than NSW, because it spread the celebrations.

My years at the Bicentennial Authority were robust. I was surprised to acknowledge how much I enjoyed managing the logistics of major events. I enjoyed access to the large cheque book, the planning, the project management and the organisational overview.

I think one of the most curious things about the Bicentennial experience is that it was like a one-night stand. It is a one-off, intense experience. You acquire on a fast track an amazing array of skills, you learn to put the show on the road, people applaud or criticise, depending on the result, and at the end of the experience there's no particular reward. The rewards are the process as it happens, and you need to savour them as you may never get another chance. Few people with Bicentennial experience have been offered the opportunity to be involved with the Sydney Olympics.

I learnt to take each day as it comes when Gordon got sick. It's been a feature of my management style and life, I think, since 1981. Some people would describe that as my pragmatism. For me it's been a focusing discipline. I really do give my best to most things I do, on the grounds that this is now and this may be all that there is. That's true for me whether I'm giving a speech or committing to a task.

My observation on many of the people I worked with is that there is a sense of bitterness that their efforts weren't recognised. I made no assumptions when I took the Bicentennial job that life afterwards would be strewn with rewards having made such a noble contribution. I took it thinking it was an exciting, interesting job. I really wanted to be part of putting the Australian stamp on the celebrations, and I liked the unknown challenge of it.

The Bicentennial Authority position also gave me an entrée into many of the boardrooms of corporate Australia. Jim Kirk and I did endless lunches at the Authority and visited many boardrooms, always with our Bicentennial video and a story to tell. We encouraged business Australia to be involved, but did not insist that they deposit their money with the ABA to sponsor events. As a strategy that worked well, and corporations responded positively. After the charges of extravagance we were unlikely to attract large licks of money, so we sought relationships. Working with Jim was valuable for me. The perspectives of a successful, corporate, mature male were important contributions to my professional development, and I'd like to think that the perspectives of a forty-year-old feminist activist who happened to be a good manager were useful for him. In any event, it was a creative and productive working relationship, and for comparison I had my close working relationship with the Chairman of the ABC, Bob Somervaille. He was of similar age, wise, doughty and very experienced, but had a very different style. I learned a lot from both of them.

One of the great successes of the Bicentennial celebrations was the arts program, which created and guarded its independence jealously. Yet when I joined I was astonished to find that there was almost no role for the ABC orchestras. Mindful that I would be seen to have a conflict of interest, but concerned that the ABC should play a pivotal part in the Australian experience, I inquired why this was so. I was told that we wanted the great orchestras like the Vienna Philharmonic and the Chicago Symphony, and the ABC orchestras weren't up to scratch. I was deeply offended by this attitude, but it was the one time when being a manager in one place and a director in another was probably a disadvantage, as I felt I could not press my views.

There was some consolation therefore when the SSO was invited, in recognition of Australia's Bicentenary, to be the guest orchestra on United Nations Day in New York in 1988. I appealed to Jim Kirk for some funds to support it, but the management of the arts program was adamant that they would not provide support. To this day I do not understand the reasons, and in any event we didn't get any. It was just fortunate that a generous sponsor, Epson, provided the orchestra with sufficient funds to undertake its US Bicentennial Tour.

Mary Vallentine, the general manager of the orchestra, suggested that I travel with the orchestra and assist with the marketing and PR. It suited my experience and I couldn't think of anything better. The tour was to take place in October/November and all the Bicentennial events were over so it was agreed that I would be the major communications consultant for the tour. The ABC Board thought it a good idea, but Jim Kirk was so concerned that I would have a conflict of interest that I was forced to take leave without pay from the Bicentennial Authority. I thought this unreasonable as the invitation was acknowledging our Bicentenary, but knew when to stop arguing with him.

Also travelling with the orchestra was Hazel Hawke. I'd suggested to Mary Vallentine that Hazel, a person whose musicianship was sound but unrecognised, would be a very appropriate ambassador. After all, presidential wives did these sorts of things. I raised it with the Department of Prime Minister and Cabinet, who said in horror, 'No, no, no. It's not possible, there is no precedent.' I said, 'I'm sure there's a precedent.' Four days later they found one, and Hazel was on her way. It was a wonderful opportunity for her and she was a great ambassador for the orchestra. In America's eyes, because we had the Prime Minister's wife travelling with us, the tour was enhanced.

One of the great moments on that tour was Hazel opening the day's trading on the New York Stock Exchange. It was an early morning start and the atmosphere was extraordinary. I was beguiled by the idea that the SSO, a publicly funded orchestra, was in the heart of capitalism, opening the day's trading with 'Yankee Doodle Dandy'.

It was a twenty-eight day tour, which included fourteen performances. I guess travelling with any band is wonderful if you're involved, and I felt involved and connected. Mary found an American specialist consultant, Margaret Carson, to manage the marketing and public relations in the USA. We met each other by telephone and got to know each other through fax. We agreed on the ground rules. She would handle the US media and I would manage the Australian, and we would liaise before committing one of our team to an interview. Margaret Carson was probably in her early seventies then and she was impressive. She knew everyone and everything we needed to know. She'd managed Leonard Bernstein, Harry Truman and Michael Tilson Thomas, and was a wise woman who it was a privilege to observe in operation.

The Washington and New York performances included Joan Sutherland and Richard Bonynge, and it was wonderful as an Australian to see the way the audiences related to them. After the orchestra's performance at the Kennedy Center in Washington, I was anxious to read what the *Washington Post* critics said. Maggie Carson was quite relaxed. 'Wendy,' she said, 'this is America. Don't read it, just measure the paragraph inches.' The measurements stacked up, the orchestra was travelling well.

When I first became involved in the tour I had rung Rupert Murdoch and asked if he and Anna would host a reception for the orchestra after the Carnegie Hall concert. They generously agreed and hosted a wonderful reception in the penthouse on the 57th floor at the Parker Meridian Hotel. Unlike our other hosts, they recognised the need for real food after the performance and provided Thanksgiving turkey.

I have many cherished memories of that tour. The UN concert and meeting Peres de Cueller, Secretary General of the UN; eating in the Carnegie Deli late at night; lunch at the Russian Tea Rooms and sitting at a table next to Kathleen Turner; going to the Opera at the Met; travelling in provincial America and finding heritage treasures; the concerts and concert halls in Las Vegas and Chicago; walking along the Potomac canals with Hazel and Ros Dalrymple, the wife of our Australian Ambassador; the reaction to Australian composers Carl Vine and Peter Sculthorpe. And of course, the music. For me fourteen concerts in twenty-eight days was heaven.

I was in regular phone contact with the family and knew when I got to Hawaii for two days' rest I had to get my energy together, as I would be facing a big moment in our family life when I returned. Gordon was now firmly booked in to have his bone marrow transplant. We had agreed that he would go to hospital when I returned. I rang from Hawaii to be told he was already in hospital. I went into panic mode and rang the hospital, which advised that he had been in for a preliminary catheter insertion but had just discharged himself.

This was not part of the agreed agenda. Nothing was to happen until I was there. I felt powerless, bewildered and extraordinarily anxious. My mind and body were so tired that when I lay down on top of the bed after that phone call at 4 o'clock in the afternoon to think about how I'd manage all this, I went to sleep and didn't wake for sixteen hours. By then the world looked a little calmer. I contacted Gordon, who said he'd just gone in for his Hickmans catheter and it would be all systems go when I returned. My Bicentennial year's major event was about to happen.

By January 1989 there were few people left at the Authority. When Jim asked if I would stay on with Bill Fairbanks to wind up the company, I agreed. I needed a year to draw breath and look for a new career. I wanted the end to be tidy. So, in a systematic and organised way, we collated reports, evaluated and audited programs and made sure that our resident historian Dennis O'Brien had the information he needed to get on with the Bicentennial book. We finalised the accounts and the endowments of the Multicultural and Youth Foundations.

It was a good year to reflect and slow down, especially as Sam was in Year Eleven and Gordon was adjusting to his new immune system. In mid-1989 I was invited by the Minister for Health, Neal Blewett, to chair the National Better Health Program, a Commonwealth initiative to focus on health promotion and advocacy. It was a broadly based program and offered an opportunity to bring the states, territories and Commonwealth together with the aim of spending health dollars more effectively on disease prevention. It was a three-year commitment and returned me to the world of health after an absence of five years. It also gave me some sense of the future and where I might be for the next decade.

CHAPTER TWELVE

HERITAGE ADVENTURES—THE NATIONAL TRUST

By the middle of 1989 things had settled down in Longueville. Gordon was back at the farm after his transplant and, apart from a mean dose of shingles, seemed to have only positive side-effects. Sam was managing Year 11, Hamish had scraped back into second-year Arts at Mitchell, and Sophie was doing some extra subjects and thinking about an Honours year at ANU. It was time I began to think about my next career and I could see nothing that appealed to me. I'd been through the cooling down period after 1988 and was trying to be realistic about my next career opportunity but I couldn't see any directions to follow.

One night I went out to dinner with Gaye Hart and a couple of friends from the Bicentennial Authority and sat next to Deborah Marr, who worked with the executive search arm of Pannell Kerr and Foster, an accounting firm. We were all talking about our next careers and when asked my intentions, my response was, 'I really don't have the faintest idea, but this time I know I want to be the chief executive of an organisation with good values.' Things were clarifying.

I wanted to grow something, to prove to myself that I could do it. I felt confident after my Bicentennial experience that I could manage anything. As I was still deputy chair of the ABC and chair of the Better Health Program, I was not unemployed, and could take some time to find something suitable. I was prepared to wait for the right job.

As we left the dinner Deborah Marr said, 'Let's have a cup of coffee and I'll see if I can help you.' Some days later we met at her office, and the brief for the National Trust job arrived by fax. She showed it to me and asked if I would be interested. When I read it I thought, This is my job. It had all the ingredients I was looking for: financial crisis, good values, a respect for history, community-based membership—for me an absolutely dream job.

I registered my interest immediately and responded to the advertisement when it appeared the following week. I was invited to an interview. It was an inauspicious beginning. I arrived at the Trust's headquarters at Observatory Hill and was met by Michelle McDonald, who said, 'Oh we're very pleased that you're an applicant for the job. Would you like to meet all the staff?' This was a very small group of six. I was nonplussed as I still belonged to the school of people who believed that job applications were confidential. I didn't want to meet the staff as a potential applicant until I had the feel of the place, but it was too late to be concerned about that.

Resigned to a loss of privacy, I proceeded on my guided tour of the building and could see all the signs of an organisation in despair. Everything about it indicated that it had come to the end of the line. The offices were like boarded up rabbit warrens, places to hide. There was no sense of openness or trust, but a collection of tiny fiefdoms inhabited by suspicious people. Predictably, my candidature was disclosed by Sydney columnist Leo Schofield in the following Saturday's paper.

It was one of the more curious interviews. There were three people on the interview panel, one remained relatively neutral, one became quite enthusiastic and one was exceedingly hostile. Regrettably it was the woman I had never met before in whom I provoked a strong sense of antipathy. I'm more accustomed to being approved of and I found this very confronting. I left the interview thinking, I could really do this job, but there's no way that I'll be offered the position. On the other hand, not many people will want it as they will see it as a dog.

Somewhat to my surprise it was offered to me. We sorted out the terms and conditions of my contract fairly quickly, and it was agreed that my starting date would be January 1990. It felt good, starting a new decade as executive director of the National Trust. I treasured the Australianness of it for the ABA and ABC experience had intensified my interest in shifting the paradigms of being Australian.

I was very excited and immediately concentrated on some intense mothering, and organised a good family holiday to keep us together for the next decade of our individual and collective adventures. Although the children were now young adults I wanted to secure the family base. I would need room to move for this would be a challenging job to succeed in. I needed my family to support me to do this job effectively. There could no longer be an assumption that I would be providing dinner every night, nor would I necessarily be home by 6 p.m. I would be home when I arrived. There would be food available in the pantry and refrigerator and it would be a bonus when we ate together. I wanted my children to understand that while they had always come first, this was my turn and they must respect it. This job was the biggest challenge I had taken on and I needed all my resources to succeed. We had to learn to live together as consenting and considerate adults.

As tends to happen when parents make decisions like this, one child will be more affected than the others. I had to be fair to Sam, who was doing his Higher School Certificate. He needed support too and I counted my blessings that we had Quentin Bryce living with us. Quentin was appointed to the position of Federal Sex Discrimination Commissioner in 1988 and asked if she could stay with me while she settled into Sydney. Leaving her loving and robust family in Brisbane was a big move. We agreed that she would stay for six weeks. Six years later she was still with me—testimony to our friendship, common values and interests. It was also fortunate that Sam was our most independent child and did not want people fussing about his studies, which he stated he was capable of organising. And I am proud to say he was.

On 28 December 1989, two weeks before I started at the National Trust, an earthquake devastated Newcastle, NSW. As I drove from our farm at Berrima to Sydney I was listening in disbelief to the radio reports. It did not occur to me that this would have an impact on my new career at the Trust. As it turned out, the earthquake proved to be an unusual introduction to the Trust in action. Dedicated volunteers were anxious about its effect on the precious built heritage of Newcastle and were attempting to identify, record and assess the damage done to the most valuable buildings. Not that everyone thought the Trust teams were helpful. Many of the city officials saw them as interfering and not understanding that 'the best thing that could happen to Newcastle was to use this as an opportunity to get rid of the old stuff so that a new Newcastle can rise like a phoenix out of the ashes'.

It was a sentiment I was to hear a great deal of in the next six months, as I travelled backwards and forwards to Newcastle arguing with the Mayor and others about the need to conserve rather than demolish. At one meeting, where the safety/demolition of the hospital and a nurses' home were in dispute, I was accompanied by Colin Crisp, a heritage engineer and a Renaissance man who could structurally conserve anything. The Newcastle City Council's engineers believed the buildings should be demolished. The tension was palpable as Colin quietly talked them through reasons for saving them. He had such a presence and reputation they had to listen, and I can think of no building where his assessment was wrong.

This was an important crisis for me to manage in my first few weeks in the job, because it went to the heart of the Trust's business. It offered an opportunity for people to examine what heritage they valued. When a natural disaster like an earthquake strikes and there is an opportunity to recreate, what is it that we hold dear? Do we want entirely new places, or is it the familiar, which holds so many of our stories, that becomes more important? As it engaged in a robust debate about which heritage to conserve, the Newcastle community exhibited all the signs of a community under threat.

To assist the debate the Trust, with the support of school principals in the Hunter Valley, organised a painting and writing competition for children to get them to express their views about heritage post-earthquake. The results surprised many people, for both the stories and the paintings revealed the importance children placed on their surroundings and how the seemingly ordinary was significant in their lives. Some children talked about the messy bit of scrub that they played in on the way to school. (Today we call it remnant urban bushland.) Some children talked about the swamps (today read:

wetlands) where they saw ducks and mosquitoes. They painted and wrote of their favourite trees and churches, and expressed their sadness when they were pulled down. Apart from the therapeutic value of the process, it was a powerful insight into how early the sense of place develops in people.

In 1995 when I was chairing the Australian Heritage Commission, we held a Commission meeting in Newcastle. Nineteen-ninety seemed light years away; here was a town now boasting of its industrial Victorian heritage, its domestic buildings, its central business district, its churches, and the railway workshop at Honeysuckle Creek. The conservation work done there was shown to us with pride. Five years can be a long time in the heritage movement.

I go *click* as I read the *Weekend Australian* of 22 February 1997. On the front is a photograph of the cathedral being conserved and the headline, 'The Renaissance of Newcastle'. Architectural historian Jennifer Towndrow writes that Newcastle is a city with a bit of everything, confident of the future. Two of its landmarks are identified as James Barnett's Customs House and the Honeysuckle Creek workshop—buildings some people wanted to pull down.

Why carry on about Newcastle? In a way the Newcastle experience became the metaphor for my life at the Trust. A lot of crisis management, long-term planning and rebuilding, and trying to mainstream heritage into city life. The bottom line for me was that heritage be seen as an asset, not a liability.

Meanwhile back at the Trust headquarters at Observatory Hill, Sydney, I had to face the fact that the Trust as a corporate entity was in diabolical trouble. Before I arrived the NSW government had intervened in its management, sacked its Council and most of the staff of sixty-five and placed it in the control of an administrator, Martin Green, from the firm Pannell Kerr and Foster. His first task was to determine whether it should be liquidated or managed out of its $2 million debt. My appointment reflected a strategic decision to try trading out of debt. It was déjà vu of the Family Planning Association in the 1970s.

From the beginning I was determined to run the Trust as an effective business operation. I had formed the opinion that many not-for-profit businesses used their status as an excuse for sloppy business practices and I could see no reason for this. We would strive for best practice in all we did. The first pressing issue was what to do about the debt that had provoked the government's intervention. Traditional fundraising was not the answer as there had already been a huge loss of confidence in the way the organisation managed its finances and no-one would invest in an organisation with an administrator in place. After consolidating the fifty-three bank accounts— that's right, fifty-three—into one place and one bank so we had some idea where the money was, I recommended to Martin that we sell one of our unencumbered buildings, the Rectory at Berrima. This property was used by Trust members for holiday letting and was an appalling example of Trust housekeeping being badly presented and maintained.

Members were outraged and asserted I was selling Australia's heritage, and they hit the airwaves to complain. It seemed to escape the complainants that we were strapped for cash and without an injection of money all the properties might be for sale. Past presidents of the Trust visited the administrator to warn him of the error of his (my) ways.

Apart from the cash, the sale offered an opportunity to introduce the idea that the Trust could not be the custodian of all historic property. We had to encourage others to take on that role. We designed a contract with covenants to protect the property and it sold above its reserve price. The world did not end: some people lost their weekender and the Trust bank account looked a lot better. Better still, the Rectory went to owners who respected and conserved it.

Martin Green and I had a glorious eighteen months working together, as we researched and analysed the organisation and selected a management team. I think of it as my extended Whitlam/Barnard period, a time when I could implement change pretty much as I wanted. Life without a board was wonderful, even though I recognised that this would be a short period and many people in the Trust could really not return to support the organisation in the way they had previously until there was a democratically elected board in place. I was also conscious that there was no room for major mistakes. I was in a position of privilege and responsibility, offered an unexpected opportunity. It was a chance to get the systems and the people right and to make some decisions that I could accept responsibility for and a new board could live with.

Also in those first eighteen months I spent a lot of time driving around NSW, inspecting the properties, meeting the people who looked after them and testing the tolerance of the members to change. This was a chance to fall in love with the Australian countryside all over again, and I met some amazing people. It was a grounding experience after the Bicentennial Authority.

I remember one woman, who was cleaning the windows of a particular Trust property, saying, 'Wendy, under no circumstances let it be known in my household that I wash windows here. I haven't washed them in my house for twenty years and have no intention of doing so, but these windows are special and I want our visitors to see this house at its best.' Like many Trust volunteers, she was prepared to give her time to do tasks that she'd long abandoned at home in order to present the house in the appropriate way. Giving time was seen as virtuous and worthy and gave the volunteers a status which the managers rarely challenged.

The status of volunteers was at the heart of the Trust's management dilemma and, surprisingly, individual philanthropy was not part of the Trust culture. It seemed that the people who volunteered time did not think it appropriate to give money. Many Trust members and volunteers resented what they called professional management. I had observed battles about curatorial influence in the Bicentennial travelling exhibition, but these paled into insignificance compared to those fought out in the NSW Trust. I expected the usual tensions between head office and the branches, but the antagonism between the curatorial view of heritage conservation and the so-called commonsense view of some of the dedicated volunteer committees were legendary.

Good taste and good conservation were not always synonymous. For some good taste and heritage ended with early Colonial architecture. Others allowed a glimpse of the Regency period, some even moved past Victoriana towards Federation. Then there were all those other seemingly esoteric groups whose time has now come. They discussed, photographed and wrote about industrial heritage and cemeteries. The Trust volunteer network had an uncanny ability to predict future conservation treasures, and of course the volunteers were as varied as the community itself. Much of the Trust's professional expertise was derived from its voluntary committee networks. Eminent people gave their time freely, and I was especially dependent on their goodwill as we had very few staff when I began working there.

In case I've suggested that my appointment was greeted with universal enthusiasm, I should hasten to say that the more conservative Trust members were very suspicious. One well known identity, after the first of his many drinks for the day, was known to froth at the mouth and refer to me as 'that woman'. The sins of my past, dealing with such tawdry subjects as family planning and sexuality, were paraded as evidence of my unsuitability, as was my feminism. I hadn't heard the old communist/lesbian tag for quite a while, but assumed it would be recycled soon.

There were other views. In February 1992 a feature story appeared in the *Good Weekend* about Australians who'd changed the face of Australia. I was one of them and the article concentrated on my role at Family Planning. During the interview, I referred to the fact that I'd had an abortion and felt no shame. I'm told this caused our identity to have more drinks and splutter more profusely about the shame I'd brought on the Trust. I could never see the connection.

In contrast, in the Trust corridors the day after the article was published one of the mature, elegant women volunteers said to me, 'Wendy, dear, I liked that story. I like to think it's better for women now. In my day we had the babies and there are friends of mine who have never even acknowledged that they had children who were adopted out and I know how much pain there has been. I think it's good for us to have someone like you who is not afraid to speak out.'

In another heart-to-heart, another older woman volunteer said, 'You know things are going very well here. You are such a good manager but it doesn't seem right to have a woman in charge. And I'm told you're earning more than my husband.' I asked what seemed wrong about it, and she thought and said, 'Well, it's not really in the order of things, you know. It would be all right if you were the deputy, as you are at the ABC, but not in sole charge.' I explained that there was an administrator and there would be a board. Would that make a difference? 'No,' she said, 'I don't think so. The fact is it doesn't seem right.' I wanted to pursue the discussion and I reminded her that the Trust movement had begun with Octavia Hill in the UK in the 1890s, and in Australia our own role models, Annie Wyatt and Helen Blaxland, were both strong and powerful women who had provided leadership to the Trust. She remained unconvinced, though she was always supportive of me.

It made me realise that the women who had built the Trust remained unrecognised in their own right and I wanted to change that. I chose Annie Wyatt as our first heroine to honour. I hung her portrait and named a major meeting room after her as my first contribution. If I had been doing it to seek approval from the members, I had miscalculated, as it was popular with the Wyatt faction but not especially with the others. I was quite shocked to realise that recognising the contribution of women was contentious, but settled for the satisfaction that I had at least stimulated a discussion.

I thought the constitutional structure of the Trust was clumsy and had too many disconnected people responsible for its affairs. Its Council included university and state government representatives, a reminder of the status accorded to association with those bodies, and in a sense reflecting the need for that support when the Act was passed in 1962. However it offered opportunities for the government to meddle and I thought it should be amended so that the Trust was quite separate from government. I agreed with the NSW government that this was the window of opportunity to ensure that the Trust's structure of governance was appropriate to the twenty-first century. Of course agreeing on the need to change did not mean we agreed on the detail, and we sought independent advice to assist us with our negotiations with government.

Martin Green hired Price Brent as our lawyers. We deliberately chose a firm which was not part of the establishment as many of those practices had been close to the in-fighting prior to the appointment of the administrator. Tim Eakin, the senior partner, and I worked with the Solicitor-General's office to achieve the rewriting of the Trust's legislation. The final result was not greeted with acclamation, the sticking points being we were too independent of government, i.e. no government appointees, and the executive director was a member of the Board. I was strongly committed to both, and the Act was duly passed.

By July 1991 the first elections in three years were held and a new Board was in place. The administrator's job was finished, the Trust headquarters at Observatory Hill had been refurbished, thanks to NSW Premier Nick Greiner, and my Whitlam/Barnard period was over. I was looking forward to working with the new directors, as I was ready for a wider frame of reference. It's a fascinating process being part of a duo managing an organisation. At one level you want it to be forever, and then one day you wake up and understand how much you miss without the wider conversation directors offer. Some of the new directors had been councillors in the previous regime and I wondered if they would find the new form of governance challenging. The most obvious difference was the status of the chief executive who was now a director equal to all others, unlike previous Trust executives who were treated as 'staff' and told to come and go at meetings.

For the general membership the election of the Board was positive because they wanted their elected representatives there. I had to realise that no matter how well I might be doing, there was no sense of democracy until members had their elected representatives in place.

Barry O'Keefe was elected President at the first meeting. He was a well-respected barrister and had a long experience in local government, so he seemed a most suitable person. I'd met him only once before the election, and while we may have seemed an unlikely combination, it was a convivial and intellectually respectful relationship.

The executive team of Stephen Davies, Jaspal Singh, Dinah Dysart, Maisie Stapleton and Chris Levins were a wonderful support to me. They were a strong, balanced and effective team. Two had been NSW Trust employees, so we had some corporate memory to help our decision-making. We had a lot of fun together and I remember with great affection their loyalty and confidence boosting when I was not appointed as chair of the ABC Board.

I have not been talking about the ABC in this context, but it was still there as a constant thread in my professional life, and of course I did borrow and reapply some of that experience to the challenges of the Trust. Perhaps it was more central than I realised, for some years later I was amused to read a comment attributed to an anonymous Trust member on the announcement of my resignation, 'She couldn't cope with the volunteers, her favourite saying was, "Oh that's the way we did it in the ABC." '

Once we had a President in place to assume many of the representational tasks that I'd been fulfilling, I thought I should concentrate on fundraising. The sale of the Rectory had helped the balance sheet, but selling assets was not a long-term solution. Prior to the election of the Board I'd been interviewing a range of fundraisers who had offered their services. I had limited experience of professional fundraisers. In my family planning days I had effectively persuaded the state FPAs to buy collectively to achieve economies of scale and establish strong commercial relationships which did not rely on favours. But setting a large financial target and achieving it was new territory. I'd made the decision that it would be counterproductive to begin serious fundraising before we were seen as a viable organisation with a new Act and a democratically elected Board.

We needed professional help and I sought the Board's support to begin a major fundraising campaign. The interviewing process widened my understanding of successful fundraising. We chose the firm Everald Compton, who seemed the most ethical, professional and disciplined, and whose feasibility study indicated a target of $4 million was achievable over five years. The feasibility study had provided interesting data on the Trust members' attitude to fundraising. They spoke of their gifts to the Trust being time, not money, and some of the wealthiest people would not consider financial contributions. It was often people outside the existing Trust family who recognised its value to our community and were willing to give money, even when they were not nearly as affluent as those who were working as occasional volunteers. It was something to do with a culture of noblesse oblige and the idea that talking about money was somehow vulgar. Some members suggested seriously that if we went back to all volunteers the Trust would be a better organisation. These attitudes also reflected the control that some members wanted, and some approached me to do deals. We will give you money if you will conserve a property in a particular way. Of course I could never agree to these and they were unsustainable anyway.

Why do I tell you? To help you understand the intensity of these passions. These were Realpolitik, not dissimilar to the passions that family planning aroused in people. Listening and watching these reactions convinced me that we needed an external high-profile person to chair the Foundation Board. An unexpected person was suddenly free of responsibilities—Bob Hawke had just been ousted by Paul Keating as Prime Minister of Australia. I decided to ask him if he would do it. I rang and asked for an appointment and he agreed to see me at the house in Sydney he and Hazel had quickly moved to. He had no idea of the reason for my visit and was intrigued that I was asking to see him rather than Hazel.

I was feeling a little nervous as I arrived. I was in fact offering him an unpaid job, and in addition he was required to make a financial commitment as part of the deal. On the other hand, I was demonstrating my faith in his leadership ability, despite the fact that he was no longer Prime Minister. I stressed to him that we valued his name and his association, and I was not asking him to attend endless meetings but to open doors occasionally. He would be able to do most of the work by telephone.

He rang me back the next day and said, 'You've been persuasive, I've always supported Australian heritage values. Hazel and I will make a donation to the bush regeneration program and I'll chair the Foundation.' To his credit, and as promised, Bob was always helpful and available.

It was important that the Foundation leadership was politically even-handed, so I then invited Rosemary Foot, ex-deputy Premier (Liberal) of NSW to become the deputy chair. She agreed and did a superb job. Our Foundation was suddenly looking promising. With campaign manager Andrew Day in place, we began planning to achieve our goals. I grew to love the game of fundraising, the planning, thinking, positioning and the thrill of achieving support for our favourite places. I was surprised at how much I enjoyed fundraising. It was an unexpected new skill and passion.

The approach we took to individuals and corporations was successful, a mixture of sponsorship, marketing opportunities and philanthropy. I was determined to persuade government to support the Trust's work. There had to be some financial recognition for the Trust's role in caring for many places in the public domain. I thought a dollar-for-dollar arrangement with government would be a strong incentive for private donors to become partners with the Trust. An announcement in 1992 from Prime Minister Paul Keating of the One Nation Program had me on the first plane to Canberra and within a short period of time we had a grant of $1.5 million on a dollar-for-dollar basis. It was the success factor that we needed, and we were on a roll.

I cherish many wonderful memories from my working life at the National Trust. It was really the first time in my life that I could please myself about my working hours. As I write it seems childish to make that statement, but it was significant that I no longer worried about Gordon or the children's needs in the same way. Many Trust meetings were held at 5.30 or 6 p.m. and suddenly this was not a problem and I could enjoy those early evenings. The Trust's S.H. Ervin Gallery, Sydney, was a joy and helped me express my love and growing confidence in the visual arts. When I arrived it was under the competent management of Dinah Dysart, but I wanted her to take a bigger role in the management of the Trust's collection and properties.

We appointed Dinah's deputy, Anne Loxley, as the gallery director. She was an outstanding young woman who brought a fresh energy and intellect to the gallery. I like to be in a position where I can provide opportunities for young people, and I am rarely disappointed. Various Trust members counselled me about Anne's appointment. 'I don't want to interfere, but it's not a good idea to have someone so young in charge, dear' and, 'She doesn't have an established reputation.' Well the latter observation was reasonable, but it is only through experience that such a reputation can be acquired. That is like saying to me it's not right to have a woman in charge. There is no evidence to support that premise, and I will not accept it.

One of Anne's spectacular coups was to bring an Aboriginal community from Central Australia to Sydney. Their work was hung in the gallery, which had been transformed by some tonnes of red sand from the Western desert, and they sang and danced as part of the performance. One morning about 10 a.m. as I drove in to park, I saw the astonished expression of one of our members as she watched the women in front of the campfire start applying paint and ochre to their bare breasts. Red sand on the gallery floor was one thing, this was something else. To the credit of those whose sense of propriety may have been offended, I received no complaints.

I loved the scholarship of the Trust, the intellect that was applied to artworks, historic collections and property interpretations. Vigorous debate was part of the daily working life and that offered a stimulating environment and encouraged a lively membership. An interest in Australian heritage was one of the great legacies of the Bicentenary, in the same way it had been in the USA, and it was fun and rewarding to be on the ground with that activity.

True to my need and/or practice of maintaining eclectic interests, I kept an outside portfolio of interest and responsibilities. When I joined the Trust I was chairing the National Better Health Program and was deputy chair of the ABC. Both involved meetings and travel, and I learned to be adept at piggybacking my interests and networking them. The ABC appointment ended in May 1991 and the Better Health Program in mid-1992 and I would not have been happy to be focused on one activity, for I increasingly understood that I am an Australian rather than a New South Welshwoman. I cannot get excited about states' rights, I want people to think as Australians. In 1990 and 1991 I attended conferences on Better Health in Singapore and Sweden and these experiences confirmed that big picture view of the world that I found invigorating. I thought my home organisation benefited from this exposure to new ideas and practices, but that may have been my justification.

I do acknowledge that arriving in a position with a portfolio of other responsibilities is different from acquiring one in situ. So in 1991, when asked by Environment Minister Ros Kelly to be part of a four-member panel to review and resolve Australia's intractable waste problem, I was concerned that the President may not be pleased if I accepted another appointment. On the other hand, the government had supported the Trust through the One Nation funding and I did not want to find myself in a politically difficult position by appearing to be uncooperative. Barry O'Keefe agreed that I would join the panel and with my colleagues Professor Ben Selinger (ANU Chemistry), Michael Davidson (NSW Farmers' Federation) and Professor Charles Kerr (University of Sydney, Public Health) went in pursuit of solutions. We held consultations in various Australian towns where waste management was a significant community issue and looked for home-grown solutions rather than high-temperature incinerators. It was a divisive political issue and in Moree, NSW, over a thousand people turned up for the meeting. I was back in the eye of the storm again.

It was during this time that community affairs were rebranded as issues management. I love to note these linguistic changes and think about the process. People in fear of 'political correctness' hate these changes and some still contort their mouths at Ms. But I am fascinated by the stories of social change they tell. For example family planning became reproductive health and fertility control, sex became sexuality and of course the great feminist name transfer was female circumcision to genital mutilation.

But I digress from intractable waste, where our journey took us to Cincinnati, Bay City, Detroit, Basel and Paris, places with interest and experience in the technology of waste management. It was new information, new values and new technology and I struggled, with my Leaving Certificate chemistry, to make sense of it. Fortunately Ben Selinger, our Chair, was a patient and friendly communicator about chemistry. And I was confident about my understanding and experience of community consultation. Across the world it was possible to see a pattern of response. Communities wanted to negotiate changes in their environment and were increasingly better informed about the science.

Click to a meeting in Cobar, NSW, where the locals were saying 'No' to a high-temperature incinerator. I arrived on the plane for a public meeting about the issue, and Premier Nick Greiner was in town. At the airport there were demonstrators wearing black shrouds. The local people wanted to discuss the matter with him, and he said, 'Speak to Wendy about this'.

A passionate man started putting the case against the incinerator and said, 'Nick thinks I'm dumb because when we were at school together he was at the top of the class and I was at the bottom. But I know more about the science of this than him and he has to listen.'

The *Exxon Valdez*, Chernobyl and Bhopal disasters have left a legacy of mistrust about corporate safety and scientific truth throughout the world, and television, fax and the internet allow us to access information to challenge what is being presented to us. We no longer believe governments and corporations who tell us what is good for us. Our solutions for intractable waste in Australia did not include a high-temperature incinerator but an eclectic mix of solutions for streamed waste types. We presented the final report to the Australian and New Zealand Environment Ministers Conference and were congratulated for our creative work.

By mid-1993 I was feeling restless at the Trust. I began to think that I had made my contribution, patterns were repeating and it was time to move, especially if I wanted another executive job, although I was not convinced that I did. Despite my enthusiasm to work hard and long, the hours were becoming tedious because of the expectations that I would be at Trust events at the weekends. I hasten to add that I had not discouraged those expectations, but I felt I was running out of steam. The financial targets I had set had been met, the fundraising was well on target and we had been the beneficiary of the substantial estate of Dr Thistle Stead, a conservation pioneer who for many years was a volunteer at the Wirrimbirra Sanctuary at Bargo, NSW. The future was looking secure and I needed another adventure. I had a yearning to go it alone, although I could not quite imagine what I would do. It's the eternal dilemma of the specialist generalist.

The Trust lawyers, Price Brent, had been suggesting that I was just what they needed to energise their practice and after a lot of soul searching I decided to become their Chief Executive in February 1994. I arranged a contract for a four-day week, as I wanted some time out to develop other interests. Most of my friends advised me against this move, saying I would be bored and I shouldn't do commercial things as the not-for-profit sector was my proper habitat. Those who approved said I needed experience in the commercial world to be a really good manager. I resented the stereotyping and assumptions that the skills were not transferable. I thought a single bottom line would be much easier, and the idea of a non-lawyer running a legal practice appealed to me.

Before I left the Trust I arranged for His Royal Highness Prince Charles to open our newest property, the Merchant's House at The Rocks. For a Republican this was a coup and for many Trust members it was a thrill, although some hated admitting it. The circumstances were curious. I was contacted by Michael Ball from The Ball Partnership, an advertising agency, to discuss a possible visit to Australia by Prince Charles. Michael had been contacted by the Palace to discuss ways in which Prince Charles could improve his image and also test the Republican sentiment in Australia. His marriage to Princess Diana was in trouble and, while her star shone, his media coverage was constantly negative.

Michael arranged for us to meet a few times and on one occasion we were joined by Commander Richard Aylard, Private Secretary to His Royal Highness. I suggested that we enhance his image in the built environment by asking him to speak at a gathering sponsored by the Trust. We were an organisation he would feel comfortable with, and this became the initial plan. Alas, by the time the visit was in the hands of protocol and politicians, Trust matters were abbreviated to a short visit to the official opening of the Merchant's House.

However Gordon and I were invited by His Royal Highness to a private black-tie dinner at the Governor-General's Sydney residence, Admiralty House, on 25 January, 1994. There were approximately twenty guests and with some of them he had connections going back to his school days. It was an extremely pleasant evening. I found the Prince a lively and engaging dinner companion and this was unexpected as he is so often presented as dull.

My four years at the National Trust were satisfying and there were victories, such as the long-fought-for introduction of tax incentives for the restoration of heritage buildings, and disappointments, such as losing the Trust's right to comment to the Central Sydney Planning Committee on the redevelopment of heritage buildings. I was pleased when *Sydney Morning Herald* heritage writer Geraldine O'Brien wrote that I was the executive director 'during the four years it [the Trust] has been making its way back from the edge of extinction'.

Leaving the Trust meant that I left behind Dorothy Capelletto, my Executive Assistant of over ten years. We had been together since AFFPA days and shared many adventures through the Bicentenary and now the National Trust. She was an integral part of my life, but asking her to change again when she was beginning to think retirement did not seem fair, so I moved on without her. These relationships should never be underestimated. Every chief executive needs a support person who is competent and trustworthy, as we don't operate as islands. I have been blessed with mine.

Chapter Thirteen

BYE BYE MISS AMERICAN PIE

In November 1993 Gordon and I went to Singapore and Malaysia for a couple of weeks' holiday. We had not been there for some time and wanted to see the economic miracles we had been reading about, and we needed a dose of Asia. We were in Kuala Lumpur when Paul Keating described Mahathir, the Malaysian Prime Minister, as recalcitrant, which interfered with our intent to have a drink with the Malay High Commissioner, who was in damage control. It was a holiday referred to by our children as geriatric backpacking because we travelled on local buses through Malaysia and checked into comfortable hotels, a perfect combination.

Before we left I had found a house I wanted to buy in Darlinghurst in Sydney's inner city. It was to be auctioned while we were away and we had a serious domestic about absentee bidding. Gordon's view was that absentee bidding was a recipe for disaster and we should wait until we returned. On matters of finance and investment Gordon usually prevails and his track record is excellent so there was no absentee or telephone bid. On our return we drove past to find it was still on the market, and I went straight to the agent to put in a bid. I knew it was mine—and female moments like these continue to surprise my husband.

I am a person who becomes strongly attached to houses. Our first house at McMahons Point I was deeply in love with, and that gave me the energy and courage to become active in Resident Action and fight for it and the suburb. When Gordon wanted to leave McMahons Point I was devastated. This was my territory and my community yet his arguments were persuasive—more sun, more space for kids to run and jump, and ours did like to do that, and so after eleven years we moved to suburban Longueville. We chose Longueville because it was a beautiful peninsula and we liked peninsulas and the way they encouraged village life. Geographically it was midway between our workplaces, mine in the city and his in the western suburbs. And most of all we loved the house, a six-bedroom Spanish Mission style house looking over the Lane Cove River. In Sydney, if you cannot afford to live in Hunters Hill, the second prize is looking at it. When we saw it in November and looked across the water to Hunter's Hill, awash with flowering jacaranda and flame trees, we fell in love. There were parks and tennis courts everywhere and a great local primary school—family heaven. It was home for seventeen years and when we sold it we left many stories in the walls.

Selling Longueville was as painful as leaving McMahons Point, but as Gordon was now committed to rural life and cattle, there was not a lot of sense in me living on my own there. While Sophie and Sam were living independently, Hamish was at home and had to be prised off the walls when we left. He felt his security base was disappearing, but we thought it was time for him to separate. These are tough decisions for families of mature children and my peer group struggles with them. The way through for us was to downsize the accommodation in the city, while ensuring that teddy bears and other significant memorabilia would be housed at the farm. Our family would have two spaces, our log cabin at Mundi Mundi near Berrima and our smaller place in Darlinghurst.

Between January and May 1994 we bought Darlinghurst, had the required garage sale at Longueville and settled me at Darlinghurst and Hamish in a flat at nearby Woolloomooloo. While they were big changes, they were manageable because we had spent a year or two preparing for them. The sale of the family home is more than a sale. It is the end of an era. I would no longer see myself as the security symbol, earthed in a special place to which everyone returns. Emotionally this was hard to let go, although intellectually and financially it was a sound move.

These changes were in progress when I joined Price Brent as Chief Executive, thus defying the conventional wisdom that one should not make more than one significant change at any one time, certainly not a house and a job. The media was encouraging when I began working at Price Brent, a medium-size commercial legal practice. The *Financial Review* and *The Australian* wrote about me being the first female non-lawyer to take on this role and the future sounded interesting. I wanted to believe my own PR.

Was I surprised when within a week as CEO there I felt I had made the wrong decision, that this was not the habitat for me? I reflected how this was the career decision I made with my head rather than my heart. Had I fallen for the rhetoric which insisted management skills were valuable only if commercially proven? The people were pleasant, I had a downtown office with car parking, and I was properly paid. What was wrong with me?

As thoughts such as these went through my mind, I began planning how I would manage the year, as there was no way I could walk out. I was hoist on my own petard. Gordon generously refrained from saying, 'I told you so.' His experiences of partnerships had meant he had counselled against this move—he thought they were unmanageable. I determined to get on with the task I had been hired for.

Partnerships are inelegant arrangements for the conduct of business. They may once have been effective vehicles for the delivery of professional services, but that time has long passed. Legal practices are commercial businesses employing many devices to compete in a competitive world. Price Brent wanted change and its partners could not agree on the leadership or direction of the change. It was difficult for them to think corporately, despite their best intentions, and there was the added complication of a merged and de-merged partnership in Melbourne.

For a few weeks I watched them operate. Each solicitor had a separate office where he/she dictated into a machine whose tape was then dispatched to the typing pool. This assumed as little interaction with the work team as possible. Each solicitor was territorial about his/her clients and would not think it unusual to refer to other practices rather than another partner. This seemed to be against all the rules of marketing and teamwork. It was really an uneasy coalition of consenting adults, based on an outmoded idea of a gentlemen's club.

Perhaps changing this might be fun after all; they knew they needed to change or they would not have hired me, so the first building block was in place. My observations and analysis of the problems in the practice, together with my private awareness that I would not be there for a long time, made me braver or more brutal, depending on your perspective. I am sure that the lack of heart involvement made some of the decisions easier.

My instinct was growing that it was time I worked for myself, and an experience in Singapore in July reinforced this. I had been selected in a group of a hundred Australian businesswomen to attend a seminar in Singapore with a hundred leading Asian businesswomen. The meeting was subsidised by Telstra and the Australian government, and was a glamorous affair. Any idea that Australian women might feel sorry for their Asian sisters was quickly dispelled. We were in the company of leading women entrepreneurs who were confident, well educated and wealthy. They also had a domestic infrastructure unknown to most Australian women. One woman I sat next to at a dinner asked how many servants I had and expressed surprise when I could account only for a cleaning service four hours a week. For her two adolescent children she had two maids, a cook, a chauffeur, and her mother to manage the household. She said, admiringly, 'I think you Australian women are so strong.' I wanted to respond that right this minute I'd settle for the money and the infrastructure rather than the strength.

By September 1994 the Sydney/Melbourne partnership had de-merged, the banking and financial arrangements were reorganised, the offices renovated (which involved relocating for three months), partner numbers were reduced to those who earned the requisite annual income, and the firm's name had changed. I learned to bill and collect debts, once I had realised that well-known names ran up huge accounts and continued to play golf on weekdays. Despite my initial misgivings, I was finding the outcomes professionally satisfying.

Somewhere around that time I started being described as a businesswoman rather than an activist. It was not of my doing, but a reflection of the times and my role in a commercial business. In professional terms I was no more or less into best business practice than I had been at the Trust; the difference was the distinction between a not-for-profit organisation and a commercial partnership. Also it was fashionable to be a businesswoman rather than a feminist: people thought they were paying you a compliment to describe you thus. At a philosophical level I didn't mind, as my feminism had begun to understand that women would not advance any further unless they moved into wealth creation. The advances of the last three decades were significant, but we neither wrote the cheques nor the legislation. Decision-making in government and business remained in the hands of men.

On my return from Singapore I took the first step to becoming an independent operator. I registered Women's Business as a trading name of McCarthy Management, our family company. It was a name I had often thought about, and when I found it was available I decided to claim it. I was not sure how and when I would use it, but it felt right and secure. Perhaps it was serendipity, but shortly after I noticed an advertisement for expressions of interest to run a series of training programs for women attending the United Nations World Conference on Women in Beijing. This had to be women's business, and I decided to express my interest. I called my friend Margaret Winn, who had wonderfully up-to-date information and experience working with women around the world, and she agreed to join me in the bid. I started dreaming about my own business.

In the midst of this process my brother Kerry died and the decisions seemed a lot clearer. Why was I doing a job that did not engage my head and my heart? Life was too short, and Kerry's death really made me stop and re-evaluate my life.

You have met Kerry occasionally through this book. He was my little brother, four years younger and for many years the only mature Ryan male, a responsibility he took seriously. He was the sibling with whom I had the closest relationship, as my sister Deborah was eight years younger. She was three and Kerry was seven when I went away to boarding school, so apart from the years we shared at Garema, our lives connected only in school holidays. This is a feature of many country children's lives, and families do adapt and develop a different type of closeness. Such was the case in our family.

Kerry was a gentle boy, and Daddy preferred Deborah's company. She was a tomboy and fearless. Kerry was more easily intimidated and bullied, and would be distressed when our parents fought. Like me he was fearful for our mother, and throughout his life he felt protective and responsible for her.

Kerry was fourteen and boarding at Farrer Agricultural High near Tamworth when our father died. I am not even sure that we had told him that Daddy was in hospital in Sydney, as it all happened so quickly. When we rang the school to tell them, the Headmaster advised my mother that it would be best if she didn't speak to him. He would tell Kerry and then help him get on with his life. He strongly recommended that he should not attend the funeral. This was not unusual advice and practice at the time, but Kerry always felt that he had been excluded from a significant family event. When he asked me about it much later in life, I lied and avoided telling him how awful it was.

Probably as for me, the death of our father was liberating for him, although their relationship was unsatisfactory and unresolved. He grew up quickly and after finishing school, like his father before him, he went to work in a stock and station agency. He was always quite sure he wanted a country life and he, like Bill (our father), was a natural auctioneer with a great flair for people.

In 1966 he was called up in the first conscription ballot and subsequently spent a year in Vietnam, an experience he would rarely speak about. I recall only three conversations, the first was the night before he was married when he told me that he occasionally had nightmares and hoped they would not frighten Susie, whom he adored. The second was to register his disgust at the news that Gordon and I had attended an anti-Vietnam march. And years later, when I was on the Board of the ABC, he asked if I would arrange for him to view the archival material on Vietnam. I did and he was pleased to view the footage. He later decided to take part in the Reconciliation march and, like many of his mates, found it cathartic, like coming home at last.

Kerry had a reputation as a party boy, quick witted, a great singing voice, was a good Rugby player and had many girlfriends. He liked a drink and people would say he was a chip off the old block. However those comments were made by people who did not understand how important it was for him to gain respect as a serious and responsible person. When he met Sue Weaver, the love of his life, he became a successful and focused family man, no doubt determined to become a better father than the one he had known.

Our political beliefs were light-years apart. He supported the National Party and saw my support of issues rather than a party as weak. He was outspoken about feminism, the Labor Party and Blacks, and claimed, at least in the last case, that his Walgett address entitled him to be the expert. We shared some very robust moments, and occasionally our mother was caught in the middle. If she supported my views he saw it as an urban plot and proof that city life had ruined her judgement. Despite these differences, we remained friends as well as family, interested in and proud of each other's family and achievements.

In 1993 our mother, my sisters Deb and Sarah, Kerry and I with children and spouses had one of the great family holidays at Bluey's Beach on the mid-north coast of NSW. We rented four beach houses at Christmas, one for each family. We met at the beach each day, had lunch, played golf and tennis, and reminded ourselves that we still cheat to win at Scrabble. Our families moved into a new mode, more relaxed and tolerant, acknowledging their connections and differences in an affectionate and accepting way.

Eight months later we were dancing and singing at Kerry's eldest son Nicholas Ryan's twenty-first birthday, held at the favourite local motel in Walgett. Family had never seemed more fun. Six weeks later we returned to that motel for Kerry's wake. He was only forty-nine.

Kerry's story is his, but it's important to me. He was the other Ryan man, and like the first one, didn't make fifty. He died from a massive stroke and it all happened very quickly. At 5 a.m. he was out in the paddocks checking stock when he was struck by an overwhelming headache and started feeling dizzy and tingling. By mid-afternoon he had been airlifted to Dubbo hospital, and was unconscious and paralysed.

Sarah, Bette and I flew up to be with him (did I mention that

Mummy had become Bette?). Deb drove over from Tamworth, and by late afternoon the diagnosed brain-stem haemorrhage was described as impossible to overcome. The bedside vigil was continuous. He was never alone. His Walgett friends filled up the waiting rooms and annexes. They were regular Aussie blokes off the land and I was overwhelmed by their ability to show their love and affection for Kerry. When they weren't with him they were telling Kerry stories in the courtyards. It redefined the narrative and made my heart sing.

I frequently thought of William Rex Ryan's last hours, alone and isolated, his funeral in a no-name chapel in Chatswood and already an anxiety about who would pay for it. Also my Nana Ryan's pain, and a brother-in-law who refused to speak to my mother, as though it was her fault.

Kerry Rex struggled for three days while we talked to him and encouraged him to hang on to his life until Nicholas came home from his rugby tour in Ireland. Did he know that it was Nick who was squeezing his arm? We all want to think so, just as we want to believe that he knew we were with him in one combination or another until he died on the Saturday morning.

Kerry's wake was a major Walgett event and it says much about my brother. The funeral service was held in the local Catholic church, whose design he liked, and there were two ministers officiating, Catholic and Protestant. He liked them both. Almost a thousand people attended and both family and friends spoke. As the service concluded, his coffin, draped with the flag of his regiment, was carried out to 'Bye Bye Miss American Pie'. The Vietnam theme writ large.

The cortège moved along the streets of Walgett where businesses were closed and employees stood outside to pay their respects. We drove past his favourite places—Wickman, Ryan, his profitable stock and station agency, the TAB and the RSL Club. Many of his regiment were present, and at the cemetery he was accorded a military burial. Kerry would have been pleased with his funeral. It had a style and flair he would have appreciated.

On the way home Hamish wrote a few verses to Kerry:

And the word did get around town,
That the legendary Kerry was now underground
So a large mustering took place
To find all his peers and children and put them in one space
For to toast K-Rex Ryan was to toast the lifeblood of the
* bush,*
Where people endured, enjoyed and lived
With a man whose heart was always in his gait.

And the memories that everyone shared
Were in the traditional K-Rex style
With his friends milling around
Sitting, smiling and laughing at his jokes,
While his spirit sailed swiftly away under town.

Over the next couple of weeks obituaries appeared in the rural press. On 20 October the editorial obituary in *The Land* described Kerry as one of the great characters in agency work, who always looked on the bright side of life, one of the best all rounders in the game. It spoke of his love of racing and his sense of fairness. Mike Wilson wrote in *The Land* on November 10: 'There must be a really big stock sale coming up in the saleyard in heaven. Last month God called home one of the best stock and station agents I've ever known to help him organise it. Kerry Ryan from Walgett was a great agent, a great bloke and a good friend. He will be sadly missed.'

He will be and is. I had been connected to Kerry for forty-nine years, longer than any man in my life. He has a special place in my memories. He was so often the counterpoint and I valued the tension, as much as it enraged me when he said 'wake up to yourself, woman'.

When I returned to work my decision to leave Price Brent was made. I advised them I would be leaving in December and offered to find my replacement. We parted amicably. They accepted that they no longer needed a change agent, that task was done.

CHAPTER FOURTEEN

WOMEN'S BUSINESS 1995

In 1995 I realised my fantasy about working from home. For many women working from home is isolating, and as a young mother I did not want to do it. I needed the stimulus of adult company and I did not want the distractions of the children and housework. But this stage of my life was different. I loved the idea of managing my own time and space and being without the emotional responsibility of employees or family. Plus I had a new house to nest in and develop for Gordon and me in the next stage of our lives together.

Although I felt I was flying by the seat of my pants for a little while, the breakthrough came when Women's Business won the contract for the Beijing seminars. Shortly after I was invited to chair the Australian Heritage Commission. It was a three-year appointment, commencing 30 January 1995, so I had a guaranteed income and two passionate commitments ahead of me. Women's Business was looking good. Then, quite unexpectedly, I was invited to be the Executive in Residence of the University of South Australia's International Graduate School of Management. The year was full.

Any concerns that I would have insufficient social contact were now disregarded. The new commitments, together with my role as a council member of the University of Canberra, would provide the public policy involvement in the areas I felt passionate about—Australian heritage, education and women. Also the bid team I had joined for the licence of the Sydney casino had been successful, so I had a commercial directorship as part of my responsibilities. I felt as though all my passions and needs were coming together.

In January 1995 we ran our first seminar for women planning to attend the Beijing Conference. I asked Sophie to join Margaret Winn and me, as her job at Liverpool Health Centre was a four-day-a-week research commitment. It was wonderful working with her and I felt proud of her competency and style. I offered her the Beijing airfare as part of the deal, and felt excited that we would share this involvement and travel together after the conference. I had written to my long-time friend from Family Planning days Lorraine Williams who was living in Shanghai, and we planned to visit her for a few days.

The Beijing seminars took us around Australia. Kathy Townsend, the Head of the Office for the Status of Women, predicted that they would be popular. I was less sure, but fortunately she was right. Margaret and I worked hard to make them interesting and useful for the participants, and in each location we found a China expert to provide reliable and contemporary information about China. We insisted that everyone eat Chinese food with chopsticks as part of the learning, and had some very funny moments chasing rice grains with them.

In the Northern Territory we were invited back to run another seminar for the Aboriginal women who had missed the first one in Alice Springs. It was a generous group and keen to work on strategies to ensure indigenous women were included in the plan of action. The women were inspirational in their commitment and struggle to be educated and participate actively in local and ultimately world affairs. So few of us have the privilege of observing, much less being involved in, that indigenous struggle. One young Aboriginal woman worked as a cleaner by day and studied at night with University of the Air on the ABC. She and her husband were equally committed to this learning and they recorded television programs in preparation for what she called 'the other side' of the desks she currently cleaned. After having trouble with the chopsticks, she returned the next morning to report that she and her husband had practised and were now chopstick perfect. That kind of response is an educator's dream.

It seemed that the bush telegraph was working across the sea to Papua New Guinea, and Margaret and I were very pleased to receive an invitation to Port Moresby to hold a pre-Beijing meeting. We said our usual group size of twenty would be appropriate, and were overwhelmed when more than fifty women came to do 'the women's business with their sisters from across the sea'. One could but marvel at their tenacity, as they walked for miles to prepare themselves for Beijing. Like their Aboriginal sisters, their commitment to improving the status of women and children was awesome. Margaret and I were staying in the local Travelodge, home to most expatriates, and the juxtaposition of that, with its armed guards, and the lives and living conditions of our group was yet another reason to be an active feminist.

In the first six months of 1995, as the Executive in Residence at the University of South Australia, I spent approximately three of the agreed six weeks in residence, in this case at the Adelaide Hilton. It was rather like being on sabbatical, reading articles I had been saving for years and reading outside my comfort zone. I asked to do some teaching with the MBA class and this was agreed. Although I found it confronting as well as stimulating, it reminded me of how I love to be in the classroom.

My travel schedule was constant and I was revelling in it. Visiting and discussing Australian heritage, talking management and business at the university and the casino, and running seminars for women was about the perfect portfolio. It was in this high-adrenaline phase that disaster struck and reminded me that nothing matters more than the people you love. And that I call Sophie's story, and is a chapter in its own right.

I have always been cautious about owing people, unwilling to be beholden to unknown calls. It also reflects my upbringing. 'Good girls are not bold girls, nice girls wait to be asked to dance, 'Don't be pushy' (for yourself that is). This can be seen as a disadvantage in business. 'She is not hungry enough', people say, and the truth is while I want to succeed, I do find it difficult to push for business.

I can recall only one instance where I ignored those refrains and made a successful career move which improved my portfolio and income. I was in residence at the Management School in Adelaide when I was called by AIC, a conference company, to endorse/approve a female American management consultant they were planning to bring to Australia for a series of seminars on Being a Successful

Woman in Business. I read her résumé and the proposed program, and called them back to say I thought we should get over Mary Beths and Mary Jos from Boise, Idaho, telling us how to be Australian women in business. I could endorse neither the consultant nor the idea. I suggested they ask an Australian woman to run the course.

The young woman on the phone was astonished. Who would you suggest? 'Well, I could do it,' I heard myself say. (After all was I not being described as a businesswoman?)

'Oh!' she said. 'Well, send me your résumé and we will discuss it in the office.'

I did not expect to hear from her again, but I sent the résumé feeling both elated and anxious. But I had read the texts and had the experience and I wanted to be back in teaching mode. I thought, the worst thing that can happen is that I will be rejected. There was something very seductive about being out in the marketplace and I was ready for it. After a few days I was asked to prepare a draft outline. This was accepted, and in a surprisingly short time I was on the circuit with a glossy A4 brochure extolling my skills. I would find out very quickly if I was worth anything in the marketplace.

For three years from 1995, I ran seminars in Sydney, Melbourne, Canberra, Auckland and Wellington. Usually the groups were limited to twenty, and until the day before I would have no idea of their composition. They often had an age range of as much as twenty years and the occupational and experience base was broad. I focused on generic executive leadership for women, but we spent a lot of time working out how to maintain a balance between their professional and private lives. I loved working with these groups. I love the rush that comes when you try to turn them into a group and the trust that builds up so that they share their experiences and help solve each other's problems.

I worried sometimes that I was not providing them with the 'how to' manual, which I knew some of them wanted, but I persuaded myself that that's training, not education, and manuals can be found on the Internet. I prefer learning through narrative, and women's stories are a powerful and reaffirming format for such learning. They help provide a script for the documentary we are making as we challenge old ideas and old ways of doing business.

These conferences took me full circle. I was back in front of a group, only this time it wasn't history or geography or sex education, but business. It still meant thinking on my feet and homework in preparation, and for three years it was an important part of the portfolio. Then one day in mid-1998 I did not want to do it anymore. I felt talked out and thought out. I needed a break.

When I started Women's Business I had no firm view of what was women's business. I just liked the sound and provocation of the name, and it provided an alternative trading name within our long-established family company McCarthy Management Pty Ltd. As it happens much of the work I have done in the last four years has been concerned with finding pathways for women in executive life. The AIC conferences, numerous speaking gigs and corporate in-house seminars, the servicing of the group Chief Executive Women, of which I was President in 1996, have all been part of the process which has developed and defined Women's Business. I remain of the view that most business is women's business. We just haven't been seeing it that way.

In August 1995, the office of Prime Minister Paul Keating rang to ask if I would join a task force on childcare. My first response was to think how I would love to have done this in the seventies, but this was the nineties. Did I really want to become absorbed with childcare? It seemed like I had only just escaped those years of balancing guilt, belief in self, and disregard for doomsayers, who knew your children would be delinquents because of your selfish need to work, rather than do your own childcare.

Yet I love children and I was as sure now as I had been as a young feminist marching for 24-hour childcare that the care of our children remains a key issue for all of us. This is no longer women's business, but it is women who must provide leadership and that is difficult when we are not high in the pecking order of our society. Also, at the time it matters most we are at our most vulnerable as new parents. I felt obliged to accept the invitation and see if I could help make headway on one of our more intractable issues. The portfolio of Women's Business was expanding.

The Child Care Task Force established by the Labor government and managed by the Economic Planning Advisory Committee (EPAC) had a brief to inquire into the childcare industry, now computed to be worth $2 billion. The Task Force decided initially to take a blue sky view of the whole sector, to find out from the people involved what they would do if they were inventing childcare now. That was a depressing start, for it revealed the paucity of ideas and philosophy in the system. Few could think outside their own narrow perspective and the various industry segments seemed incapable of working together. All the old factions emerged. The community-based childcare lobby was positive that all virtue resided with their care model, and private for-profit childcare was by definition bad. Both sectors were in receipt of significant government funds and there had been a significant expansion of the private sector. In fact we saw little evidence of high quality in private childcare centres. The sector has attracted some fairly unusual owner/operators who see it as a profitable venture and have limited knowledge of children's developmental needs, but that is the result of the system. Privately funded child care is not bad by definition.

By contrast we saw few poor quality community-based centres. The issue for parents is that these two have become opposites and that is not in the interests of families struggling to find affordable quality care. Similarly the debates over family day care and after-school care are consigned to the too-hard basket and tied up with fantasies and confused arguments about mothers staying at home. Families and children are the losers.

Throughout the process it was hard to find reasonable voices, for there were so many vested interests. The National Childcare Accreditation Council, run by Quentin Bryce, together with the consistent voice of advocacy and professionalism of the Kindergarten Union (KU) in NSW, now run by my old friend Antoinette Le Marchant (previously Wyllie) could take a broad view. Perhaps the latter's long history and high intellectual standards gave it that assurance and skill. I privately thought how lucky my children were to have attended the KU kindergartens. It also reaffirmed how beneficial it was for parents to be involved in the pre-school education of their children.

It was the most depressing job I have done and more than ever I understood the pain that Quentin went through establishing the National Childcare Accreditation Council. Sometimes she would arrive home when I was in bed and reading (those books again) and she would sit on the end of the bed raving about the hostility to accreditation that she faced every day. My stock response was, 'Tell them we accredit dog kennels. Why should children be without protection?' I don't think it helped much.

At the heart of the matter is the Australian attitude to children. We still carry a strong Anglo heritage about the place of children in our society (out of sight) and unlike the societies of many of our immigrant families, we have no strong traditions of integrating work and family life. Perhaps rural families are the exception. Modern corporate life is not family-friendly and there is little evidence of leadership to change that. Unresolved, this will cost the community dearly. Deferred birth has higher risk, well-educated women will choose careers rather than maternity and their poorer sisters will give birth for social approval. The gulf between women will widen. This was not an outcome feminism had in mind, and I find it extraordinarily sad.

Maternity, although immensely rewarding, is a social function, not a private indulgence. It is one of the great social common denominators, for it is the moment when we understand our biology and our aspirations as parents and we begin to see the future. It has the power to bind us across many boundaries. To miss out because it is devalued and seems too hard is a tragedy, for both our society and the individual.

Yet for girls of my generation so many life messages were related to pregnancy. We were fearful about falling pregnant, even if we had only a vague idea how that happened, and we had all heard of those girls whose lives were ruined because their boyfriends wouldn't agree to the shotgun marriage. They were invariably banished to other towns to see out the pregnancy and they returned to lives of service looking after their parents. They were soiled goods and no self-respecting man would want them except for sex—after all, that was how they got into trouble in the first place. It was simply a further demonstration of how hopeless they were, good only for sex.

Those messages were imprinted in our minds The changes in the messages about pregnancy since the sixties reflect one of the great social changes of the century. The ability to manage fertility, and consequently marry or cohabit for love, changed the relationship between men and women forever and correspondingly altered the relationship between women and children. It offered the opportunity to become parents when we chose, and helped make it a political issue—as indeed childcare has become. It's the reason that pregnancy remains one of the powerful themes of my life.

These were powerful forces in controlling and defining women's sexuality. We grew up being told that nice, good girls neither liked nor did sex until they were married to a good prospect.

The Task Force tried to find a middle way. Not negotiable were quality affordable care and appropriate training standards. How to fund it equitably no-one could agree on, but the Task Force recommendation was to provide the money to the families. Mid-way through the inquiry the Keating government was thrown out, and to my surprise the Howard government insisted we complete our work. It was a hollow insistence, as our final report sat on the shelf unacknowledged for months. I determined I would never do another government inquiry.

CHAPTER FIFTEEN

SOPHIE, PAULA AND ISABEL ALLENDE

Mother's Day 1995. We live in Darlinghurst or, more correctly, I live in Darlinghurst. The nuclear family has disbanded. Gordon is expanding his cattle business in Berrima and Canyonleigh and we do weekends together, as we have done since 1986. Sam lives in Canberra and is a student of politics and Asian Studies at ANU, and Hamish is working at the Sydney casino as a graduate trainee after a year at Time Life and still dreaming of a full-time career as a DJ. Sophie has finished her Masters degree in Public Health, is helping me with the Beijing project and managing a research project on postnatal depression in women of non-English speaking background at Liverpool.

We are connected and close but all living separately. It's how Gordon and I believe families should rearrange and, as I write, it works for our family. I add that rider because my life experience tells me that these situations can change remarkably quickly. I don't want to sound smug and tempt Fate. If it falls apart tomorrow it will still have been a wonderful, loving and creative family.

We all like family rituals—births, marriages, birthdays, Christmas, Mother's Day, Father's Day—and we gather for these and family holidays. Mother's Day 1995 was no exception. My gift from Sophie was the book *Paula* by Isabel Allende. I was thrilled to receive it, having read the reviews, but mentioned to Sophie that I would defer reading it as I knew it had a sad ending. Don't you find as you get older that you long for happy endings? Some weeks later I'm on a Qantas flight from Port Moresby. I'm feeling tired but triumphant.

My friend and colleague of many years, Margaret Winn, is with me. We had completed the last of our pre-Beijing workshops the night before. It had been an exhilarating time. We expected twenty participants and fifty-seven had arrived. They were a wonderful group of women and talked of their struggle to improve the opportunities for their girls. They grieve over the fact that even primary school education is not accessible to most of them, and I feel that sense of responsibility about the Australian relationship. We agree to meet in Beijing and I flash to the image of Sophie, Margaret and me in Beijing—three generations of women, all connected through values and long friendship. It is only three weeks away and I'm looking forward to Sophie meeting my PNG friends.

On my plane I decide the time has come to read *Paula* as I have a straight four hours ahead of me. I have read all Isabel Allende's novels and am looking forward to her first personal piece. I'm engrossed from the beginning. Paula, Isabel Allende's twenty-something daughter, is in a coma whose cause is unknown. The prognosis is grim and the medical advice is to keep her comfortable, but have no expectation that she will survive as the person they knew and loved. Her mother cannot accept this and sits beside her bedside trying to reach her. She recounts many favourite family stories and retells Paula's own story, in the unsuccessful hope that this will reach her consciousness and activate her mind.

It is a powerful story of a mother's love and I identify strongly. Paula was Sophie's age when she died. I'm sobbing as I finish it before we land in Sydney and I'm feeling anxious and unsettled, wondering how I would respond to such a situation. Would I think of using a similar technique? I decide positively. The power of storytelling is strong. I wish she hadn't given the book to me.

I need to call Sophie and check she's OK. She is, and we agree to meet at the Korean Bath House the following Sunday. Sitting in the bath there she tells me she is feeling tired, not quite herself. I offer the usual clichéd advice—more sleep, less alcohol, less coffee, fewer parties and more exercise, knowing as I say it that she does eat and exercise sensibly. I mention that Bette and I both suffer from a rumbly gut and it is probably her genetic predisposition. We talk of our plans for China, where we will be attending the NGO Forum at Beijing. It will be our first grown-up adventure together, and we are excited about sharing it. After Beijing we are catching the train to Shanghai and staying with my friend Lorraine Williams, who has arranged an event at the Australian Embassy where we will both be speaking about the conference. This will be our first mother/daughter gig. I'm relaxed and she is nervous about public speaking.

We enjoy our time at the Bath House and next day I leave for Adelaide, where I'm organised to spend a week as part of my contract as Executive in Residence at the University of South Australia's International School of Management. I go via Melbourne, where I have some work to do, and arrive at the Adelaide Hilton late on Monday night, looking forward to my days of reading and thinking at the university.

On Tuesday morning at six the telephone wakes me. It's Hamish, saying, 'Don't worry, Mum, but Sophie is in the emergency ward at St Vincent's Hospital. She has been haemorrhaging from the bowel. If you call immediately the doctor on duty will take your call and explain what is happening.' My guts turn to water and I move onto automatic pilot. I call the Hilton desk and ask them to get me on the first flight to Sydney while I talk to the emergency ward. The news is awful. She has dangerously low blood-pressure and has lost a lot of blood. Nobody seems to know what is wrong with her.

Her friend Rob is at the hospital. He was with her when it happened and he and her housemate David managed the ambulance journey and hospital entry with great skill. He assures me that he and Hamish will stay with her until I get there. The doctor is being non-committal, other than to say it is dangerous.

I'm in the air by 7 a.m. It's the longest trip and all through the journey I'm thinking of Paula and Isabel. Was that gift an omen to prepare me for this? Will I find Sophie unconscious?

At the airport I'd left messages for Quentin, Sophie's friend Heidi and Gordon asking them to be there. Unbelievably, not one of them was at home. I'm talking to the answer phones and becoming hysterical.

When I reach the ward I find her weak, barely conscious and wired up to everything. Her blood-pressure is all over the place. She keeps bleeding from the bowel and there's no diagnosis. She is scared and so am I. I wonder what star we've crossed and I'm overwhelmed by the powerful feelings of love and fear and determination that this is not to be a rerun of Paula. The pain is white hot and I am like a new vulnerable mother all over again.

The days blur, my friends and family rally around, the diagnosis is Crohn's disease, which I've never heard of. It's a chronic inflammatory bowel condition, but manageable when we get through this crisis. When the diagnosis is confirmed, she asks me to find out what this means for fertility—she knows she wants to be a mother. I am reassured by the specialist.

As she begins to stabilise, there's suddenly a setback and she is back in intensive care. I call my mother and Quentin. It's too much for Hamish, who starts spinning and leaves. My sister Sarah, who is six months' pregnant, arrives in the waiting room with camomile tea. I'd thought I wanted to be on my own, but I'm really grateful she's with me as the young man who had collapsed in the City to Surf fun run the previous week has just died, and his family, who have been living in the waiting room, are packing up and talking to me about it. They wish me luck as they leave. I am becoming superstitious and think this is another ominous sign.

This is a hard night and I wonder if Sophie will make it. I wish Gordon was with me, but he's had the flu and can't come in. I am angry that he thinks I can manage this alone. Sarah stays with me and we go in and out of the ward until the nurses suggest we try to sleep in the waiting room. Sophie is asleep. There's death in the air and I don't want to leave her. The surgeon is still here, but we have agreed that surgery is the last resort. Few Crohn's sufferers get through life without it and if she can survive this attack without surgical intervention so much the better. Statistically she will have to manage surgery at some stage in her life but it is better to defer.

When the surgeon goes home, I am reassured that the crisis is over. The medical staff advise us to go home and the security guard insists on escorting Sarah and me to the car. It's 4 a.m. and he is worried about our safety in Darlinghurst. I don't dare tell him I live around the corner.

In all the drama there are memorable and tender moments, like watching Hamish and Sam massage their sister's legs when they were grossly distended and swollen from fluid retention, and arguing quietly about which was the most effective way to massage. When I saw the relief on her face when the physician assured her that her fertility would be OK I was pleased that it mattered so much to her. I want my children to love children.

And when I took her home and put her in our bed, that overwhelming feeling of safety and gratitude that Sophie's story was not to be the same as Paula's.

Are we different from any other family? I wonder if somehow I'm a bad wife and mother having two family members with chronic illnesses. Then I chide myself for my self-indulgence, for we are like most others. It's swings and roundabouts, and we are still a loving and intact family unit with loving friends who helped us through.

So the mother/daughter gig did not happen in Shanghai and Sophie has still not met the women from PNG. We played out survival in Darlinghurst, and the 50,000 women who gathered in Beijing did not include Wendy and Sophie. We will have to wait until the next World Conference of Women, now being referred to as Beijing-plus 5 by the United Nations organisers.

CHAPTER SIXTEEN

AN ECLECTIC PORTFOLIO

The books beside the bed tell an interesting story. Over the years the constants have been fiction. I feel unwell if I do not manage at least one novel every ten days. In my childhood I read stories of heroic girls like *Anne Thorne Reporter*, *Anne of Green Gables*, *Verity of Sydney Town*, *Veronica at the Wells*, and endless *Hilary of the Upper Sixth* stories. By late primary I was reading the adult books that came into the house; to avoid arguments about suitability, I would swap the dust jackets. Reading was always approved of and in a childhood without the distraction of television and near neighbours, reading was my passion and central activity. I read everything I could find—*The Kokoda Trail*, *Readers Digest*, *Pix*, newspapers which came with the mail three days a week, David Jones' and Farmers' catalogues, and farm guides. It was not discriminating but inclusive—like my life, really.

At high school I read less because I slept in a dormitory and there was no opportunity to read at night. During the day, time was organised and I was enjoying playing team games for the first time in my life. After the singular existence of a one-teacher school, it was heady to have friends to sing and play with. Reading was directed and compartmentalised, and I thought many of the school texts were silly and babyish. University texts dictated my reading habits for four years and as a new teacher the need to acquire information had me reading into the early hours of the morning. For years I went to sleep next to history and geography books, and I loved it.

Childbirth and the Women's Movement moved those books right out of the way. Women were writing about universal experiences, and it was like a drug. Georgette Heyer moved aside for real life. I could not get enough. At the beginning it was all polemical and needed to be discussed with one's new friends and companions. The friends were new because of profession and lifestyle, and also because feminist writings divided us into those who were interested and stimulated by these ideas and thus kept reading, and those who thought them dull or threatening and disregarded them. Old friendships were lost or at least put on hold. Betty Freidan, Kate Millet, Germaine Greer, Ferdinand Lamaze, Sheila Kitzinger, Ann Oakley, Gloria Steinem, Robin Morgan, Juliet Mitchell and Benjamin Spock were who we discussed. They replaced even my need for fiction, and in my twenties I consumed them voraciously. The legacy of these years is the need to keep reading women's writing.

Meanwhile on Gordon's side of the bed there were books about management and money, which at the time I thought rather dull. When he wrote a good one, *The Great Big Australian Takeover Book*, I began to get the picture and vicariously started to enjoy the world of business. For a while we swapped books as we read Australian fiction, politics and social comment—Johnson, Malouf, Garner, Drewe, Ireland, Rolls, Walsh, Horne, Summers. Many of these books were available as a result of Gordon's work at Angus and Robertson, and we met many of the authors published by A&R.

The next phase was books on sex. My family planning role meant I had access to books not always available in bookstores and I had to read them for professional reasons. Our sex life showed a definite improvement, reversing the theory that quantity decreases with years of marriage. Again we read less fiction, and books on sexual theory and technique were dominant for a while. Later we thought them dull, and the need for fiction was reasserted.

Somewhere in the eighties I found myself absorbed in management texts. I am not sure how the books moved across the bed, but one day they were on my side. I distinctly remember the first time I was asked to prepare a business and marketing plan to present to the Bicentennial Authority board. I had three days to prepare and I rang Gordon in a panic to identify a book at home that I could spend the weekend with. He did, and also suggested I re-read *Up the*

Organisation by Robert Townsend, in case I took myself too seriously. It was good advice and I use the Townsend test often when deciding whether to accept a job. This, broadly speaking, is 'If you are not in it for fun or money, don't do it.' While acknowledging that my sense of fun may not be everyone's, it is a useful check as so many of the issues I am interested in do not pay in the start-up phase, and I am conscious now of needing to keep a financial balance. After all, one has to fund the other.

By the nineties the bedside authors included Charles Handy. When I read his theories on the building of an eclectic portfolio, I recognised my professional life had a form and a name. Until then I spoke of having a non-linear career, and tried to give it virtue and dignity as on paper it looked rather messy. Education here, media there, a decade of family planning, national event organiser, heritage manager. Where does this all lead, I would be asked. The truth is I don't know. Does it have to lead somewhere? Isn't it enough to be doing and enjoying it? And perhaps even making a contribution?

What Handy has done is to legitimise the non-linear careers of many women like me, not for feminist reasons but for good business reasons, and because it suits the time we live in. It also recognises that we live longer and executive linear careers may be unsustainable and unsatisfying. We need to find a new way to earn the income we require for our longer lives. It is just possible that women have found a better working life pattern than men. In my family this is normal, as Gordon has had at least three separate careers. In fact, all this time I have been developing an eclectic portfolio. I just had not called it that.

So what has the McCarthy portfolio looked like since 1995 when I left line management? The answer is it looks like a kaleidoscope of my entire professional life: teaching, public policy inquiry and development, non-executive director of both commercial and not-for-profit businesses, and membership of statutory bodies. It has evolved and keeps changing, which I find pleasing.

The other interesting aspect of this stage in my life is the chance I have had to revisit the early themes and passions of my professional life. Returning to the worlds of heritage, education and finding new opportunities to think about what it means to be female in Australia has been wonderful. Couple that with the new challenges of a commercial directorship and learning the skills of fundraising, and my life is full. It is also a wonderfully unpredicted life stage. I could never have imagined how good it feels to be free of ongoing parental responsibility. The dogs are my only constraint, and time seems limitless after the years of schooling and parenting. The simple reality is that Gordon and I can reclaim the weekend, as we did when we were first together.

Chairing the Australian Heritage Commission was a second chance; if the National Trust was the micro world of heritage, the Australian Heritage Commission was the macro. It offered an opportunity to work on the whole continent and included indigenous culture and heritage as part of its portfolio. To be entrusted with the chair of this Commission is a compliment, and when offered the task by Senator John Faulkner in 1994, I could not believe my luck. It was another chance to explore and extend the Australian experience. Although the Commission was slightly unfashionable at the time, I was not deterred, but excited about placing it back in the mainstream. Also I had seen the polling, which consistently told us that Australians cared passionately about the environment and valued their heritage.

The Commission was established in 1975 as the statutory authority for the Register of the National Estate, that list of natural, historic and indigenous places which records the places Australians hold dear. These are Australia's special places and more than 12,000 are listed on the inventory, ranging from the sublime Kakadu in the Northern Territory to cattlemen's huts in the Monaro. I think of them as our national family photos. When we lose them, we ache, for they are our sense of place and remind us of our heritage. They become the benchmark for the heritage values we subscribe to.

The Commission was a distinctly Australian response to heritage conservation and its establishment was supported across party lines. Country Party member Ralph Hunt, a farmer and future minister, said at the second reading of the Bill in 1975:

> The environment and for that matter the National Estate
> surrounds all of us. It belongs to all of us. It is not the
> monopoly of any one man. It is not the monopoly of any one
> generation, one group, one party, one government. It is ours to
> pollute, to destroy, to desecrate, or is ours to value, to
> preserve, to protect, to hand on to the next generation.

I constantly reminded myself of those words during the three years I
chaired the Commission, and alternated between offending and grat-
ifying our constituents. In my early days there I was advised by
various politicians to clean up the Register as it did not reflect popular
opinion and was merely the toy of the Canberra bureaucracy. This
view was expressed by both sides of politics and reflected, I thought,
a cringe about things Australian. It was so different from the visible
search for meaning in the Australian landscape which our cinema-
tographers were undertaking. *Mad Max*, *The Adventures of Priscilla,
Queen of the Desert*, *Storm Boy* and *Oscar and Lucinda* tell us something about our Australianness. We could be nowhere else and I
wanted in my time at the Commission to assert that Australianness.

However, the political process intervened, and a Coalition government replaced the Labor government. Much as I loved the job, I
thought I should offer my resignation as there is little point working
with people who do not trust and respect you. After a month or so
I advised Senator Robert Hill, the new Minister for the Environment,
that I was willing to exit quietly if that was his wish. To my surprise
he asked that I stay on. Rather nonplussed, I agreed that I would stay
until the end of my term in 1998. Somehow that clarified the agenda
for me, as I had been given a clear assurance that I could get on with
the job.

I wanted to provoke an emotional response to heritage, and test
the connection between the Register and popular views about heritage. We did this by running a competition in 1997 called Places in
the Heart, where we asked Australians to describe their favourite
heritage places in no more than a hundred words. The competition
was sponsored by commercial media and attracted nearly 3,000
entries. The great result from my point of view was that ninety per

cent of the places nominated were already on the Register. The entries demonstrated strongly the seamless way that people see their heritage. Natural and cultural environments come together with social values to give us our sense of place. The integrated approach the Commission took was reaffirmed, and the Register was validated.

I had my share of political heat during this time, and I need not have been concerned that Australians were other than passionate about their heritage. The proposed listing on the Register of the Holdsworthy Army area provoked strong feelings and became a hot political issue, as it was being considered as a second Sydney airport site by the Coalition government. I was accused of being a Labor apparatchik, stopping the government getting on with its business. I was not really threatened by this as I planned to get on with my statutory responsibilities—in this instance the investigation of the Holdsworthy nominations, which were arriving in multiple numbers. On the other hand, such opposition is always unpleasant and as usual the Commission was caught between three layers of government— local, state and federal. While not reaching the drama of the Franklin River in Tasmania, Holdsworthy was difficult and had the potential to explode. For we Commissioners, who visited the area and had the local Land Council take us to indigenous sites, there was no turning back. Indigenous sites, together with the exquisite and pristine bushland, convinced us that our intensive investigative and assessment system had got it right. Holdsworthy was an outstanding place and the Department of Defence had cared for it very well.

History records that Holdsworthy did not become the site of the second airport and is listed on the Register for its natural, historic and indigenous heritage. Looking back, I wonder why anyone could have ever imagined it should not be listed, but such is the nature of many heritage debates. Once the battle is won, people care even more about the place, for they have become de facto owners of the public estate, a wonderful outcome for conservation.

On Sunday, 28 April 1996 a single gunman killed thirty-five people at and around the Port Arthur Historic Site in Tasmania, a site which is on the Register of the National Estate. Most of these murders took place inside the Broad Arrow Cafe, a twentieth-century structure which serviced commercial and tourist operations on the site. The majority of the people killed were day tourists, although a number of victims both worked and lived at Port Arthur. On 7 November 1996 Martin Bryant pleaded guilty to all charges, and two weeks later was sentenced to jail for the term of his natural life for each of the thirty-five murders he committed at Port Arthur.

Like most Australians I was deeply shocked by this event, and can remember Sam calling me as I was driving to Canberra to tell me it was happening. It was impossible to comprehend; such a massacre does not happen in Australia. The morning after, Sharon Sullivan, the Executive Director of the Commission, and I started thinking about what this meant from a heritage point of view and how we could best contribute to the situation at Port Arthur. Compared with the loss of human life a heritage perspective could have seemed trivial, but my experience after the earthquake in Newcastle convinced me that neither massacres nor earthquakes should be followed by obliterating the evidence of the disaster, no matter how painful. We need our memories, and our sense of place is assisted by real evidence. In a radio interview on 7ZR Hobart, I said, 'If you obliterate it you won't obliterate the pain, and it won't take away the memories, but the gross inhumanity of it may not be remembered in the right way. And I think we just have to have a bit more time. It's very hard to speak over the pain barrier and no-one can understand better than the staff, the people who were there day in and day out, who were confronting it.'

The question to be addressed was how do Australians cope with this tragic site as survivors, as witnesses, as heritage managers, as local residents and as sympathetic nationals. Could all these interests be brought together? We decided we should visit the site as soon as possible.

On Friday June 14, Sharon and I visited Port Arthur and at a media conference called for a delay on demolition of the Broad Arrow Cafe, pending a mature appraisal of its historic and cultural significance. Against all the emotional odds, we persuaded the Tasmanian Premier

Tony Rundle to agree. Even two weeks after the event, visiting Port Arthur was a scarifying experience and I could feel my gut heaving as we walked around the Cafe. At its best, Port Arthur is full of poignant memories and I remembered how moved our family had been when we were tourists there in 1988, but the pain this time was palpable.

The immediate results of the Port Arthur tragedy were a transformation of our gun legislation, and a grant from the Commonwealth for a new interpretation and visitors' centre. The long-term results are still to be revealed, but in heritage terms the ensuing debate about what we keep and what is of significance in human suffering was important. As I write in 1999, the Broad Arrow Cafe survives and the issue is unresolved.

The most unexpected personal benefit of my time at the Commission was my contact with the heritage of indigenous Australia. Working with fellow Commissioner Bill Jonas and hearing his perspectives, taking advice from the people in our Aboriginal and Torres Strait unit and being exposed to Aboriginal ideas about wilderness and heritage were transforming. For the first time I began to understand a little about the connection of Aboriginal Australians with land, and I learned to think about that perspective when places were being considered. It also made me angry to think how I had been denied that knowledge in my education. In April 1995 an event held at the Aboriginal Embassy site in the parliamentary triangle in Canberra to mark its recognition as a site of significance attracted wide media attention and many visitors. It was an event that reinforced for me the fear people have of being different, and how ignorance highlights that fear. The public comments were so often deeply racist.

In my last year as chair, the Commission listed some special places including North Sydney Olympic Pool where the McCarthy family spent many hours of leisure and exercise time and the Homebush Bay Wetlands (remember when wetlands were called swamps?), the site of the 2000 Sydney Olympics, a nomination which initially was treated in a very hostile way. It was also the year that the Commission's authority to identify Australia's National Estate was upheld in the High Court, a landmark victory and one I could have ill afforded to lose, as fighting in court with public money is extremely high risk.

On 29 January 1998, my last day as chair of the Heritage Commission, I addressed the National Press Club on the theme 'Heritage—who benefits, who pays?' This was quite scary despite my ease with the topic, and it was some time before I could bear to watch the video. When I did look at it, I was struck by my fortune in having my friends and family as part of the audience. Sam, his girlfriend, Farida, and Hamish came to lend support. Anne Summers, my frequent walking companion, and her partner Chip Rolley were in town and dropped in. Also there were Evelyn Scott and Monica McMahon, colleagues from my National Women's Advisory Council days, and Don Aitkin and Meredith Edwards from the University of Canberra where I am Chancellor. And my colleagues from the Commission, whom I had come to value so much. It was a satisfying way to end that involvement and poetic that the ABC would broadcast it.

When people ask me what I do now that I don't have a proper job, I tend to either describe the dominant current task or say I am managing an eclectic portfolio. But lately I have begun to think of myself as a public educator and that definition is growing in my head. It sits beside the concept of the eclectic portfolio. If there is a common theme, it is about the public interest or lack of it in areas that seem so important to me. My leading passion is always education, all that shifts is the emphasis. I hold a strong belief that as a nation we should strive for a society that values life-long learning. So often I have been accused of changing my mind and this is usually expressed as, 'You didn't think that in 1960/70/80' or whatever. Well, of course I didn't; I have acquired new information and gained new insight since then. I see no virtue in the constancy of ignorance and why, as a feminist who has tried to shift the paradigms of being female in Australia, would I want things to stay the same?

So when asked by Kim Beazley, the Minister for Education, to join the University of Canberra Council in May 1992, I was surprised that my initial inclination was to refuse. I felt he was offering this as second prize to the chair of the ABC Board, and I was not especially interested in the politics of higher education. I had done that in NSW, as a member of the Higher Education Board, and doubted that the earth had moved. The compelling reason to agree was the University's leadership team of Donald Horne and Don Aitkin. Don Aitkin, the vice chancellor, had been my friend all those years ago at New England. I thought he was in the top league of vice chancellors and was making a real impact at the University. I also liked the idea that the University had grown from a College of Advanced Education and was reinventing itself. I love the chance to grow things. I decided to accept. Some weeks later I was listening to a persuasive business speaker from the United Kingdom and was impressed to hear him say that if he was looking for women to appoint to boards, the higher education sector was the first place to search. I felt childishly pleased that I had made a good decision.

And a good decision it has been, as it has been the continuous commitment for seven years and I am still learning how to do it. I enjoyed being back in the world of public education and was flattered to be asked by my colleagues to become deputy chancellor to Donald Horne.

In 1994, when Donald retired as chancellor, I was elected to succeed him. When it happened I thought, 'How can I do this? I have only a pass degree and Dip. Ed. No-one will take me seriously; this is the higher education sector.' There is that inner voice again, counselling caution when my mouth is saying 'yes, have a go'. And simultaneously I'm thinking what would my lecturers at UNE think? 'Her a chancellor? Give me a break.' But once again it's feet first. I am not going to be restrained by boundaries.

Four years later I remain Chancellor, a role I love. It is a creative task and I like the chance for policy input into the higher education sector. I find chairing the Council stimulating, and I love the happiness and ritual of graduation ceremonies.

I have had some special graduations, including conferring an honorary degree on His Majesty, the King of Thailand, in recognition of the achievement of his fifty years on the throne and his leadership in public education and democracy. This was really special, as the Palace asked that I confer the doctorate on the King at the palace in Bangkok. In a short space of time I was in the air on my way, hoping that my clothes would be appropriate, even though they would be under my chancellor's robes. In October 1996, the King of Thailand, His Majesty Bhumipol Adulyadej, became a doctor of the University of Canberra. I was petrified that I would make either a protocol or a linguistic mistake. The Thai language does not slide easily off the tongue of a linguistically challenged person like myself, and walking backwards so as not to turn my back on His Majesty is not my natural inclination. I practised both the pronunciation and the walk for days.

I had been consistently advised that under no circumstance was I to make physical contact. However, the coverage on Thai television reveals that we shook hands and I did not walk backwards. He was the most charming man with a special aura, and it was easy to understand why his people love him. When he spoke of his public education role, which was the reason for the doctorate, it was like hearing the idea redefined. The room in which this very intimate ceremony occurred was exquisitely furnished in pale pink and white, the summer colours of the Royal Family. The courtiers were dressed in white and stood in a line as the ceremony proceeded. When it was over and the King stayed to chat, I found it poignant and endearing that he identified the challenge the Thais faced with HIV-AIDS as the major current issue. He acknowledged the work of Mechai, whom I had met in my Family Planning days, and said now that he has the family planning task under control he must do HIV-AIDS for us. I cannot recall another national leader who would speak with such honesty about such a complex social issue.

I combined this visit with a visit to a PLAN community at Kong Khan in the north of Thailand (PLAN is a global humanitarian child sponsorship organisation). It was my first PLAN field trip and having recently joined the PLAN Board, I was anxious to see the field. It felt as though I was back in Family Planning, with the focus on working with women and children to improve community health. I kept wondering how I could put all this experience and learning together. That is the challenge of having a second chance when you are a more powerful person with better resources. I am still mulling over how I become more effective at these roles, but then I think of the King telling me that managing AIDS was the biggest challenge in Thailand, and I am reassured that it is OK to think as I do.

As women's rights were my driving passion in the seventies, Aboriginal rights are now. While I will never lose my sense of social justice about women, I want now to be an active citizen about Aboriginal rights. After feeling proud of our political judicial systems for delivering Mabo, I was appalled by the Wik Ten Point Plan and my passive behaviour changed to activity. I joined a small group of friends to form an organisation called WIK Ed to encourage public debate and increase the information about Aboriginality. We followed the education and consciousness-raising strategy developed by the Women's Electoral Lobby in the early seventies, and once again the public meetings in blue ribbon electorates proved a winner. People poured into these meetings in their thirst for information and understanding about Wik and Aboriginality. I kept hearing statements like 'I didn't know "they" were so educated'; 'Just think, I have never been in the same room as an Aboriginal'. One has either to weep or rage at our ignorance.

Again, the small planning group and the larger group of active volunteers for meetings and promotion worked, just as in the WEL days. It is the finest community education model to anticipate and fulfil a need. Out of this activity there were new friends and role models. Linda Burney and Aden Ridgeway emerged as strong Black leaders. Noel Pearson's attendance guaranteed an overflowing hall. It was a heady year, tempered in the end by the fact that the Wik Plan was adopted by the Commonwealth Government and caused Aborigines and their supporters great pain. That defeat, coupled with the refusal of the Prime Minister, John Howard, to apologise to the Stolen Generation meant that 1998 ended badly.

I combined my support for the Republic and my concern for the inclusion of Aboriginal Australia in mainstream life by joining a ticket for the Constitutional Convention. Father Frank Brennan, a Jesuit priest, suggested that he and I run on a ticket headed by two Aborigines, Linda Burney and Aden Ridgeway. I repressed my dislike of running for election in order to support this unlikely alliance. Like Frank Brennan, I was angry that the Australian Republican Movement had not included any Aborigines on its ticket for the Convention. This was a chance to get their names into the public arena. Well, we failed to get our colleagues to the Convention, but six months later Aden was elected to the Australian Senate, the second indigenous person and the first from NSW. There is justice in the world after all. He is there for the main event.

My evolution as a feminist led me to form a view, some time in the eighties, that unless women wrote the big private and public cheques and legislation, we would start to spin our wheels. While I believe that an executive position is the strongest, I am also pushing the view that being elected to commercial boards and parliaments matters most. As the seventies slogan reminds us, A Woman's Place is Everywhere.

When I accepted an invitation to join Women Chiefs of Enterprise, which later became Chief Executive Women, it was to support women in business. How different it was from women's organisations in the seventies, and yet the needs were similar. Women needed to support each other. It was lonely in the senior executive world and the pathways were not always clear. We needed reality checks, but these were done over lunches and cocktails in hotels and boardrooms, rather than kitchens and car pools. Commercial success was highly regarded and I occasionally felt that public policy and governance were not considered quite so significant as the private sector.

News that I was part of the Sydney Harbour Casino bid team was greeted with surprise as well as counsel that I should not be disappointed when Kerry Packer won. I kept quiet though I was confident we would win, perhaps because I was interested in being a director of a commercial company and if we won, I would have a new role. I was curious to see how different from the not-for-profit sector the commercial world is and it's hard to imagine any business more focused on the bottom line than a casino. Being a director of the

Sydney Casino, now called Star City, was certainly not a disappointment and being part of creating a business from the ground up was fun. I smile when I think that the ABC and Star City both sent me to Las Vegas as part of my responsibilities. (In 1998 I was there with the Sydney Symphony Orchestra in tow.) I was at Star City for five years and found it a fascinating business. It roughly coincided with my time as Chancellor and I often compare the two enterprises, both with an active commitment to learning but in such different environments.

Publicans, racehorse owners and breeders, directors of tobacco companies, and regular citizens regularly ask me to justify my support for a casino. I usually do not respond but for the record I am not opposed to games of chance or gambling per se, although neither is an activity of choice for me.

People love to try their luck and for most people gambling is fun. Star City is an entertainment destination—Disneyland with a gambling palace; not Monte Carlo but an attempt to create an Australian-style casino in a highly regulated environment. Licensing a casino to bring gambling within the law was, I believe, a positive act and I would rather see one well-run casino where people pay taxes than observe the proliferation of illegal gambling houses. Casinos are attractive to young people as a place of employment and perhaps that will prove to make them more realistic about gambling. The social effects of addictive gambling are well documented and they existed long before a legal casino was built in Sydney.

However, I continue to attract criticism for my casino role and in November 1997 I wrote the following piece for the Australian *Financial Review*.

A Suitable Job for a Woman

One of the hottest tickets in town in the last few weeks was to the opening of Star City. Being a director I was asked by various people to arrange an invitation or two. My male colleagues on the board were similarly approached. However the requests to me were inevitably followed by comments and questions about how someone with my background could possibly be a director of a casino.

Expressing opinions about the suitability of my role as director of a casino has not been confined to such direct approaches. At a recent cocktail party, one of my friends was taken aside and asked to explain my fall from grace. It was apparent that her responses were not important as the questioner had an established position he was eager to share.

I was acting outside my image as social reformer and betraying my supporters and prior roles: Family planning (perfectly acceptable now, though it wasn't always), deputy chair of the ABC, Chair of the Heritage Commission, CEO of the National Trust, chancellor of the University of Canberra. These are good and suitable jobs for women like me but God forbid a commercial board and a Casino. How to explain it?

Not long after at a public event, a prominent ABC broadcaster, in noting and lamenting my absence, referred to my successful time as executive director of the Trust and said that, of course, was before I went to the casino.

It sounded to many present as though I had embraced a new outlandish cult, even though I had been in this National Trust job while also being a casino board member without serious consequences. But why was this a matter for public comment?

Then there is the tendency to delete reference to this directorship when introducing me at a public event. Some months ago, at an international meeting of women entrepreneurs, I referred to the casino as a new employment option for women. A powerful and wealthy woman from Indonesia asked if I knew that gambling was forbidden by Islam and this must be bad for my reputation. I discreetly decided not to mention the Indonesian gamblers at the Casino.

It seems we are creating a new stereotype. Women can do some boards and statutory authorities, but don't mess with the big time. These are not suitable jobs for women. If some are chosen it will be because of safe specialist skills like law and accounting, not the more convivial broadly based perspectives which identify many good company directors. Such attitudes defy logic and make restrictive assumptions about gender.

The truth is I accepted the invitation to join the casino board when it was a small entity making a bid for the casino licence. I liked the idea of working with Leightons, whose skills I had admired during the construction of the ABC building at Ultimo; I love creating and growing people and businesses and I thought it would be fun to challenge Kerry Packer, especially as he is such a fine strategic player. Moreover this would be a business for the future and would attract many young people. They needed a work environment which protected and developed them. I could contribute to that.

With my experience as a resident-action activist I could help paraphrase the concerns of the local residents whose world was to be physically changed forever by the casino. Add to that the excitement of a commercial business and the challenge of designing a casino in the Australian idiom—it seemed like a great opportunity.

My professional life has been dogged by advice about appropriate professional career decisions. But there is a perversity in my character which resists being stereotyped, no matter how caring those around me believe their motives to be. Why do people not counsel my male colleagues about their Star City directors' roles?

Have we implicitly decided that some directorships should not be available to women? A casino is a people and money business. Why deny 50 per cent of the population the fun of building a business from the ground up and the opportunity of developing a career in the entertainment business of the nineties?

Charles Handy writes of the eclectic portfolio and the mix between professional and voluntary responsibilities. Perhaps that notion could replace the more restrictive notions of what is a suitable role for a woman who is interested in and curious

about the changing definition of being Australian. And could
we just occasionally be relieved of the role of God's Police?

(As I write this, Star City has been taken over by Tabcorp and my
five-and-a-half year director's role has ceased.)

Many women fundraise in the community for a variety of causes
but fundraising for women's causes is still difficult. Children, sport
and the arts do better; perhaps it reflects the tendency of women to
avoid self-promotion and place themselves last when assessing needs.
Political parties are reluctant to invest in women's campaigns. It's a
Catch 22 situation, as few women have much discretionary income
and often run the argument that women should help each other. It
was therefore with some apprehension that I agreed to chair the Royal
Hospital for Women Foundation in 1995 after being approached by
Rosemary Foot. There had been a huge community swell of anger
and protest when the NSW Government announced that the women's
hospital at Paddington was to close. People from all over NSW
objected on the grounds that there would be no women's hospital in
the Eastern Suburbs. Royal Women's had a fine tradition of service
and research and finally the state government agreed to relocate and
rebuild the hospital at Randwick. The funds allocated were insufficient and the community was asked to assist.

We initially decided to set a target of $5 million. The feasibility
study done by our fundraising team suggested we could find
$10 million and so we doubled the target. It was a great project and
two years later we achieved the target and I decided to leave. Again
I found it strange that people expected I would stay but my instinct
is always to do the job and leave the place in good shape for someone
else, or to leave when I am having a good time—the memories don't
get any better. This project reinforced how much I love the game of
fundraising.

The pile of management texts beside the bed has increased as I
branch out into new areas of consulting and governance. I do not
want to be theory-free as I take on new challenges such as the men-
toring program I am running for Citibank executives. While I feel
secure about the program, I need to do the reading and implement

the world benchmarking that such a global institution deserves. What is different is that I now need to search the world via the Internet and I can no longer plead computer illiteracy. I have finally learned to use the keyboard and the mouse.

In 1997 I worked again with David Hill. His career at the ABC had ended, and he was acting CEO at NSW's CityRail, where he was feeling frustrated that despite perfect policies in place for a decade, there were no obvious signs that women were better off. He was impatient that less than three per cent of women were driving or guarding trains, something he thought would happen after his departure as CEO in 1986. He needed a circuit breaker to help him move women into these positions and asked if I would like to help. I loved the fact that he would make that commitment publicly in a conservative union-dominated institution, and was pleased to be involved. My regret remains that the success was only modest.

A multicultural opportunity came my way with an offer from Focus Publishing to write a book celebrating fifty years of citizenship in Australia. I interviewed sixty Australians who had arrived since 1949 and listened to their stories. The resulting book, *A Fair Go, Portraits of the Australian Dream*, will I hope rebut much of the stereotyped thinking and labelling of migrants. It was a chance to explore yet again that commitment to being Australian when you are on the margin and want to find your way into the mainstream. Women, migrants and Aboriginal Australians all have that experience and observing how those groups push down the barriers continues to fascinate me.

Moving into the year 2000 my portfolio of interest, fun and responsibility includes being chancellor of the University of Canberra, chair of PLAN International Australia (a child-focused overseas aid and development agency), Trustee of the Adelaide Festival Centre, chair of the Look of the City Committee for Sydney, chair of the WHO Advisory Board of the Kobe Centre in Japan, and executive director of McCarthy Management and Women's Business. Some pay fees, some don't, but all of them are about aspects of Australian and global life I want to influence and contribute to. For me, that is what the eclectic portfolio is about.

My personal portfolio includes my family, whose company I adore, Gordon my friend and husband of thirty-five years, Sam, Hamish and Sophie, and the special people in their lives, and my extended family. But I need my friends. I could not survive without my yoga classes and the coffee and conversation that follows. Together Quentin Bryce, Lyndsay Connors, Susan Ryan and I workshop the world each Saturday morning. I hope we will find ways to do it forever, even though I know nothing is forever. Yet somehow this group weaves together our collective pasts and reminds me of the strength and generosity of women's friendships and the buzz that comes from that shared understanding.

Nineteen ninety-nine ended with a happy result of Sophie's wedding to Tony Green on 18 December—35 years to the day since Gordon and I were married. I think that is a good omen and I am surprised how attractive 'mother of the bride' sounds.

Advice Ignored to No Apparent Disadvantage

Unless you use your right hand, you will not be allowed to be a
   teacher.
Don't be bold.
Wait until you're asked to dance.
Don't be common.
Only ordinary girls pierce their ears.
I would recommend that Wendy enrols in a marriageable course
   like physiotherapy.
If you fail university, you can still be a nurse.
Men don't like clever girls.
I was always happy to stay at home with my children.
My mum stayed at home.
Do you have any qualifications other than a colonial degree?
We don't count experience overseas. (NSW Education department)
Why can't your husband support you and your baby?
If you drank at the pub on Friday nights like everyone else, you
   would have a chance.
A woman's most prized possession is her virginity. (Sir John
   Cramer, MP for Bennelong)

And in contrast, the best line of all:

A woman's place is everywhere.

INDEX